# PLAN AND PLAY, PLAY AND PLAN: Defining Your Art Practice

Janwillem Schrofer

Valiz

# INTRODUCTION: COURSE AND IMPROVISATION



The protagonist of this publication is the artist as an 'entrepreneur' who prepares himself, launches an initiative, develops and grows with his undertaking—usually a one-man operation. The word 'enterprise' aptly reflects a variety of entrepreneurship-related aspects: undertaking, venture, speculation, accomplishment, initiative, resourcefulness. The artist is constantly orientating himself, and sustains or continues transforming his undertaking. An artistic practice of this type is full of uncertainties, is speculative.

*Artist is the focus*

This publication is intended primarily for artists and art students who are steering their own artistic practice, the main criterion being to decide "where do I stand and what do I stand for?" The prime focus is day-to-day artistic practice, with the artist bridging the—apparent—chasm between autonomous and applied art, an artist who is in the driving seat. The text invites artists to make assessments, often by way of analytical models, which help him to make his own choices. An artist's existence as a form of life fulfilment is based on a fundamental choice. I do not address that one, essential 'moment', I see it as an intangible 'black-box' given. Here, it is assumed that the artistic calling and the artist's own practice can be structured, that the artist can conduct himself with others as an independent actor. Choices that have been made are bound inseparably with one's own character. You can examine all manner of choices, think about them and weigh them up, but choices should not clash with your own nature and unique characteristics—they must be in line with one another.

The publication could also be useful for curators, critics and lecturers, managers in cultural and educational establishments for artists and art students, as well as policy-makers in government and funds. However, the material asks from parties other than artists an interest in and willingness to study in more depth the tasks they face, appealing to their ability to adapt the information for their own professional field. There are few if any direct tips for those 'others' in this publication. I do not, for instance, look at artistic practice from a policy-related perspective, and restrict myself to a few remarks on art education. I am not an artist, art critic, art philosopher or curator, nor a philosopher or economist, but a generalist interested in the connection between disciplinary fields; breadth rather than depth. The material is based primarily on personal experience, an empirically inductive approach. Individual experiences of artists in their practice always form the starting point, after which I examine the similarities and differences and, where possible, distil patterns, describing and analysing them. I make use of my personal network, accept subjectivity, but get the artists themselves and various critical readers to 'test' results. When theory is involved, it is mainly from a socio-psychological perspective, with occasional excursions into sociological and socio-economic concepts. My energy and attention are driven by an unlimited curiosity about the artist—I call it 'indecent' curiosity.

### *Structure and method*

Positioning means finding a place for yourself. Taking control and not leaving decisions to others. It is a circular process: make an approximate choice, carry out work, gain experience with partners, make a more precise choice, new experience, and so on. It is important not to invest too much energy, or too often, in something that ultimately offers too little material/immaterial return on investment. That does not mean that you should keep on the safe side, because risk-taking, dealing with uncertainties and the unforeseen go with positioning.

This handbook is in three parts. All relate to choosing and improvising: the two perspectives with decision-making which are mutually reinforcing and vital to each other. The first part provides terms and reflections that augment the process of choosing and improvising. The second part contains the so-called building blocks which constitute a concrete elaboration on the terms and reflections. In the third part, 'Origins', readers are introduced to my career, and my reflections on it, to illustrate that overarching theme. Anyone wishing to know more about the author's background can begin with Chapter 9, 'A slice of life'. 250

Part I starts with 'Bonds and freedom', which addresses and challenges prevailing, sometimes mind-narrowing terms. The chapter 'Artists' positions—a large palette' takes us into the practice of art. Contrary to what one might imagine, an artist has several career options. It is essential to be alert to positioning if one is to have insight in and scope for one's own practice, but also to win respect from society and appreciation/acknowledgement from the 'art market'. The chapter dealing with that pivotal theme is the longest. It concludes with a peek into twenty-two artists' practices, combined with varying professional options.

In 'The artist and his environment, from victim to free spirit', I deal with the artist's capacity to understand the art world and, in particular, the art market, and gain control of it. The further growth and development of the artistic practice, the concomitant setting of priorities and the importance of mental and/or physical mobility are explored in 'Dynamic artisthood, growth and mobility'.

'Fabric of knowledge exchange, collaboration and friendship' tempers the idea of self-reliance and the makeable world, by indicating, alongside individual possibilities of intervention and kinds of small-scale collaboration (the predominant focus in this publication), areas in which collective action helps in surmounting social barriers and promoting common interests.

Signals from artists' studios recur in the first part, when the findings of thirty-three artists are analysed, the positions of eleven artists are dealt with, as are the twenty-two sketches of mixed practices as mentioned earlier.

In the second part, which has the overarching title 'Building blocks', concrete examples are provided of the terms used in Part I. Chapters 6, 7 and 8 examine, in turn, the development and realisation of plans within an individual and a collective route, monetary matters and the curriculum vitae as a personal mirror and a data base.

In 'Origins'—Part III—I expose my career and track record, as well as giving insight into how to acquire 'hands-on' expertise, I also analyse several generally applicable career patterns. The writing of this publication was a process that took years, starting in the 1990s at the Rijksakademie (research residency) in Amsterdam. I tapped many sources and many people contributed to the contents of this handbook. 269 Information on 'the making of' is given in the final chapter, which ties in directly with the description and analysis of my career and contains my acknowledgements.

The extensive table of contents following this introduction lists the subject matter; it constitutes a condensed summary for speedy reading.

Janwillem Schrofer, Heemstede, 2018

# CONTENTS

# Part I.

# Termin
# & Refle

ology
ections

# Part I.

This first part unlocks existing terminology relating to the artistic practice and develops new terminology. 'Bonds and Freedom' (Chapter 1) addresses the inhibitions about autonomy and entrepreneurship, and deals with amplifying themes: on choice processes, the relationship between the internal and the external world and the breadth of the artistic practice). It is a foretaste of the other chapters in Part I which supply the tools for individual positioning.

'Artists' positions—a large palette' (Chapter 2), places artists' positions plus corresponding facets of artisthood in line with an exploration of artists' studios. Artistic practice is described in three steps, i.e.:

- facets of artisthood—the internal world with personal fascinations and inspirations;
- artists' positions—when the studio door opens and the facets materialise;
- the presentation of these artists' positions in the art world.

Each position is described concisely (in this the longest chapter of the publication) and interspersed with 'real-life' examples. The chapter ends with 'The integrated artist's practice', where a 'look behind the scenes' with twenty-two artists demonstrates that very few simple, 'narrow' practices exist.

In Chapter 3, 'The artist and his environment, from victim to free spirit' the artist appears in the art market, in which he wants to get—and keep—a grip.

In order to help the artist in guiding the development of his own practice, Chapter 4, with the title 'Dynamic artisthood, growth and mobility', provides a model by way of which priorities can be identified using a personal ambition profile.

And finally, Chapter 5 'Fabric of knowledge exchange, collaboration and friendship' concludes that you are not—and in some cases should not be—on your own. For example, when embarking on special matters that extend beyond your own personal life and professional career.

The 'Reflections' are mainly intended as mental exercises, you can muse on them, rack your brains or embark on introspective exploration, making—perhaps rejecting—plans.

# 1

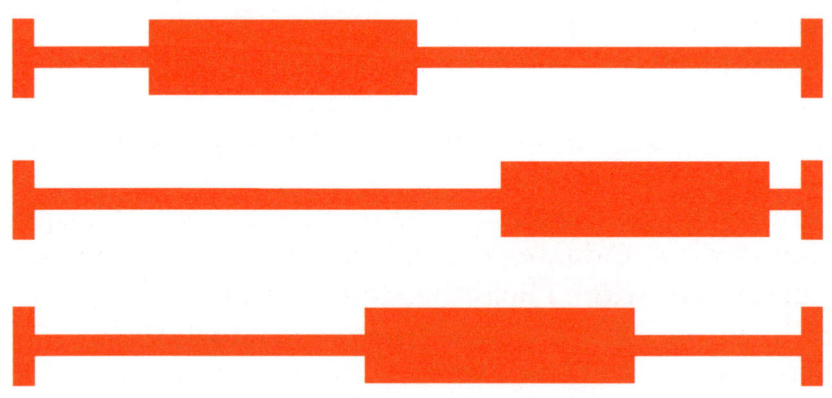

# Bonds and freedom

**A great deal has been written and said about what artists are, by those involved in the art world: policy-makers, educationalists, philosophers and other professionals. Artisthood is blithely classified into types, classifications relating to what an artist could and should do. I cannot do that, nor do I wish to. I lack the theoretical framework, and the diversity of artistic practice invalidates any attempt at external classification. Classifications can only be defined by individual artists themselves; so the variations are infinite. Moreover, such variations are not static–they are dynamic, changing as time passes, with each individual personal artistic development. This chapter deals with artisthood and the way its definition is linked to a number of stereotypes and misunderstandings regarding entrepreneurship and 'autonomy' within the artistic practice. The various sections examine what it means to determine one's own course and allow one's own artisthood to grow–in relative freedom. It ties in with choice and decision-making processes which affect both the internal and the external world. Although the various sections making up this–and subsequent chapters–are connected, they can be read separately.**

# Choice processes: where do I stand and what do I stand for?

*Choosing time and again*

With every important step in your life, you are faced, consciously or unconsciously, with the decision: do I want to take that step? Am I going to devote time, energy, money and other resources, attention, even love to it? What am I investing in my plan, my project, my artistic practice? It takes self-confidence just to dare to ask those questions: where do I want to go, along what path, and what freedom of choice do I actually have?

It proves to be a difficult task for everyone, especially artists, to chart their own course, in terms of work, in choosing one's position and in how to behave towards others with respect to one's own work. Explicit, identifiable choices and, more often, implicit choices which present themselves more or less routinely on a path already taken, merge and overlap.

The word 'strategy' is a term that is used indiscriminately for fundamental life choices as well as—incorrectly—for practical actions which may be organised differently from one day to the next. It is wise to make a distinction, on the one hand between strategy (fundamental and focused on the long term) and, on the other, tactics (incidental and modifiable in the short term). I shall return to that distinction in 'Goals, 25 strategy and tactics'.

To put the importance of charting a course into perspective, many an artist points to the impossibility of 'knowing everything beforehand', the inevitability of 'everything going differently', and the necessity of being receptive to the unexpected and the unpredictable. No choice means you are also making a choice anyway—by not choosing. Your own course plus the flexibility to improvise your reaction are two sides of the same coin: a conscious course offers the possibility to deviate purposively, improvisation provides experiences that simplify the charting of one's own course and the choice itself, in a circular process, with trial and error, is clarified.

In everyday reality, certainly at the start of one's career, the circular process often takes place as follows: choosing by trial and error, taking steps, doing work, gaining experience—alone or with interested parties—reflecting, hesitating, re-orientating, choosing more stringently and once more gaining fresh experiences, and so on.

*Positioning yourself*

Positioning means finding a place for *yourself*, establishing what position or positions you want to take up, what role do you want, where and for whom. It means taking control and not leaving your positioning to others. I first heard the phrase "Where do I stand and what do I stand for?" from the art critic and writer Anna Tilroe, who was attached to the Rijksakademie (research residency) for many years as a theory adviser and senior adviser. It occurs regularly throughout this handbook, as a mantra.

The importance of having a place of one's own is increasing, even inescapable in view of the existing social dynamic. The rapid changes that are relevant to the cultural field include:

– scaling-up: the (comprehensible) village has opened up, thanks partly to digital communication and social media;
– fragmentation: identifiable social and cultural configurations are crumbling and new ones are emerging;
– variety: 'everything's possible' and coexistent, and that also applies—despite all the hiccups and counter-movements—to multicultural variation;
– internationalisation and globalisation: boundaries are crossed, cultures and economies mix;
– turbulence: the pace and scope of changes are increasing exponentially;
– individualisation has increased considerably, though there is now a counter-movement, to recognise and develop sharing.

In the art world the phenomena of unrest, expansion and change certainly also occur: galleries come and go, there are more museums than ever, more different types of presentation venue, shrinking and swelling flows of funds, emergence of new media, and old media under strain (art magazines, for example), greater diversity of viewers and buyers, and greater numbers of viewers and buyers.

And those are the phenomena with which the western world is familiar. The need to find a place of your own—even if it is on the quiet, in your own mind—is highly relevant in culturally, socially, economically and politically constricted circumstances, under extreme, externally coercive and sometimes abominable conditions, terror of dictatorial regimes.

The artist's existence as an attitude to life requires him to set his course. Once done, further choices can be made to structure his own practice—inside, or conversely, as an 'experiment' and learning experience, outside the parameters of that course. As we have seen, direction and choices are part and parcel of one's own character. In the mould of childhood and growth in adolescence, in experiences you dared to undergo or fled from, in knowledge that made a lasting impact because it touched you. You can examine a vast number of possibilities, across the entire spectrum, think about them and weigh them up. But choices should not clash with your own nature and unique characteristics, they must be complementary. In other words: 'know who you are' and 'stay true to yourself'.

### *Freedom of choice*

The question to what extent a person is free to choose, whenever, wherever, is a philosophical one. That is not my point of departure. I focus on factors which can augment freedom of choice, six of which I shall specify.

– Set *priorities* and you are practising 'energy management', do not devote too often and too much time, energy, money on activities that contribute too little to the path your wish to pursue.

– Enhance (throughout your life) your *self-insight*, you can avoid some pitfalls. For example, self-insight as regards your origins and background, and what it means. And your strengths and weaknesses, especially your dependence on appreciation from outside (is success important?), as well as the desire and ability to be alone, or actually with others.
– *Recognise your habitus* as regards working along protracted, consistent lines or with an alternating, varied pattern; the need for a one-track focus or the need for a multiple-track approach to work, with differing, juxtaposed stimuli.
– Be aware of your *sense of direction and ability to improvise*, that makes for self-confidence—feet on familiar ground and curiosity about unfamiliar ground—helps you in choosing from what you already expect and, at the same time, alertness about the unexpected; be receptive to the unexpected. Tolerate uncertainties.
– *Deflate stereotypes*—in the art world (including that of art education) and beyond—this enhances the individual artist's freedom of choice. Debunk in order to remove inhibiting codes.
– Step back (temporarily)—step outside the social order or spend some time abroad—that creates *mental space*.

Let me amplify a little on the last point. Temporary withdrawal is not only important in expanding your personal, mental space, but also on a larger scale, creating space for innovative approaches in the visual arts. The more you are part of 'the system', the more troublesome changes or innovations in it will be. It is simpler in abutting situations, for example between visual art and other art-related disciplines, between visual art and social action, and between visual art and science. Perhaps it is better first to switch to an 'external area' in order to intervene in the visual arts field. It can also be helpful, when operating within national art circles to have a change of scenery, geographically: after a stay abroad, return home (with a fresh perspective and a reputation established abroad). Leave, in order to return.

The scope of freedom of choice is not limitless, but is formed by one's career and life experience, starting with personal origins (in the way I expose my own in the final chapter), prevailing views within one's own family concerning the dictates of government or religion, money and its importance, interaction with 'bosses' or patrons, and work ethic. You need an awareness of inner motives, such as 'desire to belong', 'desire to be' and 'desire to prove something'. So freedom of choice depends partially on the courage and ability to create space for yourself and for others, to stimulate change and innovation.

*No artistic practice without collaboration*

Other than the choices you make on your own regarding the energy, attention and resources you invest in developing your own practice, choices which scarcely involve others, if at all, almost all other choices will concern your relationship with the people around you. No man is an island, and interaction is needed for almost everything, i.e. incidental, short-lived or longer lasting cooperation. For the development of your artistic practice: where and from whom do you want to learn? For a decision on production: do you want to work alone or can you, must you work with others? For a decision on purchases: do you want to risk it with a particular supplier? For a choice about the venue for presenting your work: for whom do you want to be of importance, do you encounter actors or players with whom you have to collaborate to achieve your goal? You need to make a choice with every collaboration, with a fellow artist, gallery owner or principal. Shall we embark on it together? Will we continue, see it through to the end or is it better to stop, even at the last moment, if necessary? The following points need to be addressed every time: does this collaboration constitute enough of an artistic challenge; do you like the people; do you trust them; are the material resources (including budget) more or less sufficient to produce the work, and what is your own recompense—in money, experience, challenge, reputation—compared with the time you spend. Or: is it better to risk getting a bad name because you drop out before the end, or to continue and have an unsatisfactory result, which ultimately is not beneficial either.

In the course of collaboration—at the beginning, midway, just before completion—the focus is on the choice between 'yes' and 'no', or 'yes, provided the plan can be adjusted', or 'no, unless the conditions change'. If you are to avoid having to rethink things every time, it is useful to chart your own path, and in order to follow that path or deviate from it, to bear navigation in mind. Be aware of the direction and degree of deviation, think of vectors indicating, in this case, the direction and speed of deviation. The question as to how the source of inspiration is dealt with bears upon ethical issues, including the misuse of other people's experiences without involving them, and so denying them the chance to make use of the artist's observation for their individual or group-orientated self-reflection. That concerns the artist's personal integrity in his dealings with 'the object'.

146

## Goals, strategy and tactics

Strategy is the direction you take and the essence of your method for achieving a particular goal. The personal strategy is based on your own ideal image as an artist and the route defined for achieving your own artistic goals. It is important, when considering your own strategy, to limit yourself to the cornerstones. The fewer the better, because the 'house' would otherwise finish being bricked up.

The foremost artistic goals I encounter in interviews are:

– I want to be able to continue as an artist;
– I want continue developing my work, and myself;
– I want to exhibit my work and see how it is received;
– I want to know where I stand in the art world and what, in a broader social context, I stand for.

When you look at the personal method deployed when creating work, you encounter essential differences, between working alone (preferably in one's own studio) and, in particular, together (with other artists). And between working quickly and, notably, slowly. Is the focus on short routes or on partial steps in the course of one's life, en route to the ultimate art work. Perhaps the focus is on one track or actually involves several tracks at a time, to 'commute', to derive energy and ideas from one particular track and thus fuel the other. Invariably the step towards presence and presentation is almost an imperceptible continuation of the creative process. Sometimes the artist has an explicit point of view regarding his relationship with the public, for example if the designation does not 'just' stem from the work, but the (public) designation is also the source of the work. I shall address that in more
37 detail in 'Source and designation'. The principal cornerstones as described above have been converted into the following reflection.

***Reflection*. What are your artistic goals, and in what precedence? Do you prefer to work alone or together with others, who are they? Do you favour fast food or slow cooking? Do you need to focus fully on one track or do you favour the multi-track approach? Where and for whom would you prefer to show your work? Is it important to have an intermediary between you and your public, in other words: do you prefer to avoid direct contact with viewers and buyers, do you have no objections to communicating if required, is it important to you or even absolutely necessary considering the nature of your work and working process?**

### *Metaphor 'in the dunes'*

With respect to artistic goals, personal strategy and tactics, I like to use the metaphor 'in the dunes'.

On the horizon, behind a dune landscape, you can see a lighthouse on the left near a harbour, and, further to the right, the spire of a village church. Your first, initial choice concerns the *artistic goal*: do you want your orientation point to be the harbour and lighthouse or the village with church spire? Imagine you want the lighthouse: there will be various ways to get there, with widely divergent experiences on the way: a walk through the dunes, a bike ride or a car drive. The latter will certainly take you to the lighthouse, but you will not experience a great deal on the way. A walk in the dunes offers a maximum of experiences, but might you not decide, midway—replete from the process en route—to turn round, or switch the goal to the church spire which is now closer than the lighthouse? The cycle ride is somewhere in between.

One could describe the choice to walk, cycle or drive as a strategy decision: the personal strategy is based on one's own ideal image as an artist and on the concomitant charted route, the goal or aspiration and the working process to attain it or, in other words, is one's priority the result, the attainment and / or the process, the path? Your personal strategy is decisive for the way your artistic practice is made up.

If we pursue to this metaphor, the *tactics* are relevant: arranging a car (borrowing from a friend), renting a bike or purchasing some good hiking boots for the walk. In the artistic practice, there are things that need arranging, such as buying materials, collecting information or research, financing and sales. Such matters are covered in training and courses under the heading 'professional preparations', though the fundamental, personal strategic nature of decision-making is disregarded. Tactics can be described as day-to-day activities aimed at achieving the set goals. They take place within the strategic choice and change over time, depending on (changing) circumstances. Tactics are secondary.

A practical example by way of clarification. Only if the art market is approached through a few carefully selected, trustworthy friends—for example, in an artist collective—could this be called a 'friendship strategy'. 'Ordinary' friendly dealings with a gallery owner, art critic or principal, for instance, should be classified as tactical behaviour. One (opting for a specific market approach) really is part of you, the other (being nice) is more part of circumstances, assuming 'being nice' is feasible. The former, strategy, is more fundamental, the latter, tactics, is not as far-reaching and is more inconstant, without being chameleon-like or overtly opportunist. Back to the metaphor: you have opted for the bike ride. Dismounting to shelter from the rain or making haste because time is pressing could be described as tactical behaviour. If you turn round because the cycle path is impassable, and then proceed by car, it amounts (in this simplistic example) to a change of strategy.

A third level of behaviour is frequently mentioned: that of *operational procedure*. Sticking to the metaphor, that means filling up the car and departing, pumping up the bicycle tyres, et cetera.

So there are circumstances, as described in the foregoing, that may mean a different path has to be taken to achieve one's goal. It may also mean that, on the way to the specific goal, it may become less attractive—due to inner necessity or economic factors—and another goal becomes attractive. That will be the new focus of behaviour. So the clarification of your own goal and the path towards it, the personal strategy, need not result in inflexibility. On the contrary, it actually provides the opportunity to make new choices about your course, again and again, rather than moving onward aimlessly, the victim of external forces. It is helpful when determining your own position and deliberately changing it: to take control.

### *Decision-making and mixed scanning*

In line with the 'in the dunes' metaphor, there is a clear, helpful term: 'mixed scanning', conveying working with two perspectives. It means you are heedful of the distant goal, but also of the road towards to it, as well as of the ideal image on the horizon and the opportunities on the way, on the end result you aspire to and the working process.

Choosing and decision-making are the core components of social behaviour. To what degree can you decide your course for yourself, or to what degree is it imposed by forces beyond your control? In 1967 the sociologist Amitai Etzioni (Cologne, 1929) added to two existing decision-making approaches (i.e. 'rationalist' and 'incremental') a third approach: *mixed scanning*. The rationalist model assumes that decision-making—provided you have charted all possible relevant factors—is far-reaching or completely controllable and results in a reliable course. I do not agree. The incremental approach offers an alternative, referred to as 'muddling through', coping step-by-step and seeing where you end up, starting from little or with no control over your course. Neither that model does not much appeal to me. The first approach risks acquiring a whiff of utopia, the second is, inevitably, defensive and cautious. In mixed scanning, Etzioni combines elements from the other two approaches. It brings together two levels of decision-making: the plotting of fundamental directions or goals combined with step-by-step experiences, which are assessed throughout as to their contribution to decision-making. He demonstrates that the flexibility of this third approach is extremely useful in environments of instability, so for the art world. And for people with varying control of circumstances (artists ?). A two-track approach like this, exhibiting several layers and speeds at the same time, recurs throughout this handbook.

## Inhibiting stereotypes: the artist as an entrepreneur

Before constructive assistance can be given for the design, development, prolongation or modification of the artistic practice, several inhibiting stereotypes must be eliminated or at least qualified. They are container terms which are more confusing than clarifying, and so need some qualification. The main obstacle is the term 'autonomous art' and 'the autonomous artist', as found in the following section. But firstly, the misunderstanding that entrepreneurship is identical to business sense. The entrepreneurial artist knows where he stands, and for what, and so possesses 'strategic insight'.

*The entrepreneurial artist is a producer, not a dealer*

As a producer, an artist is an entrepreneur, but not as a distributor. In 1993 I wrote in the Rijksakademie in-house handbook 'Irksome misunderstandings about artisthood and business-orientated entrepreneurship', and it still applies. Obviously an artist needs to know what he or she makes and why: how specific is it in relation to prevailing trends, what is the approximate economic value of the work. He/she must also have good visual, possibly also written, documentation. One's own website has long been a 'must'. But that is about it, as regards business know-how, apart from keeping a record of expenses—just adding and subtracting—to know what things cost and not be cheated when pricing work. The paramount thing is to identify the characteristics of artisthood and determine what position/positions you aspire to as an artist. That will be addressed
51 in the following chapter 'Artists' positions—a large palette'.

*Business know-how and promotion*

Courses are published at regular intervals providing business know-how for artists: bookkeeping, legal know-how, all manner of marketing and communication techniques, how to write an 'artistic CV', and so on. I shudder at the so-called good intentions behind them: such boxes of tricks mainly sell illusions. Artists, sometimes with a minimum wage, hesitant about the quality and reception of their own work, are proffered perspectives beyond the quality of their work—which is misleading.

There are three persistent misunderstandings: that the artist is a seller, that selling techniques help and that there is time for sales promotion. Instrumental knowledge on selling might be useful as an escape route, if you've capitulated as an artist, having sideways mobility to work, designing gardens, organizing festivals or managing a café. But, overly high expectations from handy 'recipes' for running an artistic practice distract from essential matters, such as where you stand and what ambitions you have—they should have priority, whatever kind of entrepreneurship is involved, and similarly, for an artistic practice. Art supply is too high and demand too low—that's just the way the market is. Sales techniques help precious little, if at all, to balance the fundamentally unbalanced market conditions. An attempt to pass off poor work with a well-oiled approach will only give a temporary reprieve. In advertising, too, they realise that a poor product will sell briefly, but not over a longer period. Presentation files and such are certainly not forbidden, but are not a way to sell much more, at least at a mature level. Nor is a website of much help for sales and assignments, though the lack of a website is felt to be unprofessional.

By addressing the business and, in particular, sales aspects, you will not make the work any better. It takes a tremendous amount of attention and time to conceive and create art, alongside looking at it, reading about it and about developments in art. Not to mention keeping up to date on production know-how, such as techniques and equipment. Many artists work their fingers to the bone. Obviously, good documentation and visual material of completed projects are necessary, and testify to respect for one's own work. And of course, a clear plan reflecting the idea, approach and enthusiasm, is indispensable for mobilising others (participants, sponsors, media) for a complex project and its financing. There is no time to play the salesman. The creator has his hands full creating, but is aware—even if only vaguely—of the art world, of the force fields in which he works, and where and for whom he wishes to count. Those aspects are of greater priority than some portfolio or other.

## Inhibiting stereotypes: autonomous and applied art, the stranglehold of autonomy

Autonomous art, like entrepreneurial artist, is a container term: the Autonomous Art department in an art academy and the autonomous artist are seen to be 'different' from a decorative artist. It is worth qualifying the term 'autonomous art'—something I would like to attempt to do, from the practical rather than the theoretical angle.

## OBSERVATION: ARTIST AND DESIGNER

Vijfhuizen Kunstfort, November 2014, a round-table meeting for the project 'Op De Plaats Rust. De kunstenaar als gebiedsverkenner' (At Ease. The artist as a scout). The key question at the meeting: "Is there a difference between designing for public space, social design and engaged art?" The moderator, the design critic Lucas Verweij, spoke with the curator and the exhibitors, and sought valiantly to clarify the possible difference between artist and designer. His efforts to find a deductive, theoretical distinction did not appeal much (if at all) to the exhibiting artists and designers.*

During and immediately following the meeting, I made the following notes, a statement of sorts concerning the importance of a 'personal core', seeking alternatives for the concept of autonomy.

— An ability to interact does not mean you are 'tied' yet. If you do not have a personal core, you cannot interact, or enter into partnerships.
— If you use a sounding-board, you are not yet tied. Without a sound of your own, you have no resonance and cannot deal with sound reflected by the sounding-board.
— Awareness of the context does not tie you. You have the freedom (space) to deal with the context in your own way: by means of confrontation, integration and acceptance, or denial in full awareness of the context.
— You are not tied by a source of inspiration or by use of historical references, because you determine for yourself how to deal with the source, in independence.
— You can opt for collaboration or co-creation; you are not yet tied; the greater your independence, the better you can work with others.
— Interest in social response or use of 'social material' (it's easy enough to resort to the trendy label 'social design'), ability to deploy participation for your work does not tie you either. The deployment of tools from outside the traditional studio and the bearing of responsibility for phenomena in society does not make you lose your autonomy independence.

**— Use of research methods in the creative process–more than looking, listing or accumulating–does not make someone lose his autonomy. The same applies for the use of research methods which can help you guard your autonomy better.**

**Later, in the account on the meeting, I was pleased to read: "The curator, the participants and the public agreed that autonomy was the chief element for a successful project, in the field of art and well as that of design. It is better to listen to the landscape and its inhabitants, and include that information in the development of a project, but, in the end, you must follow your own ideas and fascinations to achieve powerful work."**

* Participating artists Danielle van Vree, Sil Krol, Ronald Boer, Henriette Waal, Neeltje ten Westenend and François Lombarts; curator Iris Dik. The subject of the symposium: What can the specific working method of artists and designers contribute to identity and development of a region, its inhabitants and entrepreneurs? What do context-orientated, temporary projects mean for the development of contemporary art and (social) design?

## *Similarities and differences*

Imagine we compare the production and development process from idea to actual product, with architects, designers or artists working on commission in public space, on invitation at self-selected locations, or working 'autonomously', primarily 'from inside'. There are more similarities than differences in a process extending from starting point, via exploration, transformation from idea to definition, organisational approach and production proper, and culminating in materialisation and sale, Moreover, the contrasts are not static, but dynamic: segregated venues for presentation are integrated, whereas connective financial arrangements from the authorities or funds are demarcated and unravelled.

When all is said and done, the financial parameters and production are the areas with the greatest differences (as yet). During the other stages of development we have so far seen more similarities and interfaces than many would expect.

It is important to realise that for every creative process (design, architecture and art), avoidance of suspense between 'self' and 'the other' is lethal. During my career, I was regularly in a position to act as a principal for designers, documentary makers and architects. As (potential) commissioned parties, they committed themselves to my brief, did not internalise independently (familiarise themselves with the subject), transformed the matter in question in accordance with their personal or a shared syntax, and not visualised from an autonomous position. If that were the case, collaboration would not take place or I would cut it short.

Is terminology 'autonomous versus applied' unavoidable because it features in international jargon? On the contrary—there is, for instance, a clearer distinction in the Dutch language between the two than in any other language. Yet in English-speaking countries, the word 'artist' covers a wider range of artists, designers and other creative people working in what we in the Netherlands could call 'fringe areas'.

*What is autonomy?*

As I was reflecting on similarities and differences between autonomous and applied work—and with the reminiscences of a patron of architecture and design commissions as well notes on the Fort Vijfhuizen project in my pocket—I felt the need to review existing definitions of autonomy. I have made a selection from 21 descriptions.

"In general, the term autonomy implies self-reliance and independence. It is used with respect to livability in the sense of structuring and giving substance to life; *orchestrating* day-to-day events *yourself*." "An autonomous person attempts to pursue things that are of importance or value for him or her, and in that way to follow his own path through life." "Autonomous people look critically at themselves and others, and determine what they consider to be good or bad, useful or useless. To think about and question such matters is part of autonomy. In that way it can be possible eventually to follow your own path of life." In private law "the principle of autonomy expresses that legal persons (must) be able to promote their own interests in *accordance with their individual preferences*". And another selection: "*right* to decide for yourself what you do"; "*independence* from an authority"; "a patient's *self-determination*; self-reliance, i.e. the ability to perform general, daily activities … independently, for example, grooming, feeding, dealing with money—for oneself"; "*self-management*, the liberty or competence to act or operate for oneself"; "*self-reliance* and *independence*".

Interestingly: the concept of autonomy occurs in political, technological, philosophical, medical, moral and psychological contexts, but is not mentioned in the general list in Wikipedia (May 2016) in relation to art. Yet the word is ubiquitous in that field: autonomous art, department of autonomous arts, autonomous artist.

Incidentally, the term 'autonomy' reinforces the myth surrounding the artist, something that is certainly useful in situations of potential admiration for art and artists. A lack of exact understanding of what takes place in art and what the artist does contributes to 'owning one's own ground' for the artist. That 'line of defence' proves to be too weak and cannot stand up to the populist claim "Give me a life like that, so much freedom and money to boot." In June 2011 the shit hit the fan in the Netherlands. Draconian government cutbacks generated downright intolerance vis-à-vis culture. Autonomy no longer constitutes an anchor in that culture war. And perhaps it is a good thing, because if 'autonomy' is appropriated as a distinguishing feature of art, it increases art's 'untouchability', making it taboo for 'outsiders' and leading to segregation rather than integration, creating distance between artists and non-artists in society, between the Autonomous and Applied Art departments in education, and between art and creative industry funds.

### *Autonomous thought, the personal core*

According to one of the definitions of autonomy, the term is suited to expressing a degree of self-reliance and independence: "for all those who wish to chart their own path of life, for instance by promoting their own interests in accordance with their individual preferences". That applies in all areas and for all human actions.

In ancient Greek, 'autos' means 'self' and 'nomos' means law; so along the lines of 'setting your own norms', with personal authenticity uniting unequivocally with social conduct. The term 'distinctiveness' also recurs, as something you may or may not share with others, or that is jeopardised by external circumstances. I like the fact that I am unable to define properly something so essential—affecting identity—that it is situated in a 'black box'; is something you must tend carefully, must nurture, acknowledge and protect. Without exactly knowing what it is.

Advice: replace autonomy as often as possible with 'personal core' and 'knowing where you stand and what you stand for'. No-one is entirely independent and completely self-reliant; autonomy is an important, but relative term. Autonomy is worth striving for, even if the beckoning horizon will always be out of reach. I would prefer to ban the terms autonomous artist and autonomous art, and only associate autonomy with an inner, personal core quality: autonomous thinking.



## Source and designation

As an artist, what is your place in the work process? Where do your stimuli come from? If they are on the inside, how did they get there, so: what are their origins and frame of reference? And if they come from the outside, how do you appropriate those stimuli and transform them, operating self-sufficiently and as an 'independent spirit'?

A few tips for determining your sources and dealing with them:

*Observation*. How curious are you? What do you look for, what are your sources? Does 'everything' stem from yourself (internal orientation, self-determined questions), with no identifiable origin, or are there external sources beyond 'me, myself and I' which inspire, stimulate or galvanise you? To what extent do you heed them, do you have a narrow or a wide outlook? You can observe nature or buildings in the city because it makes you feel good, or connect with them and worry about them. A self-portrait cannot, to my mind, be pure self-expression, a distance is created, you become someone else, who confronts you with yourself. You can also look further, at a child or an adult whom you portray in paint or film images, at relaxed or tense interaction between people on a terrace or within an organisation, at social phenomena if you are affected by economic, political, religious or social subjects and events. Do entirely unengaged artists actually exist, I wonder.

*Meaning*. Are they obvious facts or are they concealed behind a smoke screen, does meaning stem primarily from the external world or from your own internal world? I see artists as 'specialists' in identifying meaning, in transforming and attributing it, generally in visual form. For example, in a portrait revealing a characteristic of a child previously unnoticed by its parents, or else a compelling confrontation with a hidden political reality, and all manner of meanings in between. Artists can be aware of that meaning from the start, sometimes they merely suspect there is ‘something’ important and the meaning may only reveal itself after a time, even for the artist himself.

*Internalisation.* If observations, external signals or assignments from the external world (external orientation) are the inspiration, how do you adopt them, as a self-reliant individual? I was repeatedly faced with more profound questions about creative processes, authenticity and autonomous and applied work when I noted how artists, art students, teachers and critics
34 grappled with the dichotomy between *autonomous and applied work*. One way to resolve it is to examine whether the stimulus stems primarily ‘from inside’, or is mainly catalysed once the problem is defined through an assignment.

*Transformation.* The creative process has many perspectives. Including one relating to communication: what material form will your artisthood take? Are you a painter, sculptor, photographer or performer? Also, in what context does your work fit: is it a museum piece, work with a social dimension in public space, social intervention, work combining art, science and technology, and so on. The wide or narrow scope of artisthood is examined in more detail at the end of this chapter in ‘Defining
43 artisthood: the divided or undivided artistic existence’.

*Presence and presentation.* Whom are you targeting, who is your audience? At what kind of venues do you want to show your work, do you want to showcase it? In one or more positions as an artist, a broad or a narrow artistic practice? What do you want to say? What relationship comes about with your audience?

Substantive correlation between work and audience relates to the surroundings as a source, as a designation, or both. The relation between work and designation, or both, has a substantive side which also affects the material aspect (i.e. income). Do you want a narrow or a broad market approach, and in what market?

*Origin and offer*

Obviously the aspects of presence and presentation recur in this publication about the way artists position themselves, for instance when, from diverse positions, they operate in differing market settings while seeking to influence the market. In anticipation of more business-related remarks, this section first reflects on the substantive-specific correlation between source and designation. Broadly speaking, we can differentiate between mainly intrinsic and mainly extrinsic sources. In practice, a clear-cut distinction rarely exists. Intrinsic sources include personal characteristics, such as curiosity, the ability to deal with uncertainty, and fascinations (later termed facets of artisthood) which are formed in and by one's personal background. Curiosity (about what?) and fascinations (which?) right away bear upon extrinsic sources and you are dealing with circumstances in which you find or found yourself. A direct circumstance of that type is the commissioning situation, although there might also, in a less linear frame, be an external cause, such as contextual inspiration.

There are artists who employ economic matters like market, money, stock exchange and communication as central themes in their work, which often counts as social engagement. Then the economic themes are the source, but not necessarily the field of intervention: the art work is not by definition intended to be returned to the world of money, barter, et cetera. It may have different designations—just think of museums, collectors, biennials. In that respect we can pinpoint several patterns of interaction with source and designation: people in a community do form a source for the art work, but are not informed, do not know about it, unless they happen to walk into an exhibition and recognise themselves. Or: people form the source and are informed, some way or another. Or: people in a community form the source and the art work is shared with that community, sometimes they are involved in a longer-term programme. Or: the designation (museum) is foremost, the people, as a source, secondary.

The question concerning how the source of inspiration is dealt with bears upon ethical matters, such as right to use others' experiences without involving them, and therefore denying them the opportunity to make use of the artist's observation for their individual or group-orientated self-reflection. That relates to the artist's personal integrity in his dealings with 'the object'.

So something can be 'returned' to the community from which inspiration has been derived (I), or handed to art institutes, like a museum, collector or biennial (II), or to both (III). This diagram illustrates three patterns:

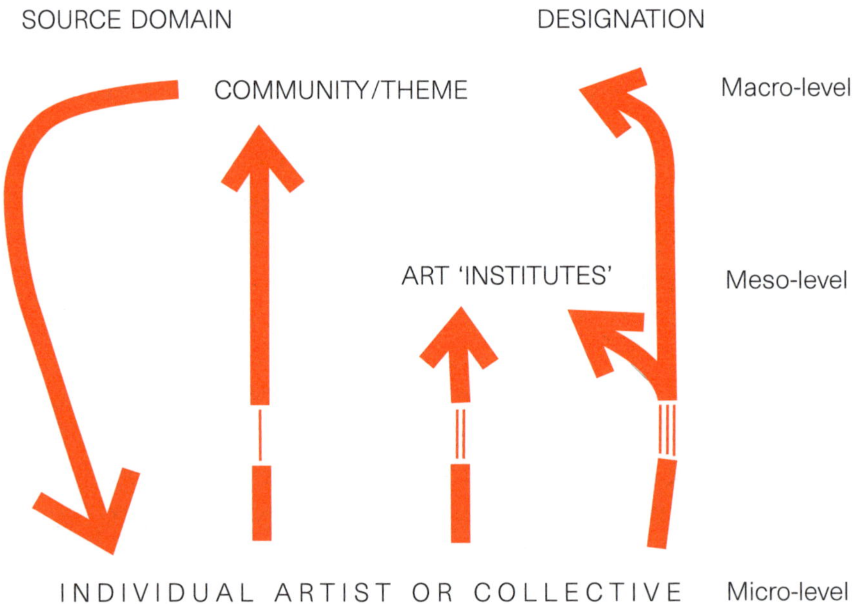


*Figure 1.* Source and designation

The micro-level relates to the individual, the meso-level to groups, often in organisations, and the macro-level (social) to themes in larger configurations.

***Reflection*. Can your sources be identified, where are they situated? How do they tie in with the designation of your work? Is there a connection between origin (source) and designation? Is one of the three illustrated routes applicable?**

The question being: how do you present yourself? As an artist in a studio, artist in public space, artist in a laboratory or otherwise? These and other artist's position (eleven altogether) are elaborated on in Chapter 2 'Artists' positions—a large palette'. 50

*Venues for presentation*

There are some very varied venues where work can be presented: in the studio, in a gallery, in a project space, a presentation facility or museum, in situ, in public space (buildings, cities, landscape) and so on.

Each has its own characteristics and to some extent provides inspiration. Here, as a start, I will concentrate on narrowing it down to the commercial aspect, saleability. It is important to consider the relationship between the work and the place/places where, and the public to whom the work is sold. There are of course many possibilities which you can just allow to 'happen' to you, but the point here is to pay more attention to the place where you would like your work to be seen, and to stay away carefully from places you would definitely rather avoid. The idea that work always—by some mysterious, obscure process—forms its own audience, is not one I adhere to. It does not only take a long time to reach the desired destination, but then you are very much at the mercy of mechanisms outside yourself, and you are obliged to go more with the flow than desirable. Naturally, there is (or will be) only an audience for good work; good work sometimes produces 'new loves' among 'insiders' as well as people who have not long been in contact with the (visual) arts. This text focuses on the extremes in the relationship between content and location, in both a positive and a negative sense; as we go along, the subtle distinctions will become clear.

The tension between internal and external world is most significant in commercial places and less in locations suited to the artist, such as art or project venues. It is possible to single out some very different types of relationship between work and commercial presentation venue:

1. With your work do you look for or are you amenable to venues that are relatively relevant to your work? Work, the internal world, comes first, and the venue, the outer world is its almost logical consequence.
2. If you base yourself on the sales location and the purchasing public it can affect the work, consciously or unconsciously. The thought that it might be the case, produces resistance from many artists; others may well characterise them as conformist followers. There are three kinds of effect from the external world:

   – influence on the artist caused by the nature of the sale location, meaning that the content of his work ties in absolutely with what is on offer because it does well commercially;
   – the artist provides a commentary on what can be seen by quoting or copying what is on offer, including sampling (intellectual imitation);
   – or the artist, by looking at and encountering a particular audience is indeed inspired to explore fresh paths and integrate them in his own work, without caving in.

3. You have ambitions regarding a certain presentation venue, but your work is not readily accepted there, yet it is where you want to be. It is important to be aware of the road/detour you have to take to achieve your goal. You probably need colleagues and intermediaries to help you break down resistance. You should not expect to earn a fast buck from work displayed at that venue—in view of the detour; time and patience are important.

4. And consequently one could add another type of relationship, in which the work comes first and the sales location is created by the artist himself. He influences the market himself via Instagram or creates places for selling work, on his own or with colleagues. Social media are ideal for sharing updates on the making and presentation of an artwork; thus being in control, establishing your own market.

***Reflection*. Which of the described relationships between your work and a sales location have occurred, when, under what circumstances and for how long? What happened then? Tell yourself about your pragmatism and opportunism, no-one's watching or listening.**

The advantage of an analytical, by definition detached approach is that it enables you to address a certain subject longer and acquire more insight before arriving at a subjective, emotional assessment and classifying normatively into good or bad. This entails three, possibly four patterns of thought: the location stems from the work, you must travel a long road to the aspired location and/or the location prompts adjustments in the work. It is vital to take a personal stance. It determines the experiences to which you expose yourself and the kind of experiences to which you shut yourself off. It also determines the risks you are prepared to take, in a material sense. And it is a good thing to know that about yourself. The ways to tie in with presentation venues and to avoid undesired situations as much as possible are a leitmotif in this publication.

## Defining artisthood: divided or undivided artistic existence

Divided or undivided existence. In an *undivided* existence/living, it is all about 'artisthood', making the work, income from the artistic profession and the ensuing business relationships. In a *divided* existence, there is often another source of income outside the artistic profession which enables the artist to pursue his profession. The terms divided and undivided are decidedly relative. If your own artisthood is defined very narrowly, for example: only work emanating from yourself, involving no question or comment from another and for which no-one ever has to help you in a practical sense—then you will often need to do something in addition in order to survive. That is referred to as divided existence. When artisthood is more widely defined, 'divided existence' is less applicable. For instance if, alongside your autonomous work, there are assignments that fit in with your existence as an applied artist. Or: alongside the autonomous work, advertising or illustration assignments form an essential part of your artisthood, since you derive important artistic incentives from such applied art—so quite apart from the concomitant earnings. Or: alongside the creation of art, teaching is of essential importance for your work, because you encounter new ideas and come up against yourself—again, quite apart from the concomitant earnings. The different professional aspects belong together, income is generated primarily in the broad personal domain and the necessity for other work as a source of income decreases.

### *Chances and risks*

Continuing in the vein of what has been said about the internal and the external world, and autonomous and applied art, we inevitably come back to the tug-of-war between artistic motives, which you could call internal orientation, and economic motives, which are more likely to occur with external orientation. With *internal orientation*, your own artistic (as well as technical) quality requirements are what count. Your own development as an artist is the chief motive. In commercial terms, the aim, where necessary, is 'minimisation of loss': how can you pay maximum attention to your own artistic ideas without losing too much time or money. With external orientation there is an encounter with location, problem definition and functional requirements (durability, vandalism-proof, etc.). In commercial terms, *external orientation* coincides with expediting the preconditions of time and money as favourably as possible. Consider profit maximisation and then see if sufficient artistic scope can be obtained and maintained within the set or acquired preconditions.

There is a potential risk with broadly defined artisthood, because the different forms of expression hamper 'consistency': coherence—for the artist himself and for the spectator—is lost. Such a wide range of activities requires from the artist the ability to shift—between concentrating on his own ideas and listening to others' functional requirements, and then 'appropriating' them. The broad definition also requires a great capacity to integrate the various forms of expression in one central artistic movement. With a narrow definition it is clearer, a cohesive picture is more likely to emerge, for the artist himself and for the spectator. With a narrow practice, judgement on quality will be passed faster and more mercilessly, and in economic terms, it is 'make or break', 'all or nothing'.

A diagram showing the interfaces between artistic 'specialisation' and economic vulnerability enables you to identify your own existing or preferred position. The search is also undeniably influenced by economic factors. If you recognise those factors and incorporate them in your personal choices, economic pressure will take you less by surprise, you can decide for yourself the scope you need to create and maintain for optimum room for the artistic process.

| | Narrow definition artisthood | Broad definition artisthood |
|---|---|---|
| Undivided existence | Very specific position, great economic vulnerability, **all-or-nothing position** | Specific position possible, watch out for 'blurring' **unforeseen economic vulnerability** |
| Divided existence | Specific position as artist, also 'non-art' income, **to reduce economic vulnerability** | Relative great risk of 'blurring', little economic vulnerability but also **risk of 'keeping too many balls in the air'** |

*Figure 2.* Chances and risks

These positions are not static: you can choose temporarily for a somewhat broader definition of artisthood because you can gain much experience from it and it provides you with inspiration. You can opt for a divided existence, because this reduces the risk of artist's block due to over-concentration on your work. Or from economic necessity, and then later decide on an undivided existence. That positioning is influenced by a personal need for concentration or, rather, for several, varied stimuli, including a feeling of attachment to the (social) surroundings and the economic necessity to obtain income. In practice, such positioning always entails mixed forms. Hardly anyone fits completely and lastingly in one 'pigeonhole'; these are dynamic conceptual models.

*Breadth of the artistic practice*

In anticipation of facets of artisthood, artists' positions and art markets in the coming chapters, as we have seen there are a variety of possible perspectives from which to consider the breadth of your artistic practice, including:

– breadth of 'the sources': input regarding origins, education, inspiration and fascination;
– breadth of 'making': the work process in terms of disciplines, methods, collaboration et cetera;
– breadth of 'presentation': the art work and the market environment in which the work will be seen, what position is the starting point of action, and the relationship between presentation and the economic necessity to generate sufficient income. I shall deal with the latter aspect briefly here.

*Involuntary breadth* resulting from economic pressure to my mind entails three forms of 'broadening'. These are not artistic 'outlets' but financial 'inlets', i.e.

– more forms of artistic expression than considered desirable for an 'autonomous artist';

– activities outside 'art' which do stem from personal competences or skills for artisthood, as developed in art education (and elsewhere), and
– activities apart from personal competences which, because of material recompense, can contribute to an artist continuing to function as such.

*Voluntary breadth* based on artistic considerations and breadth based on collaboration with friends and colleagues relate to a range of activities in which income plays a 'subordinate role'. This should be qualified because activities which originally came about from economic urgency can be artistically 'beneficial'. Some examples:

– earned income makes it possible for you to work in your studio, with less external dependence on the art market which does not yet translate into hard cash;
– apart from earning income, routine activities like postal deliveries or production on a serial basis, give you time to think about work as an artist;
– jobs in the hotel and catering sector, for example, can also be a source of light-weight social connections, counteracting 'artistic isolation' in the studio, or forming a source for observation and inspiration for work in the studio;
– assistance (paid) in the art sector (hauling, transport, odd jobs), for a gallery or for an artist, is also a possibility, but not usually very popular as initial enthusiasm wanes. In the longer term a working environment of that type conflicts with the artist's own artistic ambitions and there may well be annoyance about payment ("Such work will look good on your CV"). However, in friendly situations (among colleagues) (unpaid, non-authoritarian) such activity is not a problem.

In 'Verborgen traditie in de dataroom' (Hidden tradition in the data room) (*De Witte Raaf* 179, January–February 2016) Hermann Pitz gives a fine illustration of components of artisthood that often emerge at a later stage. He was writing about thinking spatially after having helped construct film sets—for a living: "(…) the material necessity that pushed me towards jobs outside art, has in retrospect been productive, because it introduced me to contexts with which I was not familiar. The fact that temporary film sets only had to be used for one day of filming also encouraged me to develop interventions of a temporary nature in space."

***Reflection*. Describe how broad your artisthood is. What part is voluntary, what involuntary? Could involuntary breadth supply a positive experience? Give an example from your own practice. What in your case, are possible disadvantages of voluntary breadth?**

A broad definition of artisthood is more likely to result in an undivided artistic practice than a narrow definition. Breadth can be achieved by integrating several facets of artisthood within the artistic practice, and they will be dealt with in the next chapter. Integration can be achieved by avoiding a sharp dividing line between 'autonomous' and 'applied', and then being receptive to peripheral activities which provide inspiration: people-watching, experiencing events, exposing yourself to different political, social and religious views. Or even—admittedly, in moderation and not for ever—to activities completely outside the realm of art, because they can contribute to artisthood, as breathing space, variety or source of income for 'a higher goal'. The definition of the breadth of your own artisthood is strictly personal, nothing could be more individual.

*As you bear your goals in mind, alternative routes or strategies will unfold, between origins and destination. You are a 'maker' with a narrow or broader artistic practice. It does not matter if everything stems from yourself or there are precipitating factors from outside – you think autonomously.*

# 2

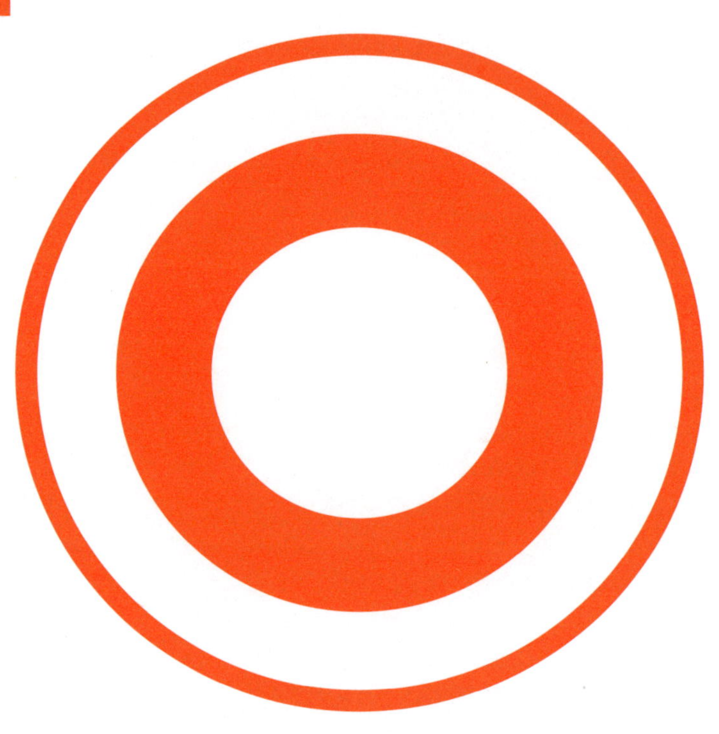

# Artists' positions– a large palette

This chapter describes the artist's positions. They indicate how the artist presents himself in public. In the 'interior landscape' of the studio, it is evident that prior to his presentation in public, an artist has interests and fascinations, which I differentiate from the various positions in the artistic practice. I call them 'facets' of artisthood, which I discuss prior to the artists' positions. In fact, many artists prove to have one or more physical studios, but all also have a mental atelier which they take with them in their mind.

Eleven artists' positions are dealt with, in conjunction with facets of artisthood: in the studio, in public space, in the laboratory, on stage, as a designer, as a writer, as a curator, as an organiser, as an adviser, as an educator and as a change agent. Some are addressed in relatively more detail because they are positions which–alongside that in the studio–occur frequently in practice, are useful for artists and are undervalued in art circles, by artists themselves and in art education. These positions are: the artist in public space, the position as an educator and the artist as a change agent. The latter is a relatively new phenomenon, at least in the West. An artistic practice can incorporate several positions at the same time.

# Exploration: signals from the studio

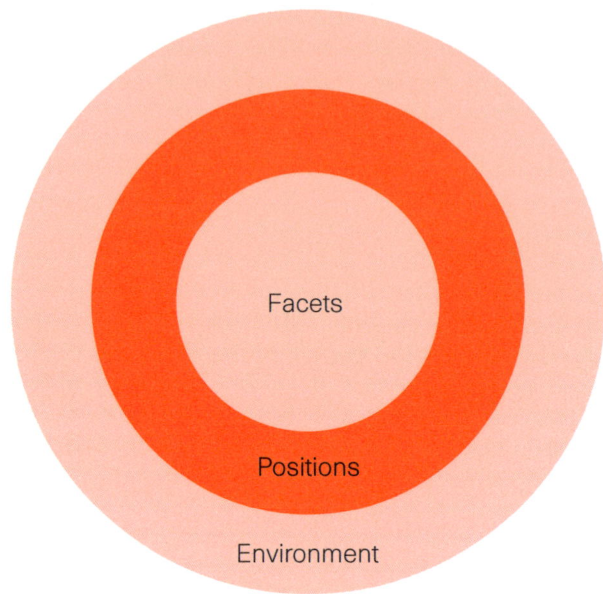


*Figure 3.* (Facets) Positions (Environment)

The information discussed in this chapter is based largely on an 'exploration' I held among artists I know from the Rijksakademie. I put the various artists' positions to them, asking them to indicate to what extent they were part of their individual artistic practice, as well as asking about the importance of and reason for each position within their own practice. The exploration is explained further in Chapter 10,
268 'Acknowledgements'.

My findings are based on responses from 33 artists from all over the world, namely: Narda Alvarado, Carlos Amorales, Tiong Ang, Mark Boulos, Olga Chernysheva, Martha Colburn, Sean Dower, Claudia Fontes, Meschac Gaba, Dora Garcia Lopez, Hans van Houwelingen, Paul Klemann, Jean Bernard Koeman, Meiro Koizumi, Cees Krijnen, Germaine Kruip, Alexandra Leykauf, Jacco Olivier, Esther Polak/Ivar van Bekkum, Michael Raedecker, Mathilde Rosier, Mounira Al Solh, Viviane Sassen, Praneet Soi, Berend Strik, Esther Tielemans, Helen Verhoeven, Maria Verstappen/Erwin Driessens, Roy Villevoye, Kan Xuan, Sylvie Zijlmans. (Eight of these artists—plus another fourteen—

will return in the 22 brief practice descriptions in 'The integrated practice'.)

Patterns of development in the practices could be traced based on the artists' explanations and by way of their work and its presentation which, in turn, are based on a deeper level—that of the above-mentioned facets of artisthood, which I shall first discuss before addressing the various positions in more detail.

## Facets of artisthood

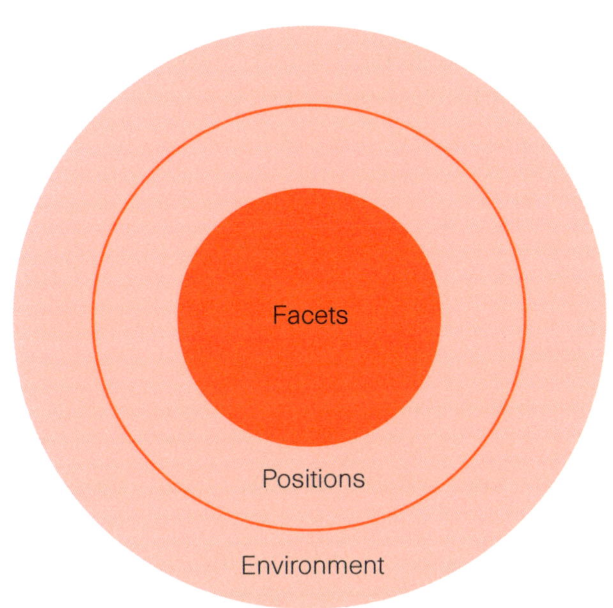


*Figure 4.* Facets (Positions) (Environment)

The starting point when considering a classification of the artistic practice that is accessible and useful for artists was the variety of positions. In the second instance, I wanted—in view of the distinction between external and internal world—to examine intrinsic motives in more detail. They are what I term 'facets' and are aspects of an individual artist's personal artisthood, like interests, inspirations and fascinations which need not 'materialise' in the outside world. With each of the eleven positions which will be dealt with extensively later,

I looked for the salient terms: facets. I describe them below with key words. It is more important to have insight into the breadth and variety in artisthood than to dig deeper into each facet. Not depth, but breadth.

Facets of artisthood and artists' positions are closely linked, the internal world and the external world cannot be sharply demarcated and I interchange those terms, sometimes with a little more emphasis on personal sources and sometimes highlighting self-presentation.

An artist 'in the studio' makes a painting, sculpture, drawing, print or photo. The object leaves the studio (or stays there). That facet of artisthood will henceforward be called *object orientation*.

An artist 'in public space' creates work there—usually in a physical environment, though possibly also in the media field (including digital media)—and also encounters technical and economic demands, and above all, the public or social dimension: the people who are involved directly or indirectly, delegated to commissioning committees via politics or via participation. The facet of the *social dimension of the object*.

An artist—the same one or another—'in the laboratory' develops work at the crossroads of art and science, often technology and sometimes 'nature'. Then, artisthood relates to the facet of *process methodology*, in relation to other disciplines.

An artist 'on stage' with a theatre, film, dance or music background makes art works, or a visual artist with an interest in the world of the theatre works in the performative domain, a form of artistic production and reception on a presentation stage. Here, the key focus is the creative and design processes, so *performativity* as action—something that is done rather than seen.*

An artist 'as a designer' is drawn to finding new solutions within the possibilities and limitation of ergonomics (usage features), economic (costs and benefits), technology (feasibility) and social aspects (social significance). Functionality is embraced (integration), examined critically (confrontation) or consciously set aside (negation). This artist thrives with multi-dimensionality, dealing with the *complexity of the assignment*,

* Quote from Nirav Christophe, Lector Performative Creative Processes at the University of the Arts Utrecht (HKU).

an all-round project or something you can call a design. When you have to take many or a great many factors into account, it inspires you; modulation and abolition of obstacles to achieve the essence forms 'the challenge of limitation'.

Many artists have two or more disciplinary strings to their bow. Combinations of musician and artist, architect and artist and so on are not unusual. The combination of 'visual artist-writer' not only occurs frequently, but also has strong public and professional resonance, from the worlds of both the *image* and the *word*.

There are artists who, possibly deploying their own work, are interested in and search for *connectedness between art works (and/or between artists)*, by developing ideas for presenting work and reflecting on it, varying from exhibitions to art-historical, art-critical or philosophical research and dissemination of its results: the artist 'as a curator'.

There are artists who know what artisthood is and demands, and who wish to create *conditions* for other artists (sometimes for themselves as well), by creating and maintaining platforms or other organisational bodies at a meso-level: the artist 'as an organiser'.

There are also artists who turn their specialism for discovering meanings, internalising and transforming them, not only into visual work, but also to giving *assistance* at a micro- and meso-level—to other artists and/or organisations, whom they advise: the artist 'as an adviser'.

Many artists—actually all of them—'transfer'. They share their insights, experience, unconventional outlook, know-how, revelations. They do that in the art work itself, without words, in explanations accompanying their own work and that of others; in the studio, an institute, neighbourhood, the street. The facet of *transference*: the artist 'as an educator'.

In addition, there are artists who deploy their critical outlooks on community (communities), their specialism for finding meaning and their representational skills—at a macro-level—for concrete *social interventions in the community*: the artist 'as a change agent'.

In discussions about positioning, other aspects of artisthood emerge, which I do not want to classify as individual facets or attribute to one position. Think of theory formulation as a 'theoretician', research as a 'researcher', innovation as an 'innovator' and change as an 'activist or missionary'. They occur with almost all facets and positions—in some positions they are evident, in others they are concealed. They are inherent in artisthood: everyone is actually an innovator or a researcher, one more so than the other. Other of these generic aspects are for example, enterprise as an 'entrepreneur', reflection and consideration as a 'philosopher'.

| |
|---|
| OBJECT |
| SOCIAL DIMENSION OF OBJECT |
| PROCESS METHODOLOGY |
| PERFORMATIVE |
| COMPLEXITY |
| IMAGE AND WORD |
| CONNECTEDNESS |
| CREATING CONDITIONS |
| EXPERIENCED ASSISTANCE |
| TRANSFERENCE |
| SOCIAL INTERVENTION |

*Figure 5.* Facets of artisthood

***Reflection*. Can you make some kind of 'patch plan' of your artisthood using these facets or fields of interest? Large or small patches, dark or light, possibly coloured patches, and especially their place relative one to the other. Do they touch or overlap?**

*Dynamic patterns*

At the start of a professional practice we often note concentration on one facet, generally 'the object'. That is partly due to a fixation in art education on 'the art work'. Invariably a person's life prior to attending an art academy is not taken into account although a variety of facets had played a part, such as with others—making music, organising projects, performing on stage. You could describe this as 'short runway take-off'. Extra-curricular activities when studying are not considered to be constructive for personal artisthood. You might say it is a form of 'narrow tunnel constriction'. In almost every artist's career, the number of facets will increase sooner or later, two, three of more, and have a different interpretation, depending on the artist. Just as one's personality is formed during one's life, the facets that were present at the start may shrivel, while tiny seeds grow into important facets. The positions you take depend on the facets you activate within your artisthood. The point is, they must be activated: facets with which you have become relatively familiar, facets which are not unknown to you, but of which you were not aware that they too could belong to artisthood, as well as facets which you had not yet identified, but, looking back, (over your life, including background, childhood, activities and hobbies) prove to form essential components within your artisthood.

The exploration among 33 artists I mentioned earlier 52
revealed the general tendency for artisthood to become broader as other facets received attention step-by-step from the studio, and other positions were developed within the artistic practice. For almost all the respondents the facet of 'transference' is part of artisthood: artist talks, seminars, lectures, discussion platforms, activities for children, meetings in one's own studio, but generally also as a lecturer or (senior) tutor or visiting lecturer in art education (Higher Vocational Education or University). That is not surprising, earlier in this publication I stated that most artists are educators by nature— 55
on account of their specialism to discover and attribute meanings—also in the art work, purely with images. 37

As is the case with many of the phenomena dealt with in this book, these patterns are not static either. As Sean Dower puts it: 'I have moved between these categories over time, perhaps due to available opportunities and personal inclination.'

Fascination for the facet of process methodology can swell and fuel one of today's increasingly important artistic positions 'in the laboratory', at the crossroads of art, science and technology.

### *Motives*

We can differentiate roughly between three motives for (re-) positioning: artistic considerations, friendship or economic considerations. *Financial motives* (spread of sources of income) will often be the trigger to broaden the practice. That broadening goes on to become an artistically indispensable component, for example in fulfilling the 'transference' facet as such, and its resonance on other facets. Positions outside the studio may be far removed from the 'in the studio' position, or else closer to it. With assignments in public space, the financial aspect is often an important reason, but before long the facet of 'social dimension of the object' becomes a major part of the artistic habitus.

In many cases the step 'out of the studio' to the position of educator—which almost all respondents took—begins with a financial motive, after which, as a source of inspiration and energy, it becomes part of the artistic habitus. In the art world, they prefer not to talk about establishing those two positions (in the studio and as an educator). When the artist as an adviser is the focus, the financial motive is nearly always dominant, regularly supplemented with one that is peer- or friend-related; in exceptional cases that facet is linked closely with the artistic habitus.

*Collaboration with fellow artists and friendship* as a motive prompting the development of other positions in the range, figures with many facets. For some artists, the peer or friendship dimension (combined with the artistic dimension) is ›60

## ADVISER, ORGANISER, CHANGE AGENT

"I have been working with Tokyo University where scholars, PhD students are looking for the meeting point between art and science" (Meiro Koizumi). And: "I'm developing projects dealing with animal behaviour and self-organisation that involves scientists at Sussex University" (Claudia Fontes). There are different ways of looking at work in public space: "Working with institutions, municipal/educational institutions is an important aspect in my practice. I am looking into ways to involve a broader public (not directly related to art institutions) in a participatory role" (Stephen Wilks). Positions in which the artist, as an adviser gives advice, as an organiser 'creates conditions' or as a change agent 'intervenes socially' can form new focal points in the artistic practice:

> *Adviser*—"Of all the points you describe, maybe the most visible in my work is as a monitoring and evaluation consultant for DOEN and Hivos" (Claudia Fontes).
> *Organiser*—"With friends, I have been making a system in Japan called Artists' Guild, in which we are trying to establish a self sustaining system that helps artists to survive in Japanese society since 2009" (Meiro Koizumi).
> *Change agent*—"My practice is shifting towards research and the development of transdisciplinary art projects or initiatives that contribute to advancement, appreciation and comprehension of Bolivian art, culture, heritage, tradition. And, I'm producing an art & development project that aims to generate jobs for artists: it is called Agency of Artistic Thinking" (Narda Alvarado). "I've been working with street kids, writing in newspapers and giving my opinion publicly in different media. Currently I am organizing a discussion platform named PARLAMENTO, where to discuss professional issues about the art world" (Carlos Amorales). And, slightly differently: "As an artist we participate in change and ignite it or act as stimulus. We also observe change and comment upon it with our work. However within my practice this is not a goal in itself" (Praneet Soi).

An example of artisthood that spans the entire breadth: "In my practice most positions are woven into each other. It comes as a natural aspect of personal growth that all these positions become available, and more importantly in productive means. I see it as an honour, but try to avoid too much interference" (Tiong Ang).

a constant factor with every single position. That is quite obvious with respect to those which cannot exist without exchange or collaboration, such as curator, adviser and organiser. And incidentally, they also contribute to the artistic dimension: "I learn so much from it, it stimulates me." "I think a, b and c [artistic habitus, friendship, money—JwS] always complement each other. If you feel good doing something, you will be rewarded sooner or later economically (I think), and anyway, while you do it, you would build good relations with new colleagues and friends who would join in the fun" (Mounira Al Solh).

### *Maslow's pyramid of needs*

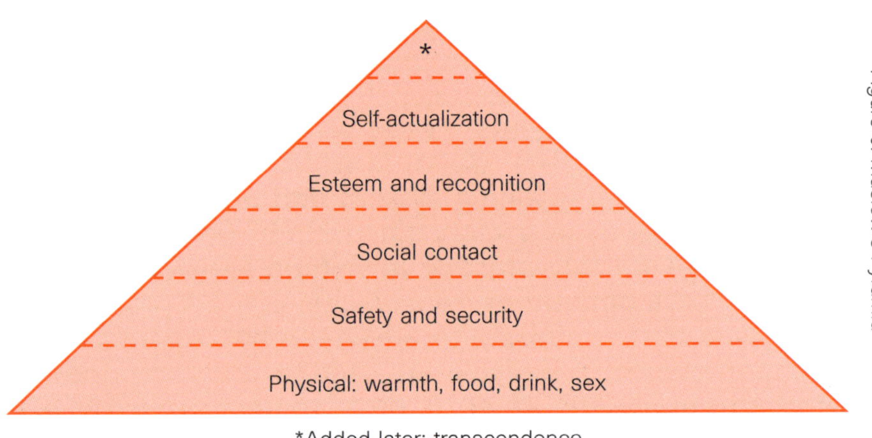


*Figure 6.* Maslow's Pyramid

Further to artistic considerations, motives of friendship and/or economic considerations, this handbook containing socio-psychological and sociological explorations would not be complete without mention of something as fundamental as the pyramid of needs proposed by Maslow (1943): a hierarchical classification which is used for charting consumer needs, for example. It is important to realise that it is not necessary to meet one need before progressing to the next. The needs in question can occur at different levels at the same time. These needs are physical (warmth, food, drink, sex), the need for safety and security, social contact, esteem and recognition, as well as self-actualisation.

The different types of needs can be linked to three types of motive for artists, listed in the questionnaire. In Maslow, the artistic, friendship and financial motives recur which play a part in adding breadth and depth to the professional practice. The artistic motive, whether a position is taken as part of the artistic habitus, primarily bears upon self-actualisation and self-transcendence (here, transcendence signifies passing beyond the 'ordinary', super-human), upon esteem and recognition, as well as social contact. The significance of peer- and friendship-related motives relates again to esteem and recognition, social contact and, in a way, to safety and security as well. The third motive about which artists were asked was that of money, and so of course refers to physical needs, safety and security, but also contributes to scope for social contact, esteem and recognition, and, if absent, can seriously hinder scope for self-development. So money affects all needs—or not?

## Eleven different artists' positions

As we have seen, the 'artist in the studio' was, and still is, the dominant version of 'the' artistic practice. A romantic ideal, often portrayed in a leaking, chilly attic heated only by an iron stove. Finances permitting, there will be money for a nude model (shivering from the cold), for whom the less-cold bed can soon offer solace, so in her interests—and the artist will make that sacrifice. A beam, or thin ray of light shines through the attic window. Is it divine light, shining upon the almost moribund genius?

A stereotype like this is not a disaster, but it becomes somewhat dramatic if that idea combines with another stereotype—like the artist sitting drowsily at the kitchen table at 11 o'clock in the morning, holding a mug of lukewarm coffee and staring aimlessly ahead, possibly making a couple of sketches and, later in the afternoon, painting "a canvas that won't get going". And then proceeding to a bar to quench his thirst in the company of similarly afflicted colleagues—

painters, generally not paintresses—with alcohol paid for with the last remaining euros from that month's subsidy.

This story relates to the position of the artist. Something must be done to overturn derogatory stereotypes of this kind, primarily by artists themselves. They can do so by providing insight into the varying positions an artist can play in the art world and the positions he can occupy in society. That is necessary if artists are to receive acknowledgement and social recognition (from the community). I believe it was the Renaissance artist, art critic and humanist, Albrecht Dürer, who said "as an artist I want to be admitted through the main entrance and not, as a craftsman through the back", to which you might add "and not be permitted, cap in hand, to have a bite in the kitchen of nice people". An 'emancipatory' act like that is associated with the acquisition of insight into and scope for one's own practice, thus creating a firm foundation: "know where you stand and what you stand for".

This handbook provides advice and in your artistic practice you receive feedback from the outside world, while you work. That is of some help, but for more self-insight you also need a
160 secret room where you can reflect and mature, in peace. Where interests and fascinations—the facets which were discussed earlier—are not yet exposed to the cruel light of day, where only an occasional confidant is admitted. No one can take that personal room away from you and you have it with you always, wherever you may be, in whatever position you present yourself: this is the mental atelier that was already mentioned.

With every position, I describe a short 'history' based on a personal recollection. In this section there is a direct linkage of the artist with one of the eleven specific positions, often an obvious association. At the end of this chapter the original
84 eleven artists return—plus eleven more—but it then emerges that there is no question of a clear-cut position. All the artists have broad practices in which two, three, four or more artists' positions become evident and converge.

### *Artist in the studio, facet: object-orientation*

The 'artist in the studio' is a position that is achieved and maintained with effort and investment. There is enough *space*, not only is there natural light but also artificial light to facilitate working long hours, behind the *door* there is a *table*, where the artist can sit, talk and eat with friends and art professionals, a *shelf* full of books and other sources of inspiration, memories and documentation, an internet connection for exploration, a *work bench* with tools, and a mobile phone within reach. The working space of many artists looks much like that. They work there alone or with other artists, with whom they share the space or where, if they are lucky, one or more assistants are working.

**Michael Raedecker**'s studio in the Rijksakademie (1993–1994, first group of artists in the Sarphatistraat building) did not have an ever-open door for advisers/mentors to come and go, and certainly not for those, ignoring the material dimension of painting, who wanted to seduce Raedecker with a theoretical discourse. He wanted a somewhat isolated spot; at that time his priority tended towards painting deriving from fashion design studies, which prior to that he had followed at Rietveld Academy. Having first worked in his own studio, he experienced a shift in the Rijksakademie period between and integration of two tactile materials: textile and paint. It did not take long for that personal development to be noticed: in 1994 Raedecker was, with the 'basic prize', one of the finalists for the Prix de Rome Painting.*

After he left the Rijksakademie I lost sight of him for a while, he was living and working in his own studio in Antwerp. Two years later he was ready for a more theoretical vantage point, left for London for an MFA at Goldsmiths, and the rest is history. Michael's practice had developed as a result of integrating his dealings with the media, but also as a result of an unconventional learning curve. He departed from the customary linear, institutional route, which starts with a BA (Rietveld), then an MA (for example Goldsmiths) and on to

* The Prix de Rome–imported from France at the start of the nineteenth century– is the foremost Dutch prize for architects and visual artists.

the Rijksakademie. He migrated from the Rijksakademie to Goldsmiths, which is a good illustration that everything happens in its own time, beyond formal educational routes, nicely upsetting the hierarchy of educational institutions: not culminating in the Rijksakademie, but as a transitional stage, an important step on the way.

255 In Part III 'Origins' three career path patterns are unveiled: passing on the baton from one generation to another, the common thread through one's own career, and intervening moments of reflection. Raedecker had several 'interim periods' before ending up in London, between the Rietveld Academy and the Rijksakademie and between the Rijksakademie and Goldsmiths, moments of transition which were perhaps decisive for his development. Moreover, during his career, there has been a constant factor: 'the alchemy of thread and paint'. And, finally, there is also a family connection, as the great-grandson of John Raedecker, painter and draughtsman, sculptor and designer of the National Monument at Dam Square in Amsterdam.

***Reflection*. Imagine that circumstances are such that you have a good studio at your disposal that you can maintain and where you can work day and night. And you have an excellent relationship with a proactive gallery owner, who does 'everything' for you. It means you do not need artistic activities outside the studio or additional activities in order to survive. What would that mean to you, and in particular, what would you miss?**

*Artist in public space, facet: social dimension of the object*

When you review centuries of art history, you see that working purely in the studio without commissions is not an 'abiding' phenomenon. The quality of collaboration between artist and principal, often combined in former days with a roof over the artist's head for a longer or shorter period—artist residencies *avant la lettre*—particularly affected the quality and volume of the art production—in other words, the 'art of commissioning' has played an important role for a long time.*

In addition to the facet of object orientation, the position in the studio which was discussed earlier, I address the social dimensions, i.e. in commissioning situations, particularly in public space. As we have seen, that position, together with lectureship, is one of the foremost economic elements in an artist's existence, alongside the substantive inspiration derived from it. Yet, in the artist's own perception—and that of many others—that position is thought not to be 'real', or insufficiently so.

The museum world and many artists themselves tend to consider commissioned work to be second rate. If you were already making such objects, alongside the 'authentic', autonomous work in the studio, you kept the two apart, in separate portfolios. There is a world of difference between the two (documentations and methods), they are separate areas with their own language. One is organic, intimate with its own signature, the other mechanical, cold and reproducible. The art of accepting commissions and the concept of autonomy in that context are discussed in Chapter 2. 31

Many artists are put off by the technical demands made on art works in public space, with respect to construction, costs, maintenance and vandal-resistance, and by interference from government employees and the population. Yet the demands affecting commissions of that type are often more concrete and therefore more manageable than the intangible, indistinct and often uncompromising codes of the inner circle professionals in the white cube of the museum. For assignments in public or semi-public space, non-professionals are frequently involved who may not understand everything, but are nevertheless curious, open-minded and have a form of silent admiration for the artist. When is artistic freedom the greater? As an artist, do you not have just as much freedom, or more, in commissioning situations? You certainly do have freedom if you can allow the question to register but not entirely adopt it, to reformulate it in

* The Roman Catholic church, kings, princes and other members of the nobility, and later on, wealthy burghers, were the most important 'partners' for artists. In Italy the name for a maecenas-patron was 'Prince'. Accordingly, writers, musicians, architects and artists referred to 'my Prince' when speaking about their patron; honour and friendship, with the artist aiming amongst other things at achieving relative freedom.

your own terms and hand it back to the principal. I shall
return to that ability in Chapter 3, in the section 'Control
145 variants'.

Today the range of work in public space—apart from informal variants like street art (graffiti and street performance)—is far greater and more varied than a few decades ago. For some time now, commissioned work has no longer been restricted to work in public space; there has been a vast increase in commissions in the areas of design, scenography and interactive media, for instance. The current trend of working in an 'art and society' context also contributes to a positive reassessment of that facet of artisthood. It can be a relief when inspiration sources in society are no longer desperately denied and the art work's 'designation' can be a legitimate focus in that society.

Yet artists are experiencing increasing strains on their commissions for appealing work in public space, commercially and often artistically as well. There are few commissions owing to the discontinuation of grant schemes and to government cutbacks. On the other hand, many, less 'generous' projects are getting going: individual initiatives and collaborations with artist collectives. One wonders whether expansion of the public space in the digital world might not, in time, create fresh possibilities and thus compensate for the downturn in work in the physical public space.

I should like to illustrate this with an example from one of the projects in the 1997 Prix de Rome 'Art and Public Space'. On 7 September 1997 there was a huge crowd at the waterside area behind the Rijksakademie. A cheerful mixture of men, women and children—I seem to remember they were eating paella, but perhaps that was because they were speaking Spanish—and especially the great numbers of people. I didn't necessarily need to know everything that went on in and around the Rijksakademie, but I was curious and asked what was happening. I was given evasive answers and heard some mumbling about a project of the Spanish artist **Alicia Framis** (Rijksakademie 1995/1996). The next day a minibus with members of the Prix de Rome* jury drove to Dam Square in Amsterdam. The square was somewhat emasculated because the beige 'penis'—the national war memorial (by John Raedecker) had been transported to Germany to be injected with chemicals to prepare it for eternal life (no joking!). It was busy in the square in front of the Royal Palace, but that is not unusual. And then something happened, something very unusual: the crowd of people started to move, a veritable throng—and from the mass a human tower arose. I think there were 187 Spaniards, from Tarragona, whom I had seen the previous evening, well known from competitions between towns and villages for making human towers, usually with a child at the apex holding a flower. They had travelled to Amsterdam in coaches for Alicia Framis' *The Walking Monument* project, with which she went on to win the first prize in the Prix de Rome. Out of the social human fabric, a monument arose that lasted only a few minutes physically, and afterwards only in the memories of those who were present, a monument as part of their collective memory: of which there is hardly any documentation.

***Reflection*. The Prix de Rome assignment in public space allowed great freedom; that is not always the case. Have you ever experienced a public assignment which was diametrically opposed to your own way of thinking and working? Discuss with a colleague, friend or fellow student how you could reformulate the question so you would like the idea of the project.**

### *Artist in the laboratory, facet: process methodology*

A topical niche in artists' positions is again a practice combining art and science, or art and technology, or art, science and technology. Recently new cross-overs have been taking place at the interface between science and art, between university and studio, usually with a high theory content and, when connected to the natural sciences, with a considerable technology content. The studio practice has a technological

* Tiong Ang, Saskia Bos, Jan van Grunsven, Sigurdur Gudmundsson, Hermann Pitz and myself as chairman (without the right to vote).

side, for example technological research when developing colours—just think of of Anish Kapoor's patented black. An artist can be a researcher for tactile work, for his own scientific projects or with a complementary projects or work together with scientists when developing new technologies.*

The observation and study of nature have been part of the artistic practice since the Renaissance. Nowadays technological progress enables artists to modify nature. BioArt provides an example of how artists, inspired by process methodology of scientists, can proceed. Artists not only work in and with nature, but also use nature as an avenue for developing new scenarios; the laboratory as a place for consideration and exploration of the future. A parallel niche is that of (electronic) audio art. Since the 1960s the Netherlands has been an international pioneer in that field, with proponents including the composer, artist, curator, sociologist and art historian Paul Panhuysen (1934–2015), the founder of the Apollohuis—a space for experimental music and visual art in Eindhoven. And the composer, theatre maker, theorist, musician and visual artist Dick Raaijmakers (1930–2013), who was attached to the University of Utrecht and the founder of the Sound and Vision faculty of the Royal Conservatory and the Royal Academy of Art in The Hague. They have inspired generations of artists up to the present day.**

The artist in the laboratory uses the term 'research' more than his colleagues in other positions. Apart from the fact that artists sometimes incorrectly label what they are doing as research, the object of their research—what is being 'researched'—is not defined. There are great differences between introspective research into one's own *personality* and research into ammunition for inspiration, such as source research or research into optimising the personal *working process*, into *techniques* and *media* or *working methods*. Or research into ways of refining the *commercial process* (buying, production

* The approach using a technology component–if we momentarily pass over Leonardo da Vinci, the scientific artists of the Middle Ages and the eighteenth/nineteenth centuries–ties in with a movement from the 1960s. It has its roots at MIT in Boston (Otto Piene and others) and later institutes of art and technology, including what were then new media. For decades there has been a strong network in which institutes like V2_ (Rotterdam) and NIMk (formerly Montevideo) and STEIM (Amsterdam) have played a part within the Netherlands; internationally, it involves many places in Japan, the United States and Europe. Think in that context of an institute like ZKM in Karlsruhe and festivals like Electronic Art in Linz.

** Sense of Sound, 40.000 m³ geluidskunst', www.dordtyaart.nl (2017).

and presentation). What I mainly have in mind in the case of the artist in the laboratory, working with interfaces between art and science, technology and often nature as well, is the hunt for source areas in science, technology and nature and the identification of working processes that are influenced by systems analysis.

There is a cast-iron international network of places for development and presentation of and for artists working 'in the laboratory'. Once you have gained recognition among the 'in crowd'—and risk being smothered with appreciation—it is often hard to present yourself in different worlds.

**Maria Verstappen** has been working with **Erwin Driessens** since 1990 as a multidisciplinary artist duo. After completing their studies at the Academy of Fine Arts in Maastricht they both went on to the Rijksakademie's Art Media Studies department (1989–1991). Their work is generated by independently operating processes, often inspired by physical and chemical processes in nature, and resulting in constantly new and original forms. At some stage our paths crossed, when a project was being developed and implemented which entailed a series of cut-outs visualised as models with a specific perspective on museum galleries. We discussed suitable platforms for presenting the work and tried to get several international art magazines to offer them 'free artist' pages, a phenomenon that was not yet common at that time. Initially it did not materialise, but with a somewhat more modest approach and additional financing from a Rijksakademie budget, it did succeed. The Driessens/Verstappen working method can better be described as more appropriate to the laboratory than the traditional studio.

***Reflection*. Imagine you operate entirely in the world of the laboratory. Projects follow one after the other, you race hither and thither, and there is sufficient income. What facets of artisthood would you miss?**

### *Artist on stage, facet: the performative domain*

The 'artist on stage' could develop in two directions. Either these are artists with a background in theatre, music, literature or cinematography and integrate that background in their visual work. or else they are visual artists who concentrate on performance, sound art, texts, film and video art, and present themselves on platforms of theatre, music, literature and film. The works are invariably made in collaboration with others; there are also solo practices: performative work by one person, sound work made on your own; while film-makers are often less 'solo'. The results vary from actual performance, to an art work with theatrical quality or the building of a physical stage.

In this context, stages are physical spaces for performative (art) activities, not economic platforms for the artist's reputation. This position would seem to offer relatively large scope for experimental, trial-and-error development. Initially, a cautious start, step-by-step in a small, safe circle before being judged in the spotlight at a highly critical level. On that platform you 'become', in interaction with spectators under 'experimental' conditions.

During admissions in 2005 **Guido van der Werve** signed up, having followed a great many, varied studies, including the Conservatory and the Rietveld Academy. I remember video works with a car crash, falling trees and ballerinas in the street and on a small balcony, always with compelling classical music. Only later—much later than the artists in the admissions jury with their exceedingly keen approach to selection—did I discover deeper layers in his work beneath the jokiness and 'compulsiveness'. It was a decisive moment for me when I saw his work *Nummer acht (Everything is going to be alright)*, the Icebreaker. That, and many subsequent works, made it increasingly easy for me to 'read' the older work with ballerinas, car, trees et cetera: a retrospective discovery of authenticity. I believe that with Van der Werve, the strictly personal source can be found in his own background and course of develop-

ment, as will be addressed in 'Career patterns'. Van der Werve did not want to become an artist like his father and brother, who both painted, but a professional pianist. However, breeding will out, and he made his way from the stage to creative (visual) art with a large palette: performances, films, photography, books and compositions.

***Reflection*. Do you or did you act, make music or dance? Is that still part of your work as a visual artist? If not, is there some way to develop and perhaps integrate a performative facet in your artistic practice?**

*Artist as a designer, facet: complexity of the situation*

One of the possible distinguishing characteristics of the artist's position as a 'designer' could be formed by technical and organisational prerequisites, as addressed in 'Similarities and differences between autonomous and applied art'. With respect to the 'artist as a designer', think of how 'complexity' is dealt with, with a series of conspiring, sometimes conflicting factors: economic (cost-benefit effectiveness), technical (feasibility), ergonomic (usability), social (social relations), ecological (durability and environment), et cetera.

For this position it is important that the artist internalises or 'appropriates' the questions, that the assignment undergoes an 'autonomous' transformation, without the artist having to fear (understandably but unacceptably) that the assignment might fall through. A submissive attitude like this could indicate a tendency to risk-avoidance when collaboration is involved.

In 1999 a majestic young woman crossed the Rijksakademie courtyard, a 'ballerina' with charisma, conscious of the theatrical space in which she was walking which she created with her very presence. **Germaine Kruip**, a finalist for the Prix de Rome Theatre and Visual Arts, was working in one of the temporary Prix studios for artists from outside the Rijksakademie. The jury* began its judging during the final round in her studio, with a multi-interpretable photo of a scampering child: playing on a grassy field or running away from gunfire to the edge of a safe

* Ritsaert ten Cate, Arnout Mik, Michelangelo Pistoletto, Tom Stromberg, Peter Zegveld and myself as chairman (without the right to vote).

wood. The jury then went for a walk in the neighbouring Oosterpark: had the soldier drinking tea chosen to sit there of his own accord or had Kruip put him there, was the couple necking on the grass staged or was it true love, the junkie with the dog, and so on. For days you have a 'third eye' for what you see, for what it means, what is behind it. That kind of perception, interpretation and visualisation crosses through disciplines in Germaine Kruip's work. She does not shy from complex processes when creating 'as a designer'. The front and the back of the coin she designed in 2005 to mark Queen Beatrix' silver jubilee, depict from different angles the moment the queen took the oath twenty-five years earlier. According to the committee the design transcends the majestic and, on account of the way it has been executed, is of importance as a documentary record.

***Reflection*. Get a friend to give you a design assignment with almost impossible requirements. Make a counter-proposal using a sketch or prototype. Use the friend's reaction for a new counter proposal. Are you fed up with it or has it turned out as you wanted? Would your friend want to own it?**

### *Artist and writer, facet: image and word*

The combination of artist and musician or artist and architect occurs regularly. Visual art and architecture are not miles apart either, but other combinations, such as artist and writer appear—at least to the outside world—to be far more prevalent. However, artisthood and authorship coincide to such a large extent and on such a high level that I am devoting space here to the facet of 'writing' within artisthood. At the Rijksakademie alone there are countless artist-writers among the Dutch residents.* Writing within this position is not about an explanatory text accompanying visual work or directly related to curatorship (frequent), but authorship that is prominent in the literary field, with resonance in the publishing world and with readers.

* Hans Aarsman (1951, Amsterdam–RA 1978/1981), Maria Barnas (1973, Hoorn–RA 1999/2000), Tijs Goldschmidt (1953, Amsterdam–RA 1979/1981), Jannie Regnerus (1971, Oudebildtzijl–RA 1995/1996), Frank Starik (1958, Apeldoorn–RA 1987/1989) and Anton Valens (1964, Paterswolde–RA 1990/1992). Also encounter the combination of poetry and drawings, for instance in work by Iris le Rütte (1960, Eindhoven–RA 1983/87). A 'combination' also found among the present residents, like Nicoline Timmer (1975, Vriezenveen–RA 2012/2013).

Even if, as an artist-writer you are working in two separate markets, the two types of presentation are often compared, especially from the visual arts perspective. “Lucebert [the artist] writes beautiful poetry, but…”, “Jan Wolkers’ fiction is better than his sculptures and paintings”.

It is possible to make a small systems analysis-type sequence of the various relationships between authorship and artisthood, based on the artist’s position and the market setting. A diagram will illustrate this.

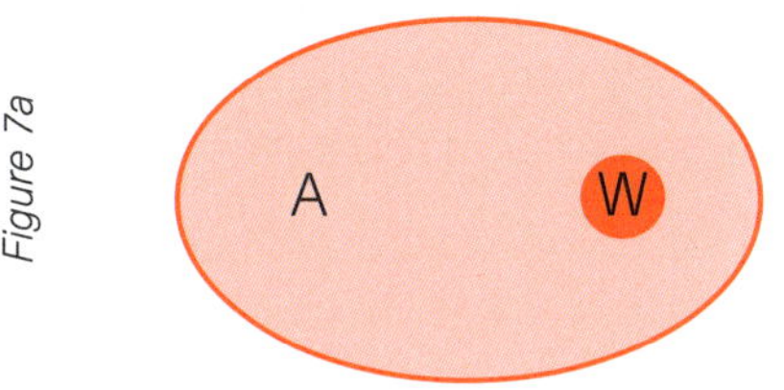

*Figure 7a*

Artist (A), who also writes (W) about art, focused on the art world. Artist is dominant, writing is secondary and embedded in the artistic practice; it does not relate to any individual artists’ positions.

And the series with two individual positions:

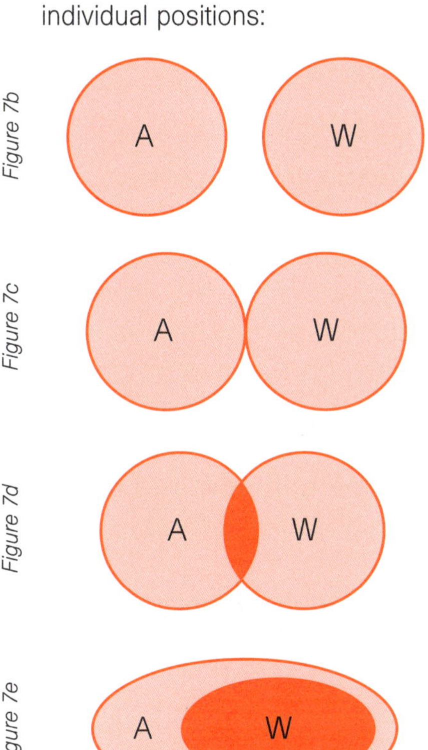

*Figure 7b*

Artist and writer, in two market settings, with their own dynamic and criteria.

*Figure 7c*

Ditto, but induction takes place: inspiration either by accumulating energy in one area for better concentration in the other. In that case, writing in relation to the studio can generate peace and quiet and reflection, like when you go for a walk.

*Figure 7d*

A new, third area comes about, a symbiosis of the two which is hard to define beforehand.

*Figure 7e*

Total integration, the two become one.

An example of an artist and writer from the Rijksakademie is **Jannie Regnerus**. She paints, draws, makes projects in public space and site specific, is a film-maker and takes photos of her travels to Japan and Mongolia, for instance. On 9 September 1996 a group of people from the Rijksakademie were in a plane on their way to the Venice Biennale. We sat together, it was the first time Jannie had flown, and it was her 25th birthday that day. Someone—I don't recall whether it was me—asked if the 'birthday girl' might be allowed into the cockpit. In those days hijacks were not an issue and Jannie could watch from the sky, from the cockpit until we landed at Marco Polo airport. It was the start of her extensive travels. Her books include *De volle maan als beste vriend, reis in Mongolië* (The full moon as your best friend, travels in Mongolia) (2005) and *Het geluid van vallende sneeuw, herinnering aan Japan* (The sound of falling snow, a memory of Japan) (2006).

***Reflection*****. Look for an old text you wrote as a child, adolescent or young adult. Does this text bear any relation to your visual work? Do you still write, and if so, for whom?**

### *Artist as a curator, facet: connectedness between art works*

There are artists who, alongside their work in the studio, are interested in bringing together and presenting other artists' work, and in how those works interact. Many graduands from art institutions already took part in group presentations during their studies when one of the participants took the responsibility to take a step back and look farther than his/her own work. That person tries to get an overall view and discover similarities and differences, the things a visitor, professional or not, will experience.

A role of that type requires curiosity about other people's work, the trust of the participating artists and, preferably, an appealing idea or concept. The 'role' can develop into an artist's position as a curator. Or as a gallery 'manager'. The 'duties' of the artist as a curator combine substantive and organisational components. There a variety of modalities concerning the surroundings and the position as a curator: the curator and nothing else, artist and curator, or the artist becomes a curator because connectedness and theoretical reflection prove to have pronounced personal qualities. Or because—as you continue to work in the studio—it is a way to escape loneliness, or else it provides a platform that ties in better with your personal qualities and offers greater prominence. And lastly from another angle, the curator who becomes an artist or turns the exhibition into an art work of his own out of the exhibition.

Having taken a access route via teacher training, (VU Open Teaching Methodology), followed by the Rietveld Academy and Croydon College of Art, London, **Jan van der Ploeg** took the next step in 1983 together with two friends. They split up the Dutch post-graduate field, as it were: one took on Ateliers '63 in Haarlem, another the Jan van Eyck Academy in Maastricht, and Jan van der Ploeg went to the Rijksakademie because he had heard that someone (Schrofer) had just been appointed and had new plans, intending to overhaul 'the old institute' radically. In the three years he was working in what was then the 'Monumental Arts' department, headed by professor Harry op de Laak, we regularly spoke—about his own plans and about the institute's transformation. Even though, after 1992, part of his artistic practice moved to Australia and New Zealand, it was not difficult to follow his studio and public space work, particularly when, inspired by the platform activities of artist friends 'down under', he began curating exhibitions himself. He started in the family sitting room and later in PS Project Space, based on substantive coherence and affinity, and on generous reciprocity with friends.

***Reflection*. Have you worked as a curator, on a small or large scale? Did you enjoy it? Was your own work included in the presentation? Was that problematical or actually very productive?**

**And if you had done it before, what did you learn from that, are there now conditions you would like to discuss beforehand? What are they?**

*Artist as an organiser, facet: conditions for other artists*

During the workshops on positioning by artists (see 'Coun-
252 selling of artists: sources of experience') that I run at art academies, one of my opening questions to graduands is: are there students here who already belong to an artist collective or are considering launching that kind of initiative? Who have on occasion organised an event with a visual component, a presentation of work or a VJ performance? Or have thought about setting up an artist residency to change something in the art world together with others, or in a community? Someone who, during couch-surfing, chance shared meals and casual conversations was inspired to go beyond pleasant incidents of that type? When an artist organises such activities he winds up in the position of an organiser. And in fact that is what you are doing if you succeed in being hospitable in your own studio or home. The word 'managing' is closely related to the concept of organisation. It amounts to 'getting things done through others', which plays a part in a set-up in which a contribution is required from others.

The position of organiser, as well as those of adviser, educator and change agent which are discussed later, makes use of the ability to combine involvement, empathy and distance, to be well-up in the material, and outside, between and above it. In those cases you will have to find a way, as an artist, of dealing with the antithesis between participation and observation. It may be necessary, with constellations like this, to formalise, even ritualise interaction. Patterns of interaction return in the
145 following chapter in 'Control variants'.

After 1995 a quarter to a third of the entire population of artists in the Rijksakademie came from Africa, Asia and Latin America. From countries with an uneasy social structure, political turbulence and economic instability, from countries where the position you occupy in society matters, where, as an artist, you 'can make a difference'. Many of those artists were grateful that, partly thanks to their period of working at the Rijksakademie, they could interact with and enter the international, Western art world; to be seen in the celebrated art market. But, at the same time, they wanted an artists' platform in their home land, to organise discussion, action, collaboration, training, communal work accommodation or a residency. That went on to be organised at various places including Mexico City, Buenos Aires, South Africa, Cameroon, Mali, Mumbai and Jakarta. Places organised for and by artists, in their own country as a countervailing power vis-à-vis the West-dominated art market in which they—the artists—could also be a part; artists' initiatives interconnected via the Rijksakademie Artists' Initiatives Network (RAIN, www.r-a-i-n.net)* In that way they became organisers, and often educators or change agents as well (see the description of the change agent).

Since 1993 I have been following **David Bade**, who that year—immediately following Ateliers '63 (which was still in Haarlem)—won the Prix de Rome Basic Prize Drawing.** The 'Prix' was our main common ground. In 2007 I invited him on the jury of what by then was an (again) updated Prix.*** In the past twenty years I have seen how Bade, as an organiser, has embraced the facet 'creating conditions' for others, insiders and outsiders in the art world, in the street, in museums, in art education in Curaçao and Europe, and enters into collaborations with people and institutes. The foundation in 2006 of Instituto Bueno Bista (IBB) in Willemstad on Curaçao was a milestone—it was a 'Silent Zone' in the Netherlands. IBB is an art and artist centre, a training programme for young people from an underprivileged background in material and artistic terms, in a 'neglected' Caribbean region. IBB is not part of the RAIN network, but does serve as a preparatory training route for art academies, in the Netherlands for example. It not only educates but also, with the knowledge of what is needed to travel a rocky road, supports students during their studies in Europe and later when developing their artistic practice in the Caribbean.

* Individual initiatives received guidance from the RAIN network founded in 2000 by the Rijksakademie with support from the Ministry of Development Co-operation: support for their (local) initiatives in Africa, Asia and Latin America, promotion of exchange and collaboration, as well as emancipation of artists on peripheral 'silent zones' in the South by way of penetration into the Western art world.

** Jury: Ben Akkerman, Christiaan Braun, Frank Vanden Broeck, Martin Disler, Thomas Schütte and myself as chairman (*Prix de Rome*, 1993, Rotterdam: 010 Publishers).

*** Jury: David Bade, Angela Bulloch, Chris Dercon (chairman), Jean-Marc Bustamante, Barbara Visser and myself as jury secretary.

***Reflection*. Organising is collaborating. Discuss with a colleague, fellow student or friend what was your very worst experience of collaboration. Why did it just about succeed, or not? Is there an example of a project in which collaboration actually produced something very positive? What was it? Will these experiences be of influence when you organise projects in the future? How?**

### *Artist as an adviser, facet: expert advice*

There are artists who are asked, on account of their artistic quality and insight into artistic practice, to advise in selection processes in a jury, in allocating grants in a committee, or in awarding assignments. Their 'artistic eye' is of great importance for such decision-making. And that appears even more important for outside experts assessing final exams in art programmes.

In line with activities of that type, some artists assist others—independently or as part of a collaborative venture—in the role of project manager, helping to realise artistically and technically complex projects. A form of specialist professional practice in which artisthood is a vital ingredient. This is not routine, procedure-actuated, technocratic support, but a requires good eye, knowledge of artisthood and curiosity about uncertainties concerning working together as a good colleague with artists.

The meeting to launch the RAIN network, artists' platforms set up by Rijksakademie residents from Africa, Asia and Latin America, was held at the start of 2000 during a two-day seminar in Amsterdam and at my home in Heemstede, converted into a conference facility for the occasion.

**Claudia Fontes** (Rijksakademie 1996/1997) was a forceful protagonist and antagonist in the establishment of RAIN, and had a lot to say. She was to be the founder and driving force of the TRAMA platform, active in various cities in Argentina, in order to fill the gap in art education in particular. A project with the essential features of a temporary collaboration, i.e. purposive concentration of energies and ideas, with a distinct start and finish. In line with TRAMA, which continued in people's minds and in documents (as a legend) after Fontes had formally ended it a few years later, she began working with organisations in the culture and development fields. Quoting from her response in the field research: "Of all the points you describe, maybe the most visible is my work as monitoring and evaluation consultant for DOEN and Hivos" (Dutch international support organisations).

***Reflection*. At home, when you were a youngster, did they listen to your opinion, did they do anything with it? Are things different now, with fellow artists or students? Do other people approach you, or do you go to them for help and advice?**

*Artist as an educator, facet: transference*

Artists are educators, not primarily on account of passion or love of beauty, which do of course help. But because they (here he goes again) are specialists in discovering hidden meanings, transforming those meanings into visual work or texts, and returning the meanings to others in society. In works deploying the power of the image* the artist reaches the highest level of 'transference', the central facet of the position as an educator.

In actual fact almost all artists are educators in the broad sense, sometimes, in a narrower sense, as teachers. In *education*, in schools: primary and secondary education, with teaching certificates; in higher vocational and university art education, as a visiting lecturer, teacher, tutor, principal lecturer or as an external expert, for example as external examiner appointed by the state, or in higher education as an artist-in-residence at a university, for example. Also, they may be in *artists' initiatives* and platforms, in a museum as an educational employee, in *socio-cultural work*, in cultural or community centres. And further: in a *health care* institution, for instance as an occupational therapist (with specific further training), or else have a role in informal sectors, undertaking activities in the *neighbourhood* (see also change agent) or giving lessons in the *studio/at*

* Consider a well-known example from the recent past: the photo of Kim Phuc, the Napalm girl, in Vietnam (1972), which gave a decisive push for the swelling opposition among the opponents and the growing hesitation among proponents of the Vietnam war and causing the whole situation to overturn and everything changed.

*home* to children and adults who do not wish to make art their profession. The expansion of the total playing field within the position of an artist-educator and especially as a teacher in the above—seven—fields of transference produces among artists and art students the cry: "But that's something I do think is interesting to do!"

The said exploratory field research reveals that almost all the artists who were approached deploy their transference qualities across a broad front: in their own studio, in art centres and museums, collectively and individually, in education, particularly art education. Incidentally, every artist is, to a lesser or greater extent, also his own propagandist. In other words, not only transferring meanings outside himself, but also of his own, personal meaning: "Where do I stand and what do I stand for?".

Some diagrammatic variants are given below of the position as an educator in relation to artisthood (in and from the studio), in this case as a teacher.

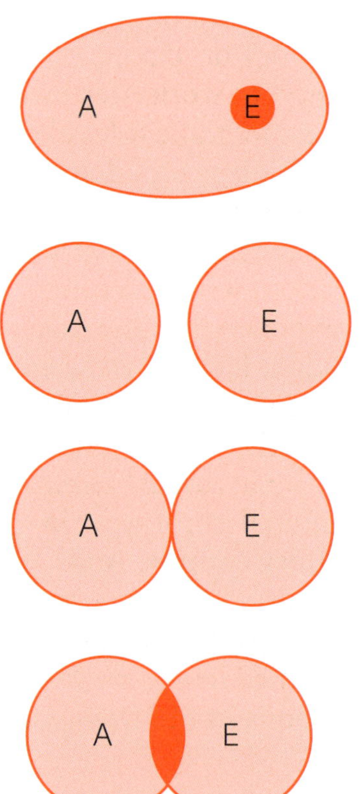


Artist clarifies his own work, in the studio or in a museum. *Figure 8a*

Artist and educator, functioning in two worlds with their own criteria, a divided existence. *Figure 8b*

Induction derives from teaching. When you work with young people you tap energy ('Dracula effect'), draw inspiration (unexpected ideas) and your imagination is fired when you meet as yet unknown worlds of ideas. *Figure 8c*

A new area comes about from synthesis, it can be just about anything: setting up a course, organising artist talks, founding a new academy, publishing on teaching methods, etc. *Figure 8d*

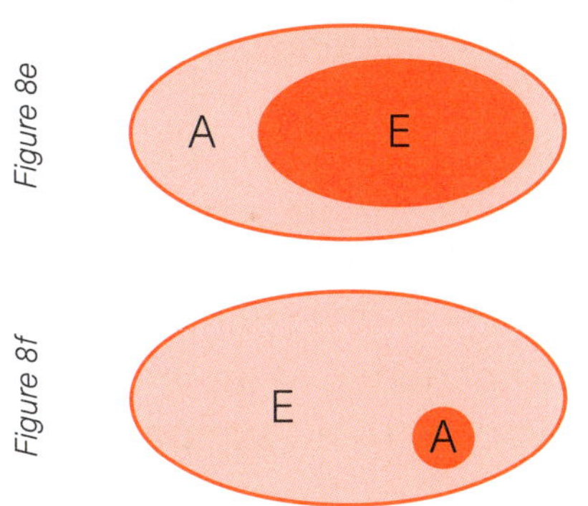


*Figure 8e*

Active artist' practice, embedding fully the educatorship

*Figure 8f*

Educator who incorporates his own work in teaching, but scarcely presents his work on public, professional platforms.

For me, **Sylvie Zijlmans** (1964) is an example of an artist with the position as an 'educator' in her palette. She works together with her partner Hewald Jongenelis, and often also with her children Una and Igor. Sylvie followed the teacher training programme at the Academy of Fine Arts and Education in Tilburg and graduated in Fine Arts. Her lecturer, Marlene Dumas, got her into the Rijksakademie at what was then the department of painting (1987–1989). Those were the early years of the revamped Rijksakademie before it moved from the Stadhouderskade to the Kavallerie-Kazerne (cavalry barracks) in Sarphatistraat. I looked Sylvie up in her studio in the attic of the old building and from then on followed her work, career and life. She taught at the Dutch Art Institute in the ArtEZ Master's programme and for many years at Gerrit Rietveld Academy. In recent years the Jongenelis/Zijlmans duo have worked on a project in Amsterdam-Noord—The Magnetic North—comprising sculpture, film and drawings which was centralised in a monumental, dramatic installation at Museum Boijmans Van Beuningen in Rotterdam in 2017. Local, universally familiar social matters have been translated expressively into performances which were made and 'acted' on location and in collaboration with residents of the Noord district. This interpretation of the 'transference' facet generates a smooth transition between the position as an 'educator' and the following, and final, artist's position, that of the change agent.

***Reflection*. Do you recognise your own experiences in the above fields of education–ranging from teaching to guiding in a museum, from socio-cultural work to a children's studio in your home? Are there as yet unknown areas among the domains of transference that particularly arouse your curiosity?**

*Artist as a change agent, facet: social interventions*

The artist as a change agent. The profile of that type of artist is extremely complex: he needs a 'hard core' of his own, perseverance a prerequisite, flexibility indispensable, ability and willingness to communicate necessary, and without an original 'vision', why start. Of course, knowledge of art and of social processes is needed, and—it goes without saying—considerable intelligence.

I thought that the RAIN platforms (between twelve and fifteen of them) in Africa, Asia and Latin America at the start of the present century—brought about thanks to an initiative of artists during and after their residencies in Amsterdam—were unique. In recent years, at meetings of ResArtis (a world-wide collaboration of artist residencies) it transpired that incredible numbers of new artist-driven, grass root residencies have started in the last five to ten years, particularly in Asia. Places where critical intervention in society has taken place, starting from a critical artist collective. Involving different and new forms of economic cooperation, social networks and political models that are bottom-up rather than bureaucratically top-down.

The archives of the Museum of Arte Útil (art that has a social use as a tool of change) contain more than 500 case histories from the past and the present in which artists made or make a difference (www.museumarteutil.net). A project initiated by the Cuban artist Tania Bruguera in New York and presented temporarily in 2014 at Van Abbemuseum, Eindhoven. Artists can make a difference by thinking out-of-the-box and with their specialism for meanings. They can play with bureaucracies and ritual rules, create fresh openings and assume the role of the joker, if required. It is logical to expect an artist who fulfils, as a change agent, an important missionary role, can be seen as an example to follow. As a sign of hope. He demonstrates that there is a way out of economic poverty or cultural deprivation. Someone like that can (also) be a role model for a larger community.

Take an example from 'real life': in 1995 **Hama Goro** from Bamako in Mali went to the Rijksakademie. He continued in his studio in the Netherlands to work with dyes made from bark and other natural materials—the stench was incredible, reaching far into the corridors of the 'cavalry barracks'. He used them to paint on textile, in the Bogolan technique. He returned to Mali at the end of 1996. In his two years in Amsterdam he had taken two major steps: detaching himself from tradition and using the technique on hard panels. After working on flat surfaces he went on to create spatial, three-dimensional objects. It might seem like a logical step, but in his cultural context it was a quantum leap. During a studio interview, I noted that he wanted to set up an artist collective in Bamako with some friends. We discussed it, made sketches of the building, drew up a business plan and looked for finances. Goro's Centre Soleil d'Afrique opened in 1999 and was the first project to be supported by the Prince Claus Fund (www.soleildafrique.org). Hama Goro and fellow artists offered artists and art students from Mali a space, executed assignments at the airport and at the presidential palace, and in that way became an example for a large community and especially for many young people. This was a route that he had no doubt already taken as a youth in the Dogon valley and that he continued and consummated in Amsterdam, his compelling plea being: "I just don't want to sit at the roadside selling bags to tourists." Soleil d'Afrique is part of the RAIN network.

***Reflection*. Do you see the 'interventions in the community' of the artist as a change agent as conflicting with the position of the artist in the studio? Why–or why not?**

| | |
|---|---|
| OBJECT ORIENTATION | ARTIST IN THE STUDIO |
| SOCIAL DIMENSION OF OBJECT | ARTIST IN PUBLIC SPACE |
| PROCESS METHODOLOGY | ARTIST IN THE LABORATORY |
| PERFORMATIVE | ARTIST ON STAGE |
| COMPLEXITY | ARTIST AS DESIGNER |
| IMAGE AND WORD | ARTIST AND WRITER |
| CONNECTEDNESS | ARTIST AS CURATOR |
| CREATING CONDITIONS | ARTIST AS ORGANISER |
| EXPERIENCED ASSISTANCE | ARTIST AS ADVISER |
| TRANSFERENCE | ARTIST AS EDUCATOR |
| SOCIAL INTERVENTION | ARTIST AS CHANGE AGENT |

*Figure 9.* Facets and artists' positions

***Reflection*. a. To which facets (left part of the diagram)–the 'fascinations' that are still not visible to the outside world–would you like to pay more attention? What might that mean for the development of your work? b. Describe briefly your current position/positions as an artist. Use your answers to earlier reflections in this chapter on artists' positions (right part of the diagram). c. Look to the future. Can you see certain positions (as yet not materialised) that you would like to adopt or extend?**

## The integrated practice

Some positions are easy to combine, others less so. Sometimes there is a 'hero', who manages to unite all the positions, like **Michelangelo Pistoletto**: in the studio, work in public space, on the stage, as a mentor of artists' projects, an educator as a professor and head of the sculpture department from 1991 to 2000 at the Fine Arts Academy in Vienna (where we met) and, crowning his artistic existence—the curator/organiser/educator at his own Cittadellarte—Fondazione Pistoletto in Biella, as a change agent inside the art world and outsidc it, as wcll as a role model. He unites art and society, art and science, art work and spectator—who becomes part of his *Mirror Paintings*. Ever since that first meeting in Vienna we have been in touch and worked together on the Prix de Rome (Theatre and Visual Arts) when Pistoletto was a jury member in 1999, and later at the Rijksakademie where he became an adviser. We exchanged ideas on setting up and opening his impressive undertaking—Cittadelarte—and on possible changes at the Rijksakademie.

In the previous section we saw how a facet takes shape in a position; here we will examine how broad and mixed artists' practices can be. Initially we reviewed 22 artists, eleven of whom were already featured. Each was invited to introduce one of the positions, examine the underlying facet and supplement it with a personal memory. Now we take a wider look, rather than focusing on one aspect. We are interested to show that hardly any artist presents himself in one position only.

I have addressed the multi-practice of artists to contrast with the focus on one position, but I have nothing against—

and actually admiration for—artists who deliberately opt for one position and can express in it their entire philosophy and the various, concomitant facets.

The choice of these artists was not a random one. I asked several who were involved in the Endowment Fund established by the Rijksakademie to participate in this handbook, outlining their artistic practice by way of a work (usually donated) and a short description of activities and the various artists' positions within their practice. They were selected because theirs were felt to represent a variety of practice types. A more detached viewpoint has been taken for the overall picture (snapshot) of each artist's practice compared with the eleven personal descriptions. The artists add colour through their works and quotes accompanying them.

Snapshots follow of the practices of Carlos Amorales, David Bade, Driessens & Verstappen, Marlene Dumas, Claudia Fontes, Alicia Framis, Meschac Gaba, Ryan Gander, Antony Gormley, Hama Goro, Sigurdur Gudmundsson, Hans van Houwelingen, Joan Jonas, Germaine Kruip, Matt Mullican, Michelangelo Pistoletto, Jan van der Ploeg, Michael Raedecker, Jannie Regnerus, Auke de Vries, Guido van der Werve and Sylvie Zijlmans.

The portraits of artists who have mixed practices reveal the range and breadth of artisthood. It might seem like a plea for the *homo universalis* as a new ideal artist. *Homo universalis*, literally universal man, refers to someone with skills that cover several areas. This ideal primarily developed (under the influence of humanism) during the Renaissance, based on Leon Battista Alberti's statement that "a man can do all things if he will" (he was himself many things, including a writer, artist and architect). This harked back to the classical Greek scholarly and educational ideal, with general schooling geared to comprehensive development, thus doing justice to the 'true' human nature. Leonardo da Vinci is generally cited as the 'prototype'.

## CARLOS AMORALES

Carlos Amorales, born in Mexico City in 1970, moved at the age of 22 to Amsterdam where he attended the Gerrit Rietveld Academy (1992–1995) and later the Rijksakademie (1996–1997). His practice deals with a wide range of media, including typography, through which Amorales challenges Mexico's socio-political conditions. The primary association is: the artist as a change agent, aiming at social intervention.

His first project was *Liquid Archive* (1998), an archive in which the artist stored images and typefaces, either found online or created by him, and continuously rediscovered and reused in his artworks. This archive represents to a certain extent the basis of his *studio* practice of collecting, storing, remixing, influencing and remaking visual shapes. Amorales' work revolves around this activity of reactivating shapes or symbols, moving them to unusual visual contexts, to address complex political issues through neat colours (black and red) and disturbing, surreal forms (*Black Cloud*, 2007)

The political dimension of Amorales' artistry extends to social intervention through art, in which the artist operates as a *change agent* in a specific environment. In *Los Mutantes* (2000), street children living in El Caracol (an NGO) in downtown Mexico City are dressed up as tourists and equipped with a camera; their task was to shoot and document the lives of other children. In this artwork, Amorales, intervenes in the outcasts' microsociety of charities and NGOs from which it is difficult to escape; once you become a 'professional victim' there is no future outside that secluded society. The street children were given the opportunity to 'mutate' the perspective to change their own self-depiction.

The aesthetic research on language and images in Amorales' oeuvre is not only confined to the realm of galleries, but is also intertwined with social change. *Nuevos Ricos*, in collaboration with the composer Julian Lede, is a music label *designed* by Amorales himself which distributed 5 albums challenging the entrepreneurial attitude, a central focus of our capitalist lifestyle, investigating the commercial spirituality of contemporary society.

Amorales operates in varying spheres, including *educational* ones as a guest lecturer or adviser to artists, he is closely connected to the world of galleries (Annet Gelink Gallery), museums (amongst others MALBA in Buenos Aires and Migros in Zurich), and biennials (Venice Biennale, Moscow Biennial) as well as the documenta (in 2009).

> "The archive contains a wealth of templates all of which contain nocturnal, dark, aspects. With this figurative inventory, including hybrids, hermaphrodites, wolves, skulls and apes on their knees or creeping along, Amorales creates surreal, mythical worlds which are analogous to horror films and thrillers."
> (*Global Contemporary*)

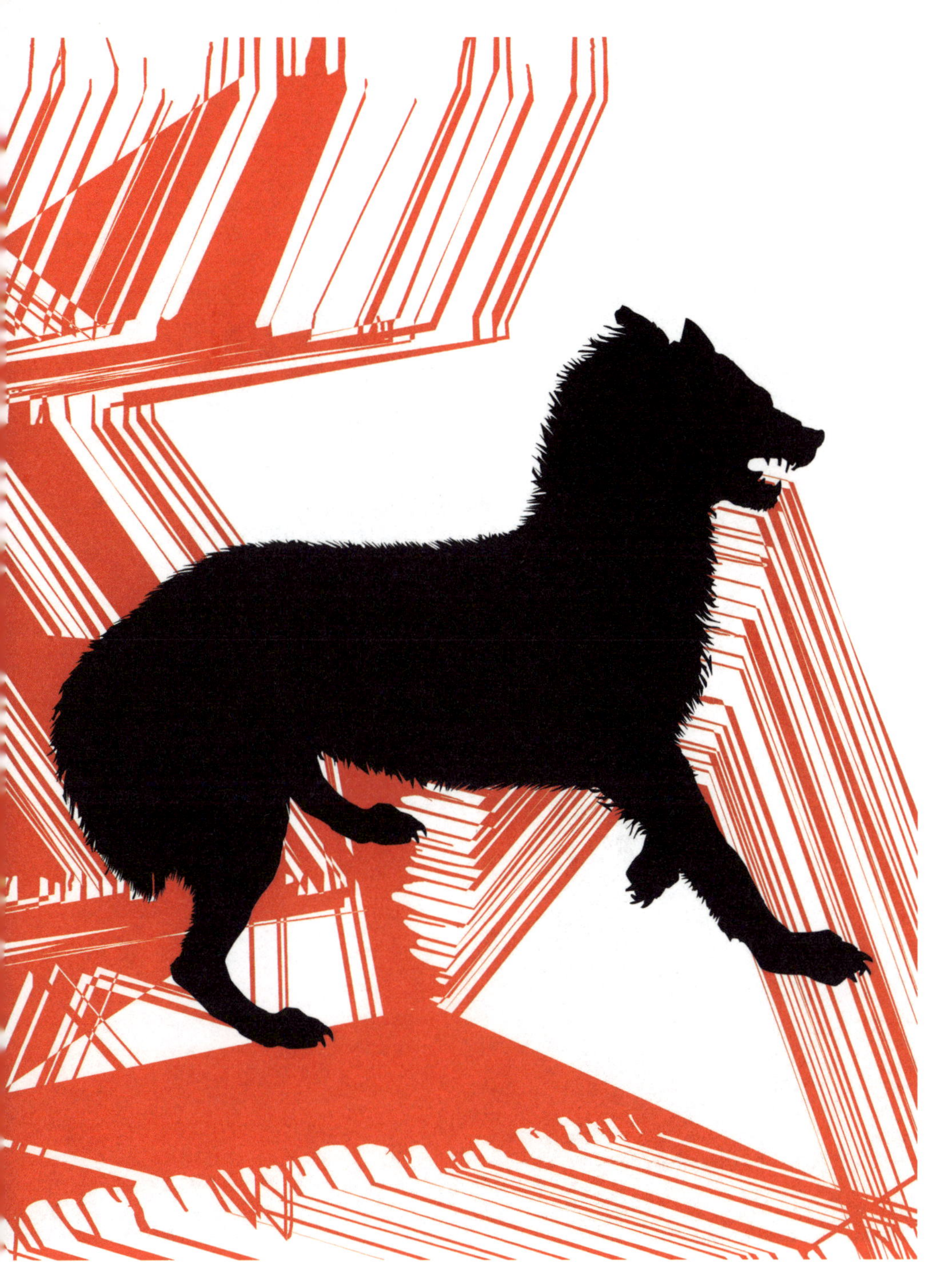

Carlos Amorales
*Scared Wolf Painting*, 2010, oil on canvas, 200 × 140 cm

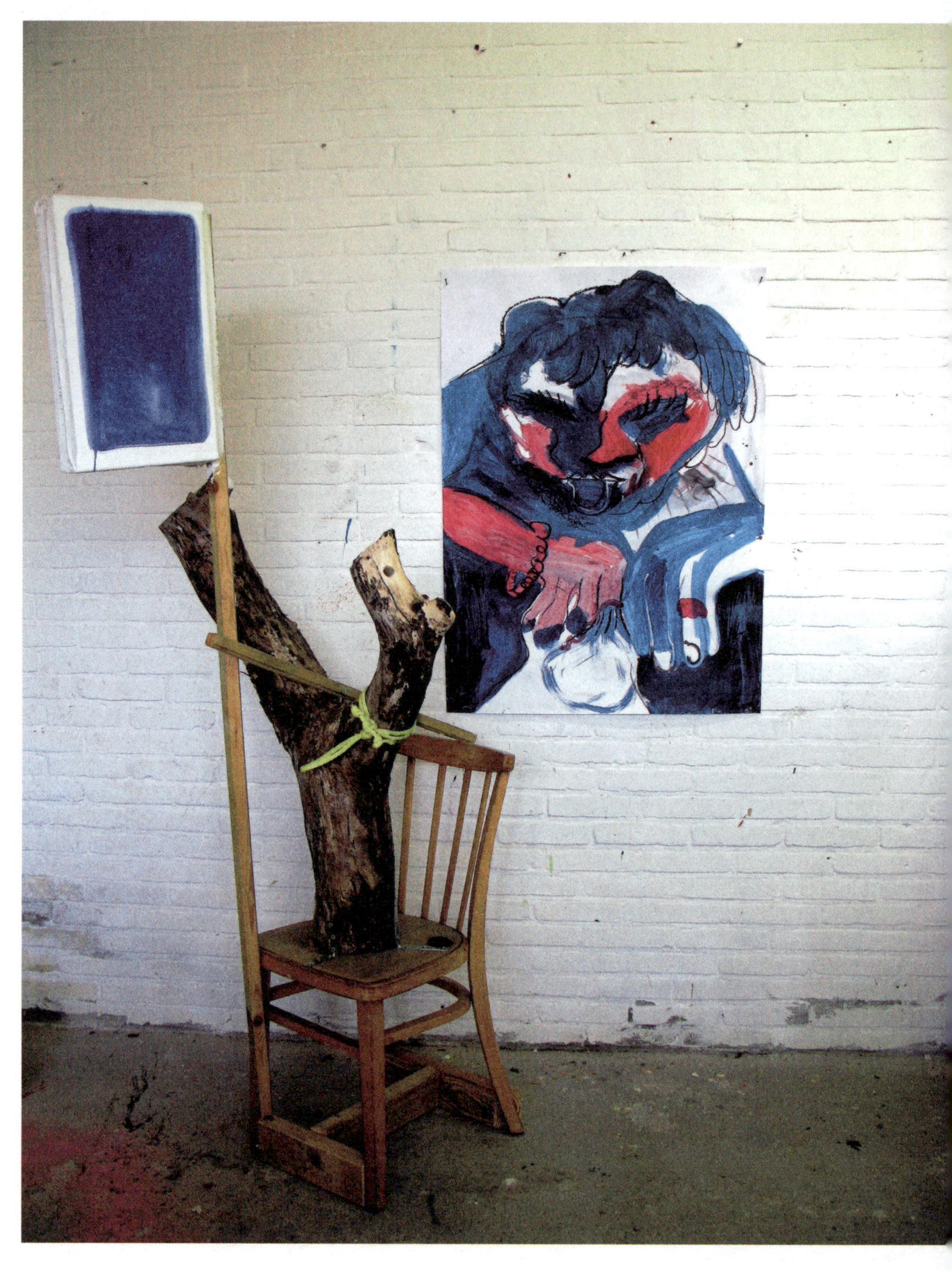

**David Bade**
*In the Pocket*, 2010, mixed media installation, c. 184 × 120 × 110 cm

## DAVID BADE

David Bade, born in 1970 in Willemstad (Curaçao), works and lives both in Curaçao and Zaandam (NL). He followed the programme for art teachers at Hogeschool Holland, followed by participation in Ateliers '63 in Haarlem (1993–1994). In 1993 he received a Prix de Rome for drawing. While he is currently associated with the artist's position as a change agent focusing on social intervention, at that time the physical *studio* was the preferred and only locus for his practice dealing with the creation of art objects. Bade started a successful career that led him to participate in important events, including the Venice Biennale (1995). Once established in the international art world, he was invited to participate in the educational project 'Onze Vader, Ons Moeder' in Museum Jan Cunen in Oss (1998). The artist worked on an exhibition with young vocational training students, coordinated and coached them in his first attempt to integrate the public (collectively) in creating and co-producing the work. Because of his personal enthusiasm for the project, Bade decided to take a further step in order to construct a personal environment within which to organise and educate, founding the art organisation ArteSwa with the Curaçaoan art-historian Jennifer Smit and his brother. Later, he returned to Curaçao on a more permanent basis, inviting a group of mostly Curaçaoan artists and designers originating from the Netherlands to instigate a project involving inclusion and development of local creative forces. The success of this first ArteSwa project led him to settle in Willemstad, from where he started engaging in debates with local people in order to understand Curaçao's cultural and social needs. From those discussions the long-term friendship and partnership with Tirzo Martha came into being. In 2005 they *organised* a project for the Curaçao Carnival together with the Capriles psychiatric clinic. Patients from the clinic and other people were, and still are involved in the project, organised by Bade and Martha. The success of this project and his experience in artistic tutorship within schools are at the basis of the Instituto Buena Bista (2006), an *educational* institution for all creative youngsters from Curaçao and elsewhere. In addition, the IBB hosts three artist-in-residence studios and facilitates their projects in order to stretch the island's artistic horizon, as well as starting a collection of contemporary artworks by resident artists. In this context, young artists have the chance to develop their skills and share ideas in a friendly, social and imaginative environment. Bade's practice of inclusion and organisation is aimed at releasing the imaginative power of people, in order to involve them in re-imagining their social environment. Bade uses his experience to advise, as he did as a member of the Prix de Rome jury in 2004 and 2007.

"His three-dimensional work is the result of an impulsive, associative process. The works have an informal, sometimes quirkily fun spirit, partly achieved by inviting members of the public to join in and help make a piece. Bade has an interest in producing a tightly finished product; the fragile, malleable and fleeting nature of the materials used in his installations underlines a working method that centres on the creation process itself." (*Global Contemporary*)

## DRIESSENS & VERSTAPPEN

Maria Verstappen and Erwin Driessens form an artistic duo based in Amsterdam. Erwin Driessens was born in 1963 in Wessem (NL) and Maria Verstappen in Someren (NL) a year later. They met whilst studying sculpture at the Academy of Fine Arts in Maastricht between 1982 and 1987. In 1989, both started at the Rijksakademie in Amsterdam. Since 1990 they have constituted an artistic duo that is prominent in the field of generative art. Their practice embraces different media such as sculpture, software, robotics, installations and photography, focusing on processes of growth and transformation.

Art and science, nature and technology are at the core of their artistic investigation in their mental atelier as well as in their physical *studio*. Nature is often perceived as an unstable, organic, open system while technology as a stable, closed system, even though 'openness' in nature is the result of precise and deterministic processes which cumulate over time, giving the illusory perception of a chaotic system. Verstappen and Driessens' practice revolves around conditions of unpredictability enabling an artwork to unfold in an unplanned way from computer-calculated environments in order to create an open process with technology, an artificial nature. In their practice, this fundamental facet of stability and instability is not only central in the *laboratory* (which is their main position) but also in public space and in their design and education activities.

Artworks like *Glow* (2014) and *Membrane* (2005) bring the generative image projections to a monumental scale in *public space* (the former on a 25-metre tall tower in Maastricht, the latter is a pavilion at the Museumplein in Amsterdam). In both artworks a computer-generated image unfolds on a physical structure whose characteristics define the space of the digital illusion. Technical constraints are also at the basis of the *design* project for the commemorative coin for Crown Princess Amalia's birth. The complex specifics of a coin can limit artistic freedom for design yet Driessens & Verstappen took advantage of the limited space to create a dynamic image unfolding in three images at once. The creation of opportunities for experiment and imagination is at the core of their *educational* activities which, aside from professional lecturing at festivals and symposia, include teaching children.

> M.V.: "One could say that in nature everything is also very precise and deterministic, but the complexity of all the elements that interact with one another and feedback relating to one another is so great that we experience it as uncontrolled, whimsical and open ended." (email received on 13 July 2016 from Driessens and Verstappen)

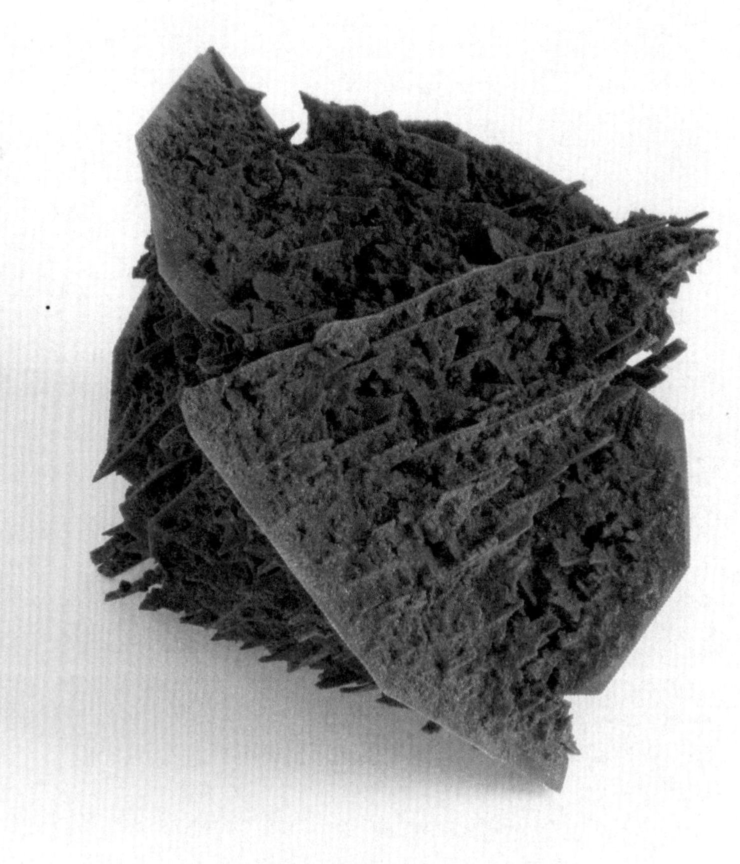

**Driessens & Verstappen**
***Accretor #ru4944*, 2012, 3D print in acrylic, 20 × 20 × 20 cm**

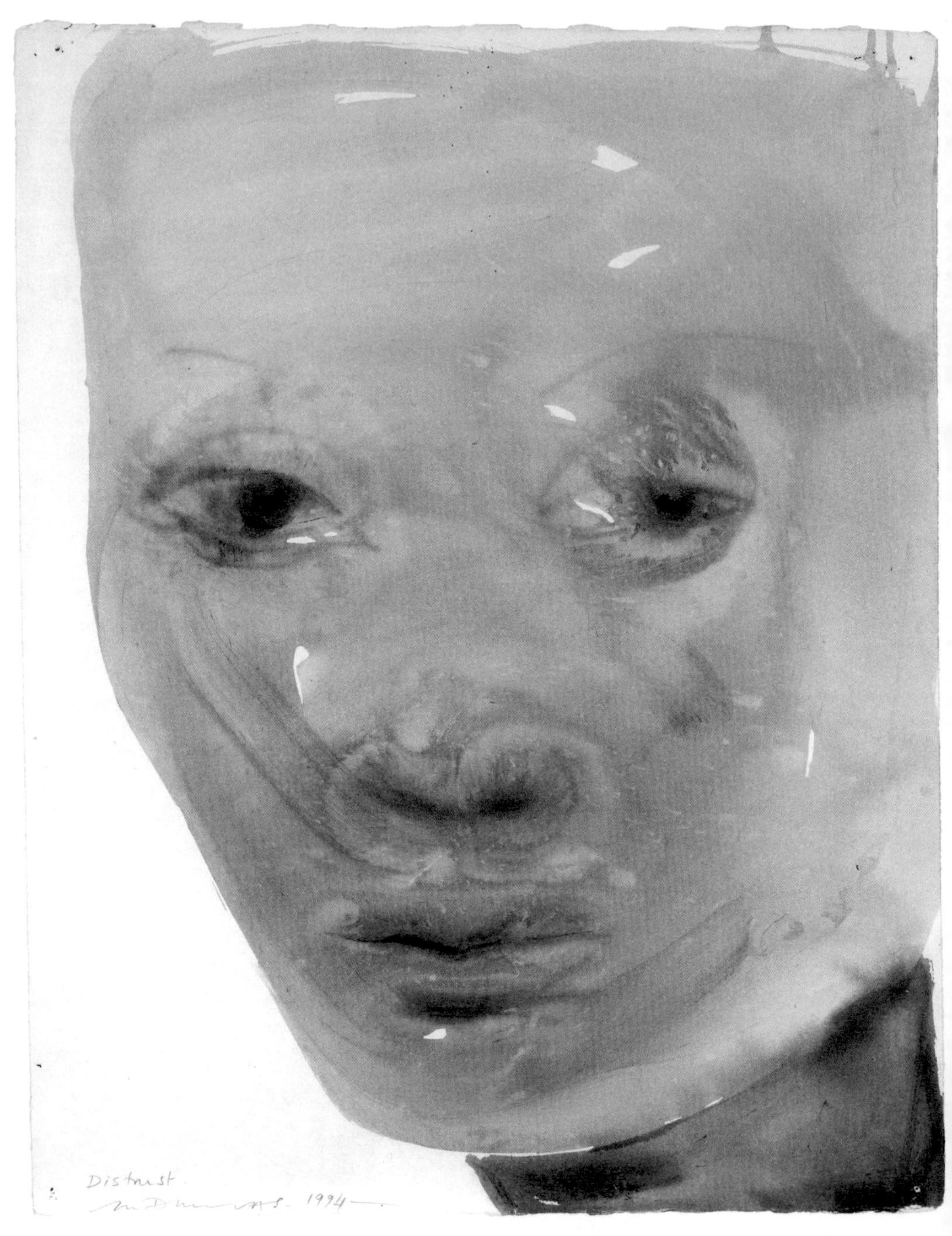


**Marlene Dumas**
***Distrust*, 1994, watercolour on paper, 65.5 × 50.5 cm**

## MARLENE DUMAS

Marlene Dumas born in Cape Town (SA) in 1953, currently lives and works in Amsterdam. From 1972 to 1975 she attended the University of Cape Town (fine art) before moving to the Netherlands. She participated in the programme for aspiring artists at Ateliers '63 in Haarlem between 1976 and 1979; the following year she studied at the Psychological Institute, University of Amsterdam.

Dumas' practice is based on the investigation of the image of the human body, dead or alive, coming from art history or pop-culture alike. This forms the starting point for her paintings. Her visual sensibility in studying and internalising an image in order to give certain details back to the beholder, blowing-up or zooming, cutting or adding, makes her work an investigation of the sexual, racial, social nature of images. Her *studio* is a space for individual reflection and creation. Dumas has a huge archive of images, cut out of newspapers, magazines, postcards and so forth that constitute the primary source for her work. Most of the images are accompanied by texts contextualising them, and that helps the artist's understanding. Only a few images of this archive have become a painting but the study of all of them is the backbone of the creative process in which personal experience and sociological culture merge into her artistic production. The space in-between documentation of reality and the construction of the painting is where the tension lies, highlighted by a minimal and dry painting technique.

Her focus on the image and on the creation of paintings, collages and drawings did not prevent Dumas from experimenting in other directions. She has also always *written* about art and these writings are published in the book *Sweet Nothings* (1998, updated version 2014). In 2000 she was asked to make a tapestry for the Constitutional Court in Den Bosch. In 1998 she *designed* a set of playing cards. Recently she received a *public commission* for an altarpiece for the Annenkirche in Dresden, realised between 2014 and 2016. Throughout her career she has accompanied her practice as an artist with *educating* at various institutes in the Netherlands, including the Rijksakademie and De Ateliers in Amsterdam.

> "The relation between art and female beauty, art and pornography, female models and models of art has been a constant theme for Marlene Dumas. Her work is characterized by a sensual and gestural technique that is also swift, dry and minimal, as if under pressure to leave only what is necessary. (...) Images from high or low culture or from anonymous acquaintances, the images are all familiar to us." (*Global Contemporary*)

## CLAUDIA FONTES

Claudia Fontes, born in 1964 in Buenos Aires (AR), now based in England, attended the National School of Fine Arts Prilidiano Pueyrredón and Art History at Buenos Aires University, after which she gained a grant for Taller de Barracas. Later she participated as an artist in residence at the Rijksakademie in Amsterdam (1996–1997). In her artistic practice she investigates alternative perspectives on society and culture, often linked to the decolonisation of individuals and groups.

Interest in shifting perception is expressed in her artworks and social actions, which started at an early stage of her career in the *studio* with the creation of art objects and outside the studio. Since then her practice has developed into a *progressive* engagement within the *public sphere*. Fontes won an international competition and her understanding of intricate social relations led her to decide to reconstruct the portrait of Pablo Miguez–victim of dictatorship, tortured and thrown out of a military plane over the water some 13 years earlier–commemorating all 'desaparecidos': *Reconstruction of Pablo Miguez's Portrait* (1999), placed in Rìo de la Plata.

The participatory characteristic of her practice and her comprehension of complexities are at the core of her *advising* activity, unfolding mainly in the art world. From 2000 to 2006 she ran (and founded) TRAMA a platform of cooperation and friendship between artists in Argentina through debates and workshops, to make the local art scene more democratic, inclusive and cooperative. It meant also–as an *educator*–filling the gap in art education in different regions in Argentina. This project was included in the broader scope of RAIN, a global platform for artists who came from the Rijksakademie, of which Fontes was a prominent *organiser*. Acting as an adviser she is able to encourage a shift in perspective, thanks to her evaluating cultural programmes in the field of international cooperation, by cultural funds like DOEN and Hivos. The former is focused on artists, with the objective of sustaining creativity and artistic freedom, whilst the latter is a platform to support cultural organisations and institutions that fight against poverty, corruption and human rights violations by means of art production. While she was operating as an adviser, she was also expanding her position as a change agent. Moreover, Claudia's broad artistry, including the continued studio practice, has resulted in her representing Argentina in the Venice Biennale in 2017.

> "This attempt at reconstructing an image became an exercise in collective memory building, in which Pablo's relatives, friends and 13-year old children took part. In exercising the right to memory, we all tried together to dismantle said perverse semantics and give evidence to a fact, which unfortunately is still widely denied."
> (www.claudiafontes.com/work/Reconstruction-Pablo-Miguez-portrait)

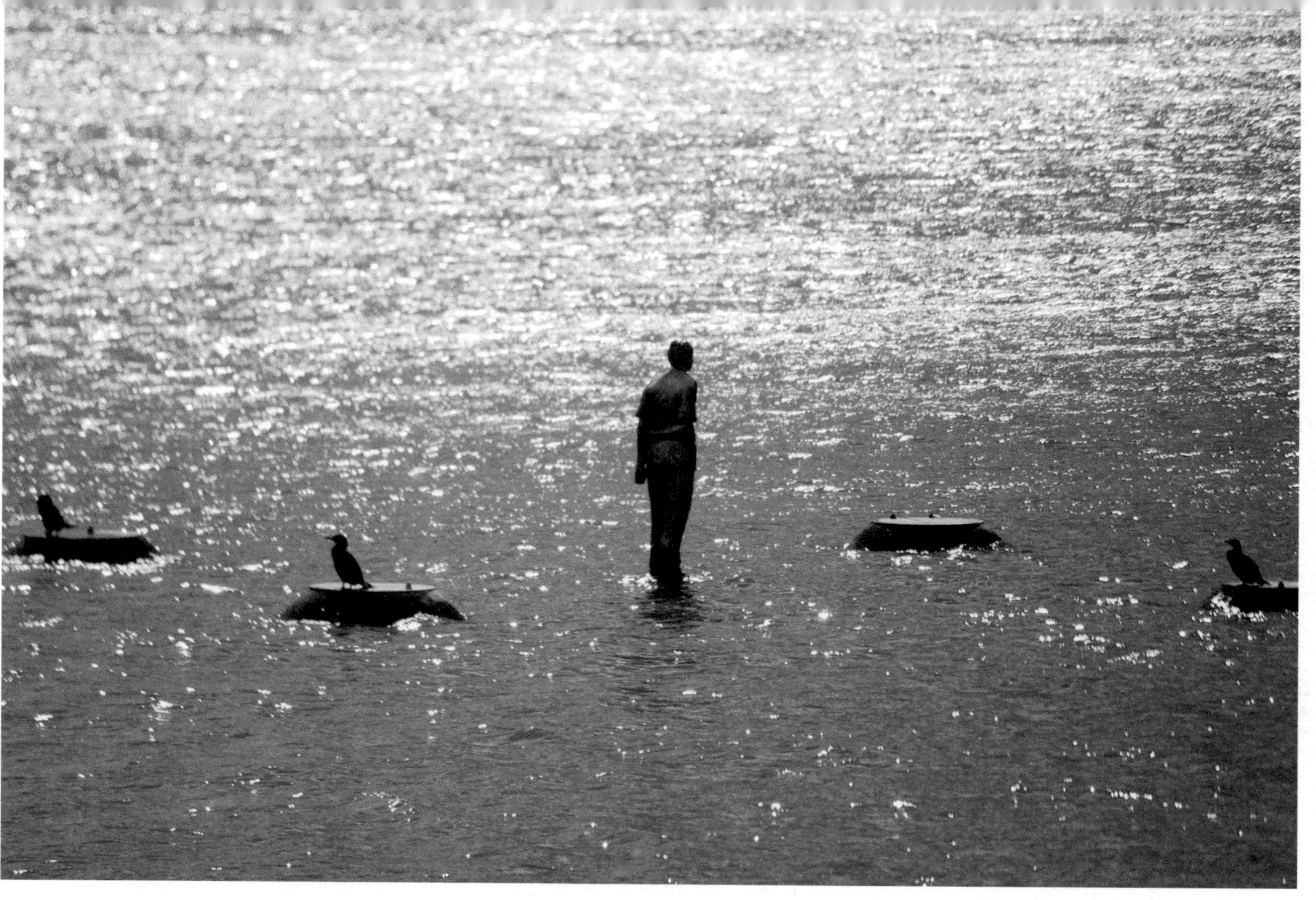

**Claudia Fontes**
*Reconstruction of Pablo Miguez's Portrait*, 1999, installation, 170 × 50 × 70 cm

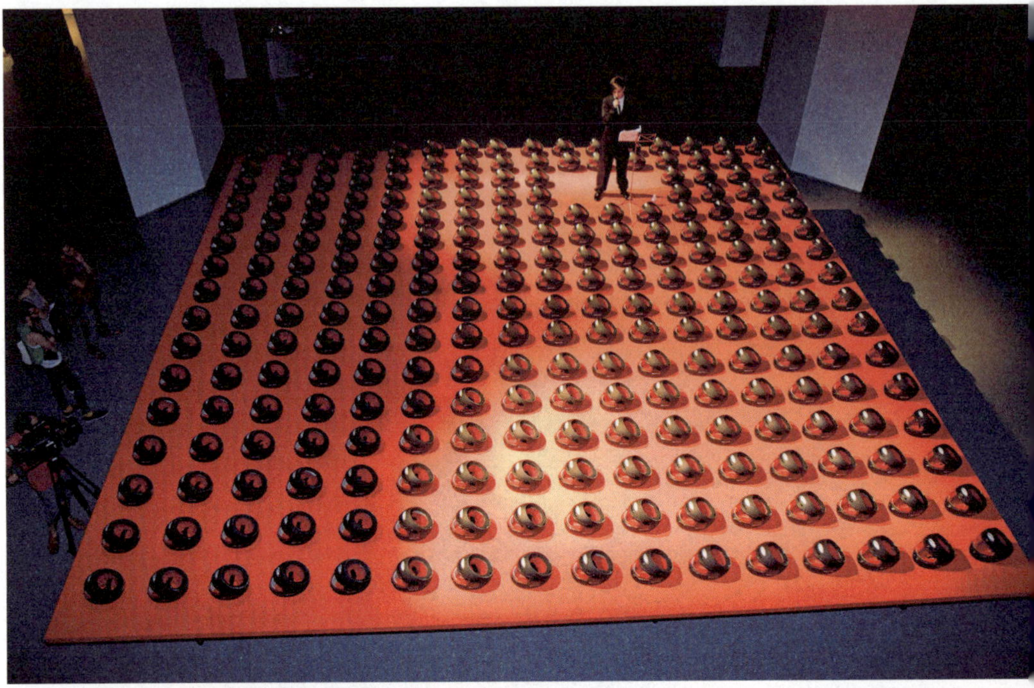

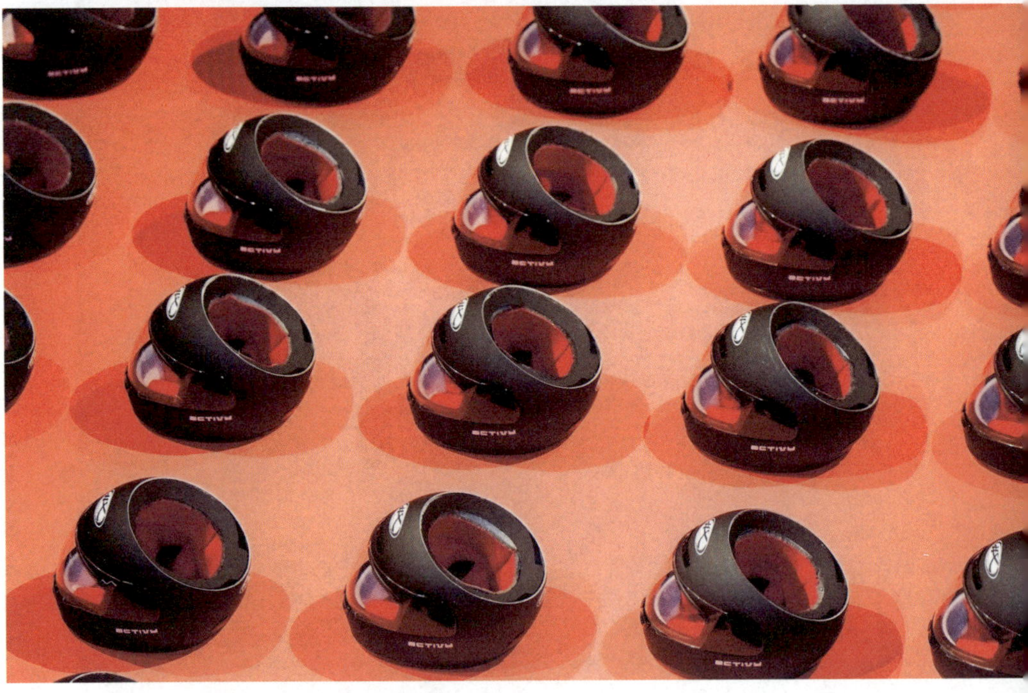

Alicia Framis
*Guantanamo Museum*, 2008, installation of 274 helmets, DVD, table and speaker, c. 800 × 800 × 40 cm

## ALICIA FRAMIS

Alicia Framis, born in 1967 in Barcelona (ES), currently lives and works in Amsterdam and Barcelona. She obtained a BFA from both Barcelona University and Ecole Nationale Supérieure des Beaux-Arts in Paris followed by attendance at the MFA institute at Institut des Hautes Études, also in Paris. Later, in 1996 and 1997 she was a resident at the Rijksakademie in Amsterdam.

Her practice, with a strong interest in the social dimension of art objects, touches upon different media and artists' positions, from architecture and design to performance and sculpture, having as a common thread a strong engagement with societal dilemmas, crossing boundaries between disciplines. While her research is developed in the *studio*, the preferred locus in which her practice unfolds is the *public space*. One of the first awards this artist won was the Prix de Rome for Public Art in 1997, with *Walking Monument*, a *performative* sculpture in Dam square in Amsterdam addressing political, historical and memory issues. In another public artwork *Billboard House* (2000–2009) Framis *designed* a rudimental house with billboards then placed it in natural contexts, engaging with contemporary social challenges–in this case the need for shelters for immigrants. In *Loneliness in the City* (1999–2000) Framis catalyses social forces to discuss solutions for *loneliness* in urban environments in an itinerant pavilion of her design. It travelled around, stopping in squares where people could freely participate and have the chance to discuss the problem of solitude in contemporary society. Transferring ideas is part of her practice, both in creating platforms for social cooperation, where she plays a role as a *change agent* thanks to her capacity to organise and deal with complexities, both socially and technically.

> "She explores the legacy of horror of places such as Auschwitz or Alcatraz and analyses the historical process of sites with such a terrible past, questioning if they can be become a tourist attraction. ... Framis assures us that, in the not too distant future, Guantanamo Prison will be transformed into a museum." (*Global Contemporary*)

## MESCHAC GABA

Meschac Gaba was born in 1961 in Benin, living and working in his *studios* in both Rotterdam (NL) and Cotonou (Benin), where he was raised and educated. Though initially a painter, his tendency to experiment with different, often unconventional, materials was clear from the beginning of his career. Between 1991 and 1996 he worked in Benin until he moved to Amsterdam, where he obtained a residency at the Rijksakademie. There, Gaba initiated, developed and presented for the first time his famous artwork *Museum of Contemporary African Art*. It is now composed of 12 rooms, all assigned to different functions, which constitute an alternative museum to the dominant Western institutions. *The Draft Room*, the first of the 12 rooms of this museum, was shown at the Rijksakademie during the Open Studio in 1997. The first public exhibition of another of the rooms called *Architecture Room*, was shown at the Gate Foundation in Amsterdam in 1998. During the curatorial process the artist designed unconventional rooms for his museum, like the *Game Room*, where people could meet and interact while gaming. The museum for Gaba represents not only a place for conversation and display but also for study and research. Gaba's rooms have been separately exhibited internationally but one part remained the artist's property: the *Library*, now belonging to his project (MAVA: Musée de l'Art de la Vie Active) in Cotonou. The acquisition of the complete museum by the Tate Modern marks a moment of further shift, widening Western-centric perspectives within that institute.

As an international artist he tries to change the perspective on African art, while as an artist and citizen of Cotonou he tries, with local experiences, to change the ground for the understanding of contemporary art in that community. In this regard some of his art-works, sometimes in the form of *performances*, were displayed in the streets of the city. He wants to shift the perspective from art as object to art as *social project*.

*Curatorship* is an important part of his practice, connecting creative forces and people, but the production of art objects is equally active. The artist produces pieces that document contemporary reality and in order to do so, is often helped by craftsmen and other professionals from the local community.

> "Gaba invites visitors into his museum as active participants. His rooms often feature money: shredded banknotes from Benin, Holland and Switzerland. For Gaba, money represents the skewed economic and cultural relations between the West and Africa in the world economy." (*Global Contemporary*)

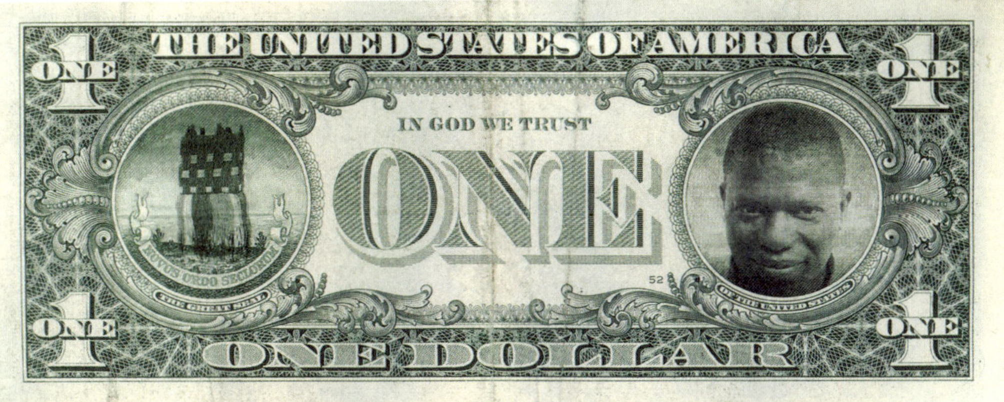


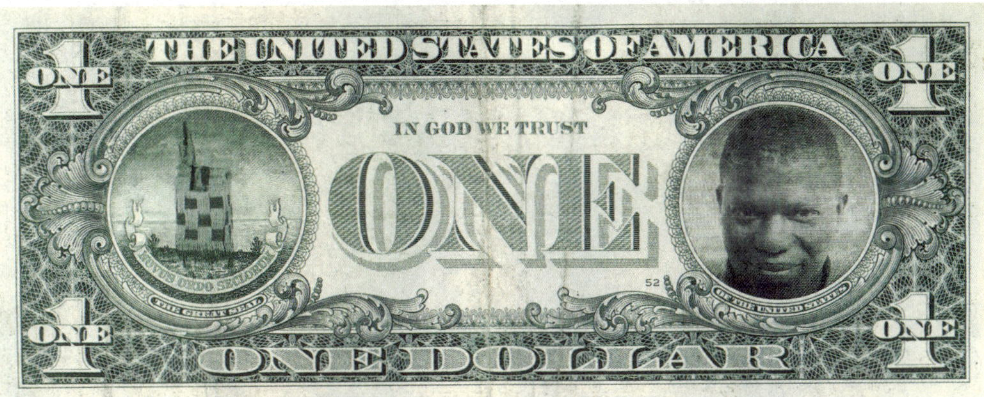


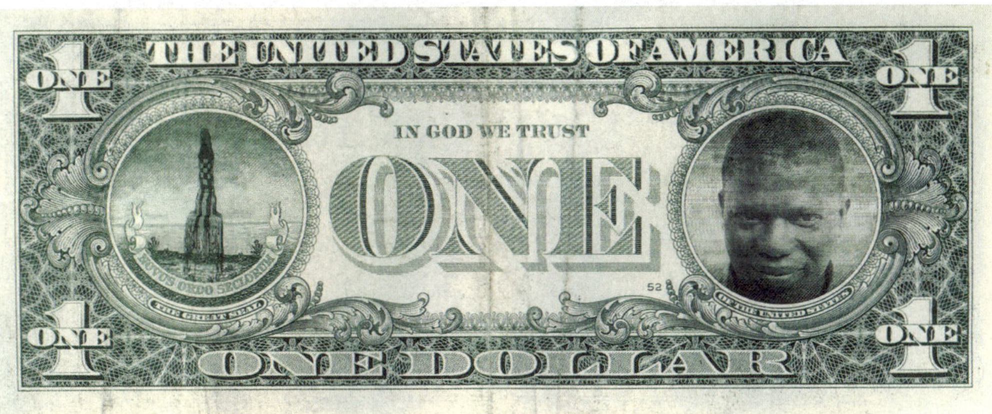


**Meschac Gaba**
**_Artist with American Inspiration_, 2004, digital prints, 46 × 109 cm**

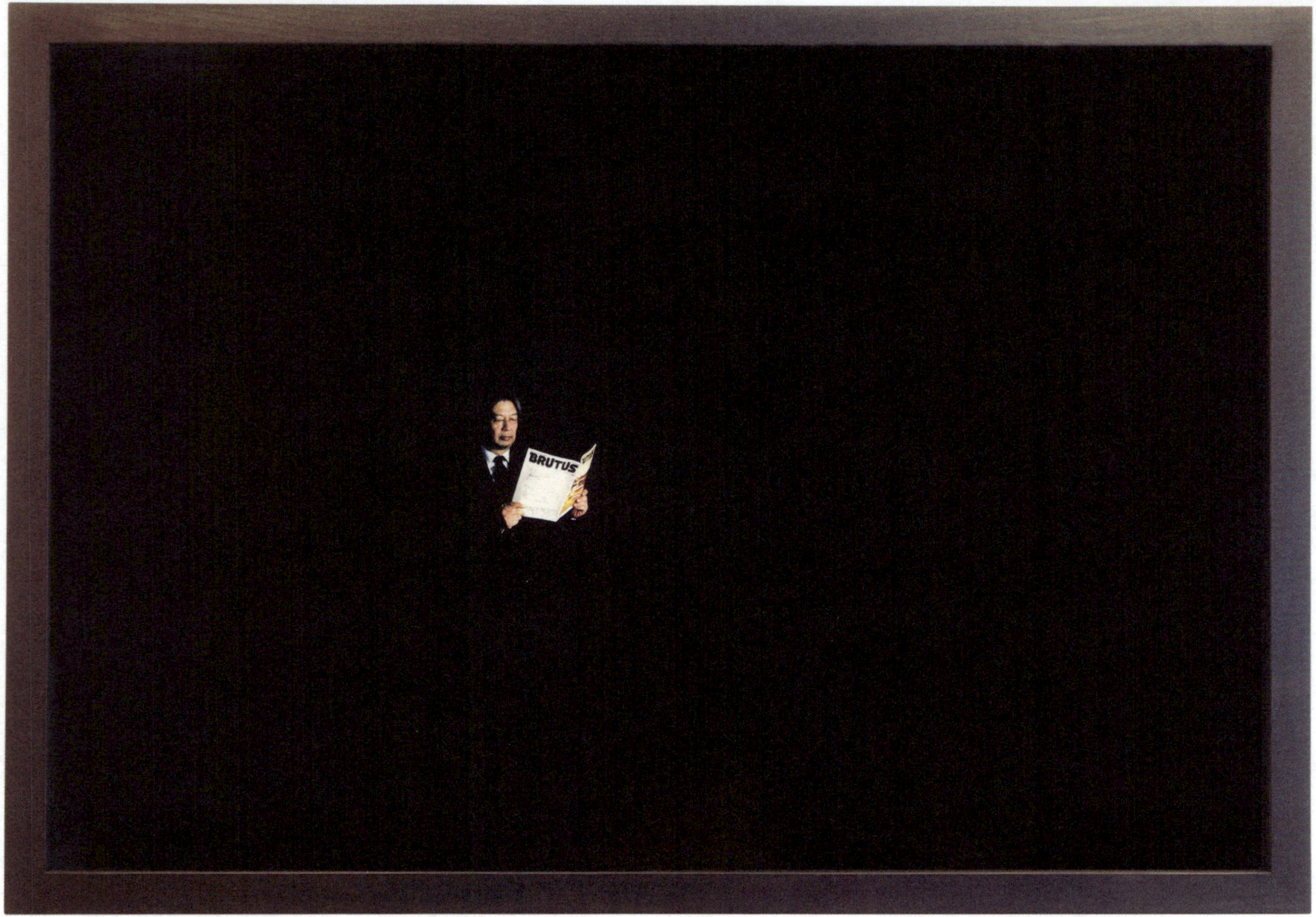

**Ryan Gander**
***A Portrait of Mr Sato Attempting to Differentiate Between Santo and Aston in the Darkness*, 2010, c-print, 100 × 150 cm**

## RYAN GANDER

Ryan Gander was born in 1976 in Chester (UK), currently living and working in London and Suffolk. He studied Interactive Art (BA) at Manchester Metropolitan University from 1996 to 1999 and a year later he attended the Jan van Eyck Academy in Maastricht (NL) as a Fine Art Research participant. In 2001 he moved to Amsterdam where he was a resident at the Rijksakademie until 2002. In 2003 he won the Prix de Rome for Sculpture.

Gander's work unfolds through a variety of media such as installation, video, advertising, sound and literature which he uses to reconfigure aesthetic parameters in order to dismantle art-historical conventions, in a process of permanent reflection on his own practice. His oeuvre is characterised by crossing boundaries and a merging of styles, to the point that there is no evidence of a personal 'vocabulary'.

The creative process begins with an investigation and analysis of multiple topics which are elaborated through archiving and documenting. The *studio* is a space for team-work, as Gander does not produce the artworks himself, but hires different craftsmen for different projects. In effect, the variety of interests and media in his practice and the high rate of production demand a broad set of technical skills. Gander's success has led him to exhibit internationally in many venues, not working solo but allowing him to organise and coordinate considerable numbers of people. His aptitude for *organising* is not only confined to managerial activities but extends, on a relational level, to connecting people and especially artists. In 2007 he founded and directed the non-profit temporary gallery 'Associates' on Hoxton Street, where artists who have never been exhibited in London had the possibility of being presented in a solo show. 'Associates' gallery offered the entirety of their sales profits to the artists in order to empower them, not only by offering a space for collaboration and friendship, but also offering them economic empowerment.

Gander's drive towards creating conditions which induce artistic creativity to blossom, led him to conceive, together with creative consultant Simon Turnbull, Fairfield International, a project in progress for a residential art *school* in Suffolk (UK) for young artists with both artistic excellence and a need for financial support.

> "Ryan Gander connects prosaic historical facts and events with a large collection of fictional and semi-fictional elements. ... The finished pieces are often minimal, but they suggest a variety of positions of reference, from the utopian impulses of the early twentieth century to contemporary popular culture and mundane aspects of everyday life."
> (*Global Contemporary*)

## ANTONY GORMLEY

Antony Gormley was born in 1950 in London (UK), where he lives and works. Between 1968 and 1971 he attended Trinity College in Cambridge, studying archaeology, anthropology and history of art. He travelled in Asia from 1971 to 1974, where he witnessed and experienced Buddhist practices (which began to play a role in his artistic research in the following years). After his return to the United Kingdom he attended the Central School of Art, Goldsmiths and the Slade School of Art in London, between 1974 and 1979.

Gormley's practice is grounded in the *studio*, the locus where work is developed, produced on a large scale, stored and distributed. The physical studio–the studio's architecture–matches with Gormley's mental atelier: most of the building is given over to technological research, production and experimentation, while in a smaller room Gormley develops the concepts of his artworks in a space for personal reflection, meditation and calmness, often making drawings. The art object is developed in the studio. Gormley produces many sculptures for relatively intimate spaces including museums and commercial galleries, but his work often acquires a social dimension in *public space*: *Angel of the North* (Gateshead, England), *Another Place* (Crosby Beach, England), *Inside Australia* (Lake Ballard, Western Australia), *Exposure* (Lelystad, the Netherlands) and *Chord* (MIT–Massachusetts Institute of Technology, Cambridge, MA, USA), to mention but a few of his famous public sculptures. The setting of those pieces is not only in cities but also in nature; the relation between the artist's body and space is the core of his artistic investigation. His work has developed the potential opened up by sculpture since the 1960s through a critical engagement. Both his own body and bodies of others confront fundamental questions of where human beings stand in relation to nature and the cosmos. Gormley continually tries to identify the space of art as a place of 'becoming', in which new behaviours, thoughts and feelings can arise. Other artworks, like *One and Other* (2009), are strictly related to urban space, in which the artist staged a transformation of live human bodies into art pieces by giving people the opportunity to stand and perform on the fourth plinth in Trafalgar Square. Gormley has often collaborated with architects and choreographers, including Sidi Larbi Cherkaoui and Damien Jalet, to realise a dance performance, *Babel (Words)*. His contribution entailed *designing scenographic structures*. His multifaceted practice comes into its own as he copes with these complexities.

> AG.: "There is a lot of experimentation, but the *Domain* series really got going when I realized I could describe the space of the body as a matrix formed from eight lengths of stainless steel in a reversal of the Greek pointing system, with rods resting on the internal surface of a body volume. They are put together with a loose set of rules: one end of each T-connection should always be touching the skin or boundary." (*Global Contemporary*)

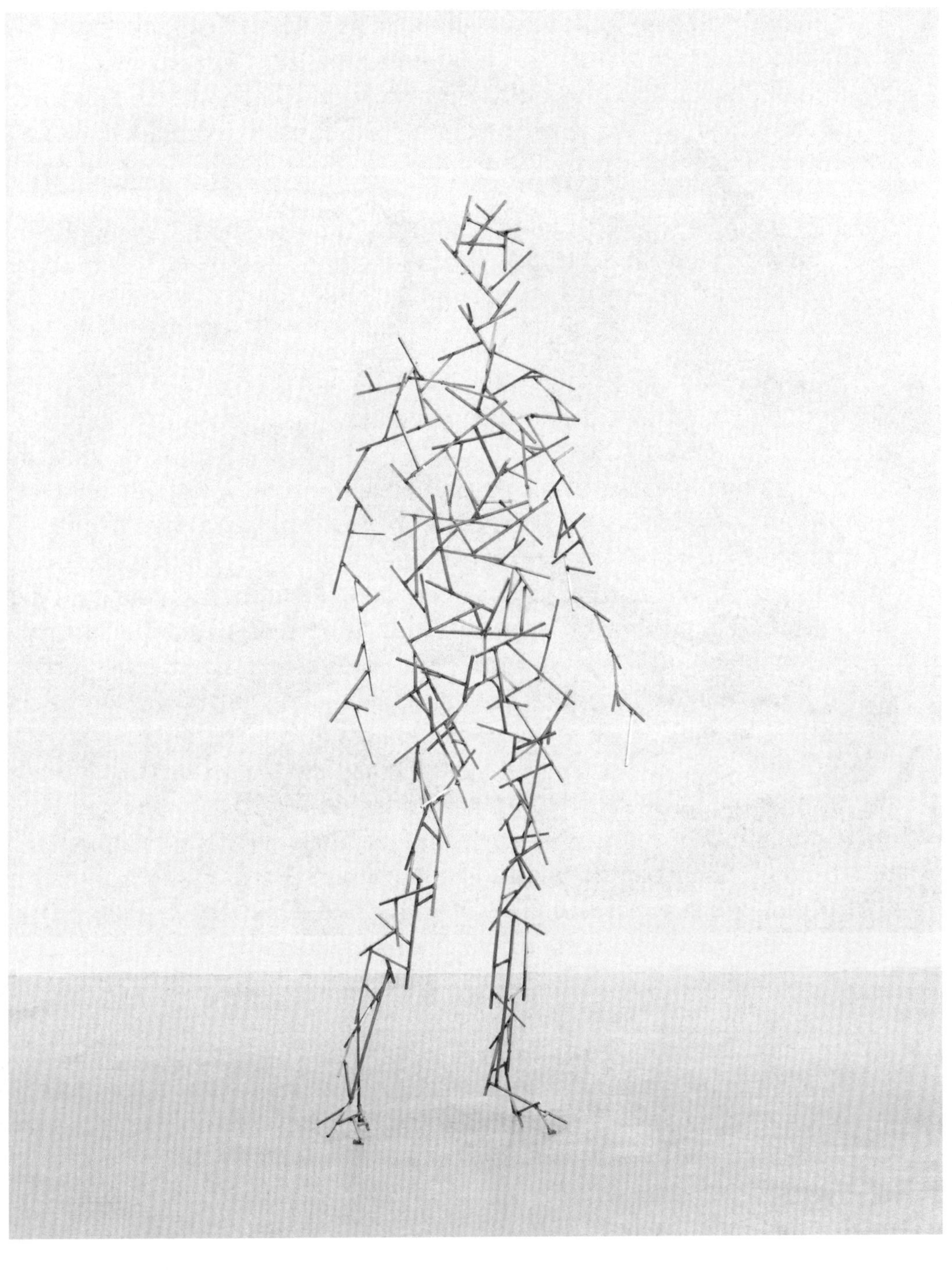

**Antony Gormley**
***Domain LXXI*, 2009, 4.67 mm square stainless steel bar, 189 × 71 × 42 cm**

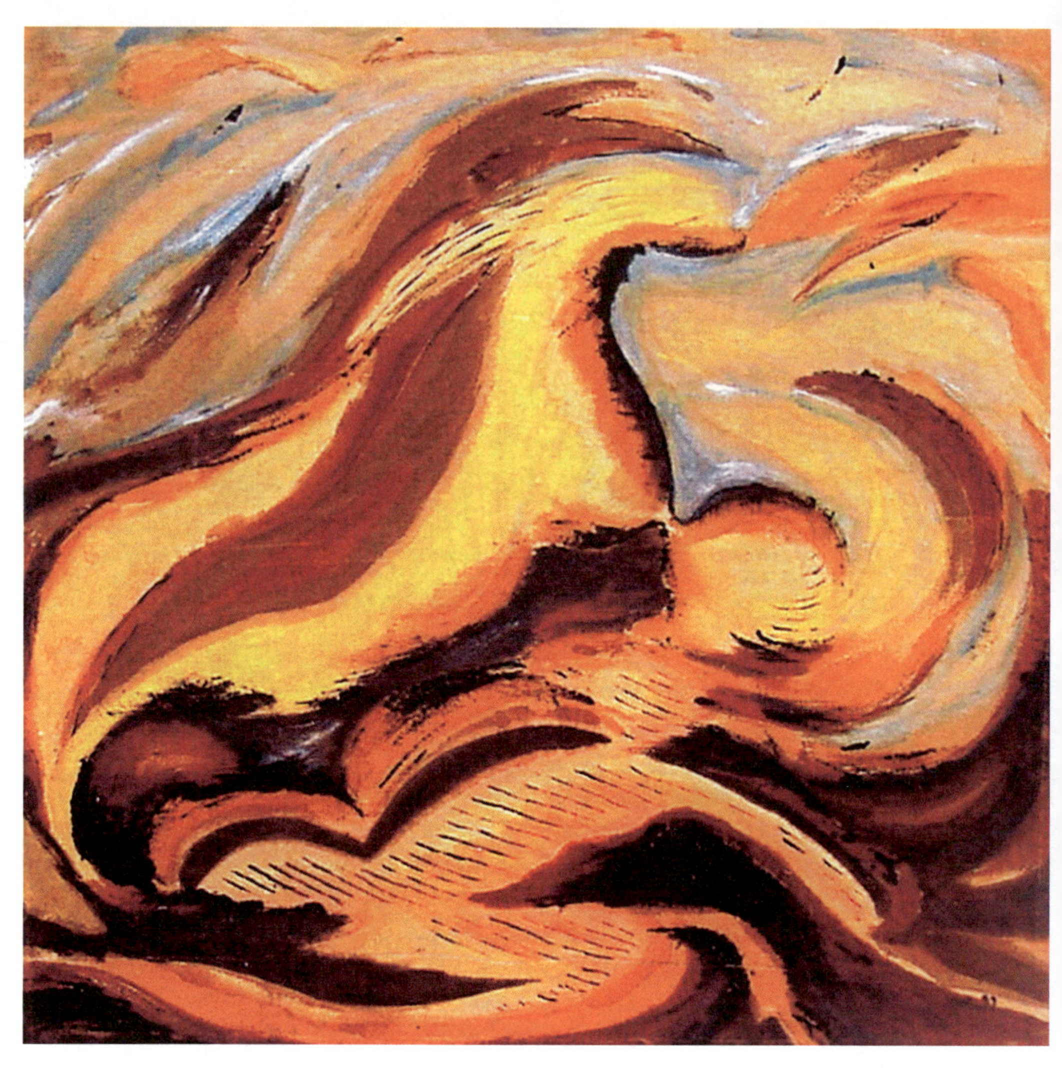

Hama Goro
*Puissance*, 2011, bogolan and acrylique, 145 × 120 cm

## HAMA GORO

Hama Goro, born in 1963 in Dinangourou in the Dogon area in Mali, lives and works in Bamako (ML). In 1987, he graduated in drawing and visual arts from the National Art Institute of Bamako. After working in a collective with friends he moved to Amsterdam and attended the Rijksakademie in 1995 and 1996. At that stage of his career the *studio* was the locus where he painted social, economical and political subjects using a traditional Dogon technique with colours prepared from natural pigments. Goro's artworks are characterised by natural chromatic tones. In contrast with this traditional paint-on-canvas method, he began applying the Dogon technique to furniture decoration, allowing him to distance himself from tradition. His period in Amsterdam helped him to perceive Mali from 'the outside', leading him to take a critical position towards his country and, upon his return, to engage with African society in a more socially committed way.

In 1999, he founded the centre Soleil d'Afrique in Bamako, whose mission is to foster and host artistic projects by local people. At the centre he works with friends to realise cooperative artworks. International artists were also hosted in residencies, where they had the chance to teach and learn simultaneously. To help this project succeed he took further steps in education, attending a course in Management in Artistic and Cultural Action at the Conservatoire des Arts et Métiers Multimedia Mali in 2007. Goro's engagement with society through the arts unfolds in his activity as an *organiser*, *educator*, *adviser*, *curator* and a *change agent* as well. Aside from directing the centre Soleil d'Afrique, curating its exhibitions and teaching younger artists, he co-founded different platforms for artistic solidarity and support for African artists such as KYA network, Aterial Network and RAIN. His various activities are by no means separate from his studio practice, but are complementary to it.

> "Just before the events that threatened to jeopardise the very existence of our country (Mali), the state was struggling to impose its authority. This inspired me to translate on canvas an adage from home to challenge the people 'on dit celui qui a été bien rassasié de lait maternel de sa maman qu'il se manifeste.' (It is said that he who has drunk too much of his mothers milk, let him say so). So for me this work could inspire Ministers and officials who gathered in the conference room."
> (email from Hama Goro received on 29 July 2016)

## SIGURDUR GUDMUNDSSON

Sigurdur Gudmundsson was born in Reykjavik (IS) in 1942, currently working and living in Xiamen (CN), Amsterdam (NL) and Reykjavik. Before moving to the Netherlands he attended the Icelandic College of Arts and Crafts in Reykjavik until 1963. Once in Holland he participated in Academie '63, later Ateliers '63 in Haarlem in 1971. His practice developed through different media including performance, photography, painting, writing and in recent years his focus has turned mainly to sculpture. In 1966, he joined Fluxus which strongly influenced his most famous series of artworks *Situations*, a series of photographs with the artist himself as the protagonist, but which are not self portraits. Initially *staged* as 'happenings', the photographs are both documentation and central pieces of the project. Gudmundsson wrote a story through these images, in which the photographs do not stand alone, but compose an absurd narrative of everyday situations relating to nature, a strong element of his work. *Situations* are 'conceptual poems' in which existentialism and lyricism are tied together by both the human element and objects, in which visual and written narratives merge. His activity as a *writer* further developed in recent years in the publication of several Icelandic writings, including three novels: *Tabúlarasa* (1993), *Ósýnilega konan* (2000) and *Dýrin í Saigon* (2010).

Nature is also a core feature of his various sculptural works installed in public spaces throughout the Netherlands (as in the case with *Red Secret*, 1998) in the choice of materials, that are usually metal, wood or stone. Gudmundsson's practice is not limited to the creation of art objects in the *studio* but includes many roles the artist has within society: he has been an *educator* at Academy of Art and Industry in Enschede (1978–1986) and later an adviser at the Rijksakademie, he is also part of the Dieter Roth Academy, based in Seydisfjordur (IS) and the co-founder, in 1978, of the Reykjavik's Living Art Museum, a space that fosters experimentalism in art. He is often an *adviser* and more often an *organiser* behind the scenes, as in the case of the Chinese European Art Center (CEAC), artist residency and presentation platform in Xiamen, China.

> "Documented and undocumented performances, photographs, drawings, prints, sculptures, installations and even musical compositions. ... Gudmundsson's work is still distinguished by poetry, romanticism, philosophy and he demands the viewer to be a poet, a romantic and a philosopher."
> (*Global Contemporary*)

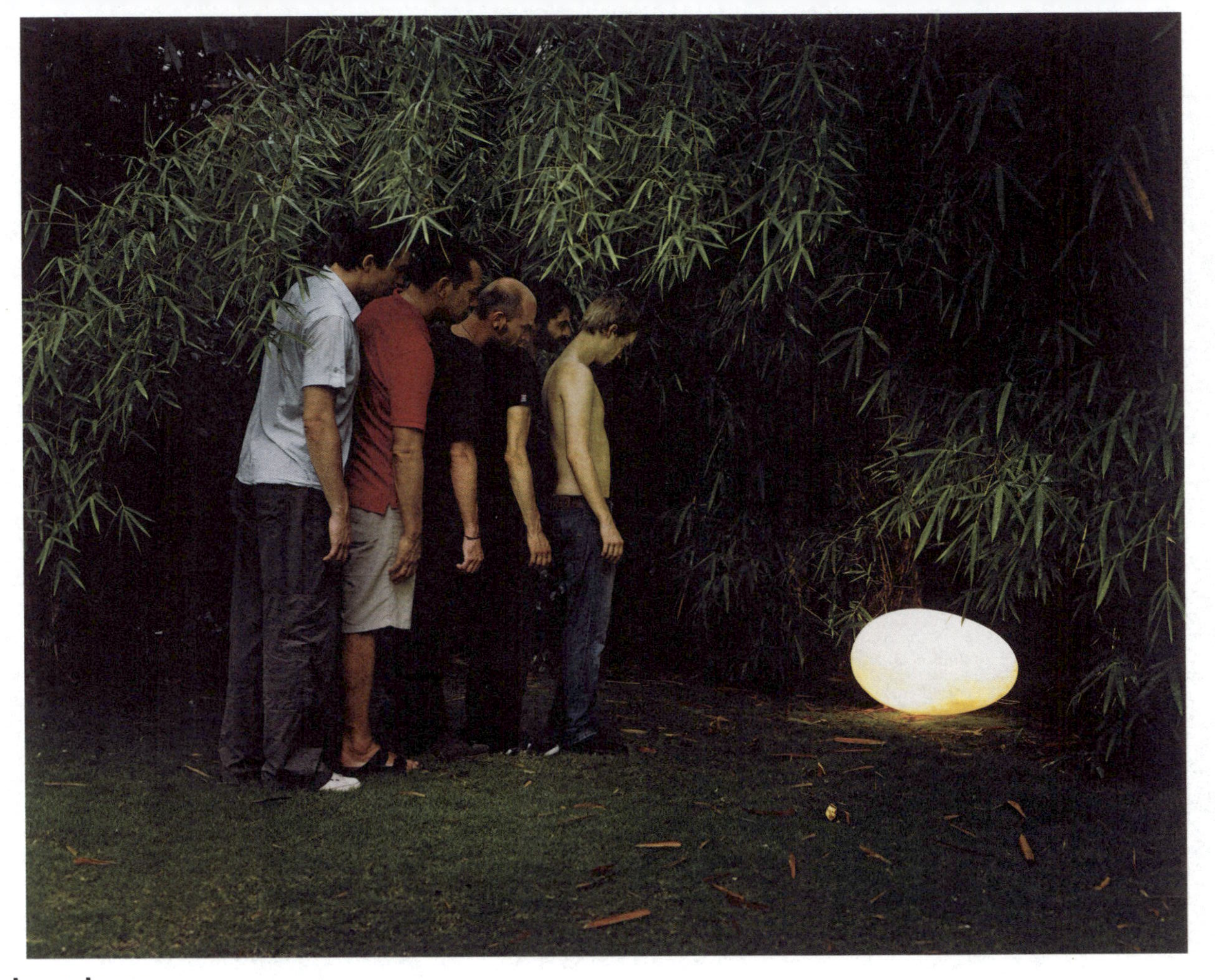

Sigurdur Gudmundsson
*Five Males and an Egg*, 2007, c-print on aluminium, 120 × 150 cm

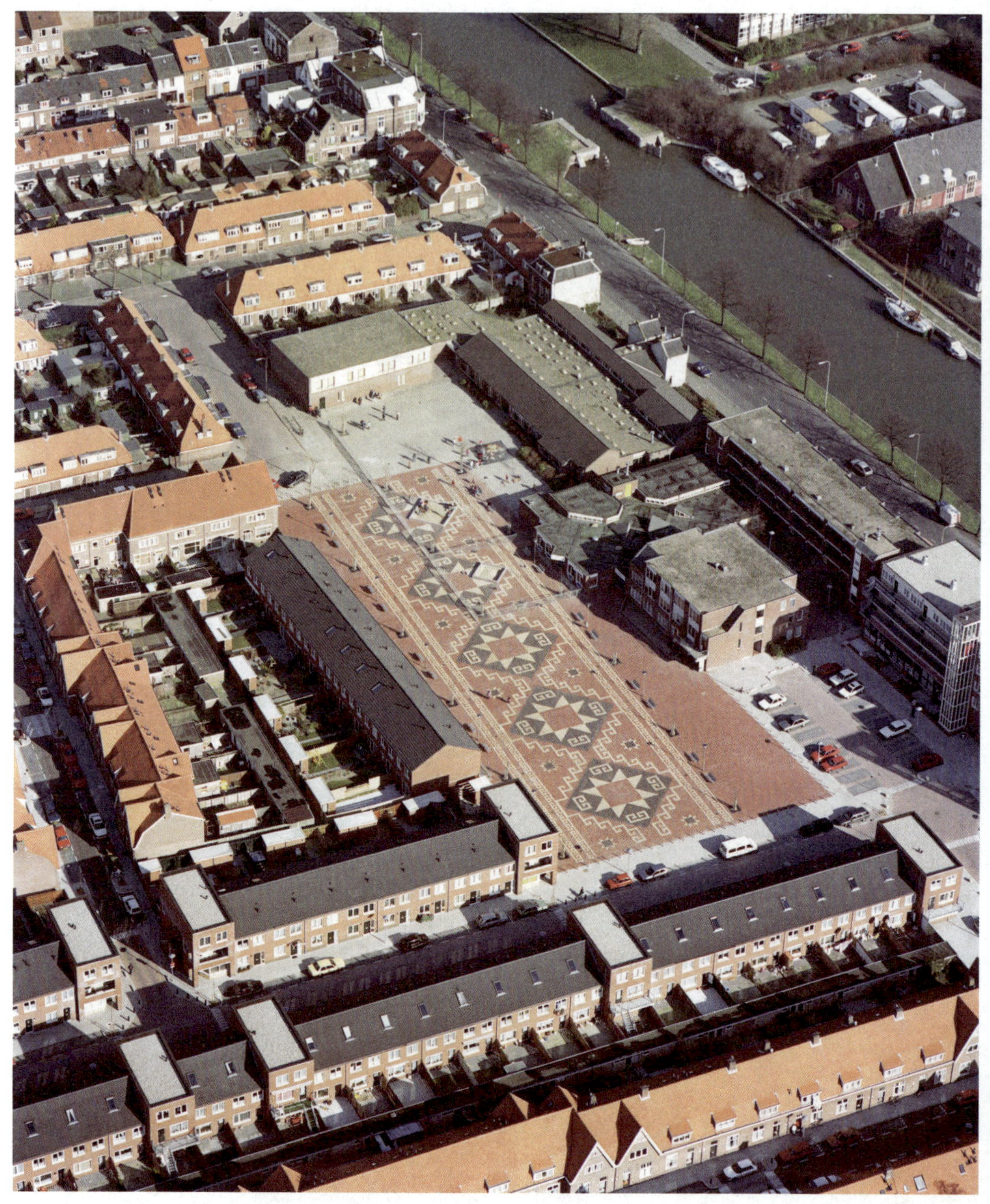

Hans van Houwelingen
*Het Tapijt*, 1994, bricks

## HANS VAN HOUWELINGEN

Hans van Houwelingen (born Harlingen, NL, in 1957) works and lives in Amsterdam. He attended Academy Minerva in Groningen and later the Rijksakademie, Amsterdam (1985–1988) during which time, in 1987, he won a Prix de Rome prize for sculpture. His practice started with the creation of sculptures in the studio, focusing on art as an object, mixing his traditional background and contemporary conceptual notions. Soon he also began to produce artworks for public space, often commissioned by municipalities that invited him to deal with architectural and social complexities of environments, like the Amerhof in Utrecht (1994). In this traditional working class neighbourhood he created, a brick Persian carpet, by Moroccan designer Hamid Oujaha, overlapping two schoolyards facing the square, demonstrating the complex inter-relations within that area.

Van Houwelingen's ability to tackle complexities is clear also in projects on the micro level, such as the design of coins, in which a visual and conceptual design needs to be dealt with and understood within specific technological constraints: the commemorative coin for the Peace Treaty of Munster and the commemorative coin for the marriage of King Willem-Alexander and Queen Máxima. He also designed two military medals for the Kanselarij der Nederlandse Orden (Chancellery of the Netherlands Orders of Knighthood), on the occasion of the King's marriage in 2002 and installation in 2013. Precisely on account of his deep understanding of the limits and possibilities on the macro and micro level, both socially, politically and technologically, he has become a long-time adviser for the Ministry of Finance coin production, bridging between coin artist-designers and the technical producer at the Royal Dutch Mint.

His experience in such fields, in art and non-art institutions as well as public space, together with his working method of observing, researching and being involved, are the basis of his broad activity. It resulted in the Wilhelmina-ring sculpture oeuvre award in 2014 and his membership of the Royal Academy of Art in 2015. His task there includes counselling and advising politicians in the cultural field. Recently Van Houwelingen simultaneously reintegrated making objects in the studio, revisiting more classical art markets. His practice can be understood as political in the way it engages with debating on issues both artistic, cultural and social.

> H.H. "The beauty of monuments is that there art and politics meet. You work in each other's fields. That is delicate."
> (*de Volkskrant*, 2 September 2011)

## JOAN JONAS

Joan Jonas, born in New York City (USA) in 1936, currently lives and works both in New York and Nova Scotia, Canada. She obtained a Bachelor's Degree in Art History from Mount Holyoke College, South Hadley, later attending classes of drawing and sculpture at the School of the Museum of Fine Arts in Boston. Joan Jonas graduated in Sculpture (MFA) at Columbia University, following simultaneously Trisha Brown's dance courses and thus approaching performance as a medium. From 1968 she became a pioneer in the field of *performance*, combining different media, turning to video performance art in the 1970s. A voyage to Japan with Richard Serra in 1970 led Jonas to discover Japanese theatre and thus *the stage* began to play a role in her work. Her sculptural background working in the studio contributes to her understanding of space, a fundamental feature of her work, in which the sculptural dimension of her body and the stage have a basic importance.

Jonas creates the scenography for her performances which usually consists of an installation composed of her sculptures, the stage on which the performance unfolds, as in the piece *Mirage*–first shot in 1976. Her dimensional and spatial sensibility also reaches the space in which her pieces are displayed, as in the case of *Reading Dante II* (2009) in the Arsenale at Venice Biennale, for which she *designed* the lamps hanging in the room to illuminate her installation. Jonas' practice extends to *education* where, thanks to the recognition gained for experimentalism and innovations of the video medium, she taught New Genres at UCLA in 1993, then in Stuttgart in 1994 and later Visual Arts at MIT in Boston. In the Netherlands she has been an adviser at the Rijksakademie in Amsterdam. Joan Jonas represented the U.S. in the United States of America Pavilion at the Venice Biennale in 2015.

> J.J.: "They were ephemeral because they were performances. But I also made them several times in different places. I made them over and over again because for me it was not about one gesture, was about developing something as, for instance, the sequence of images and actions."
> (vector e-zine)

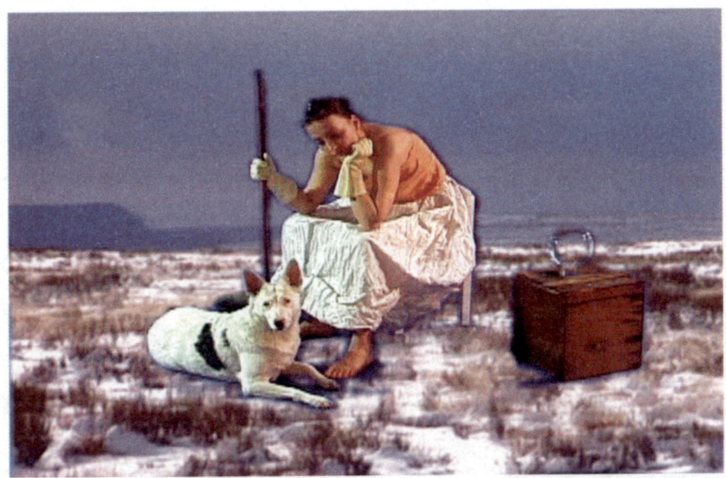

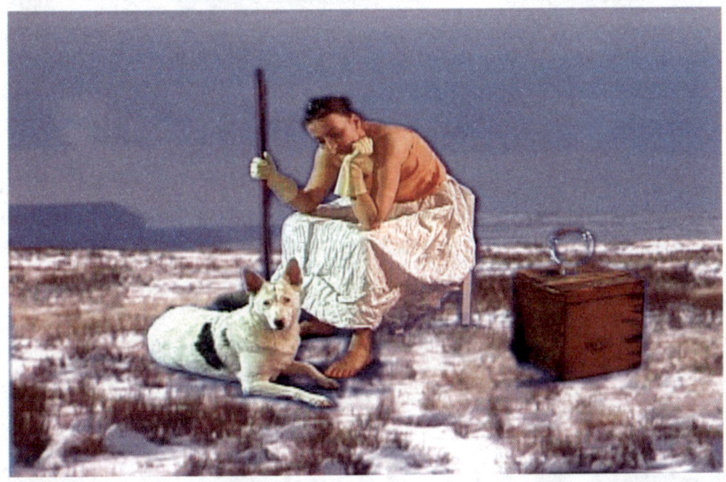

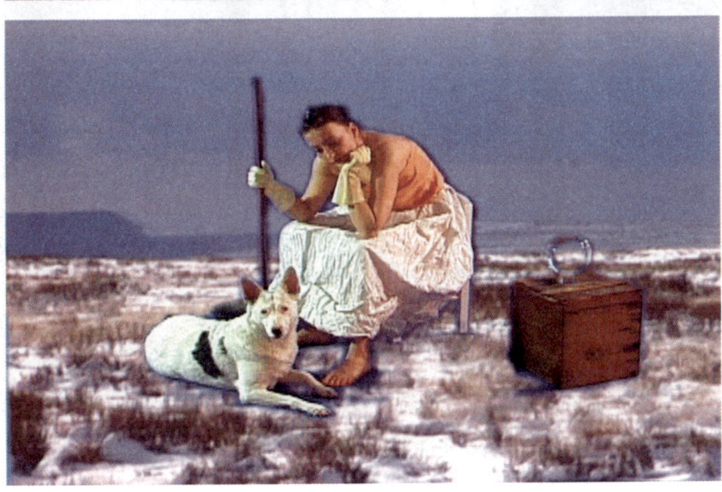

**Joan Jonas**
***Melancholia*, 2004–2005, single channel colour video, continuous loop (5'11")**

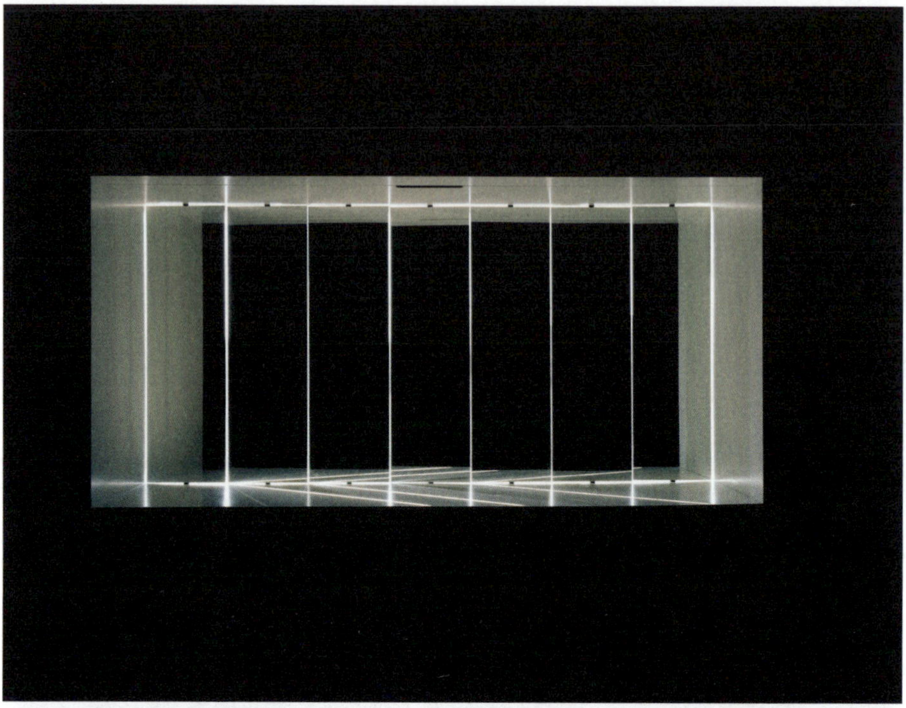

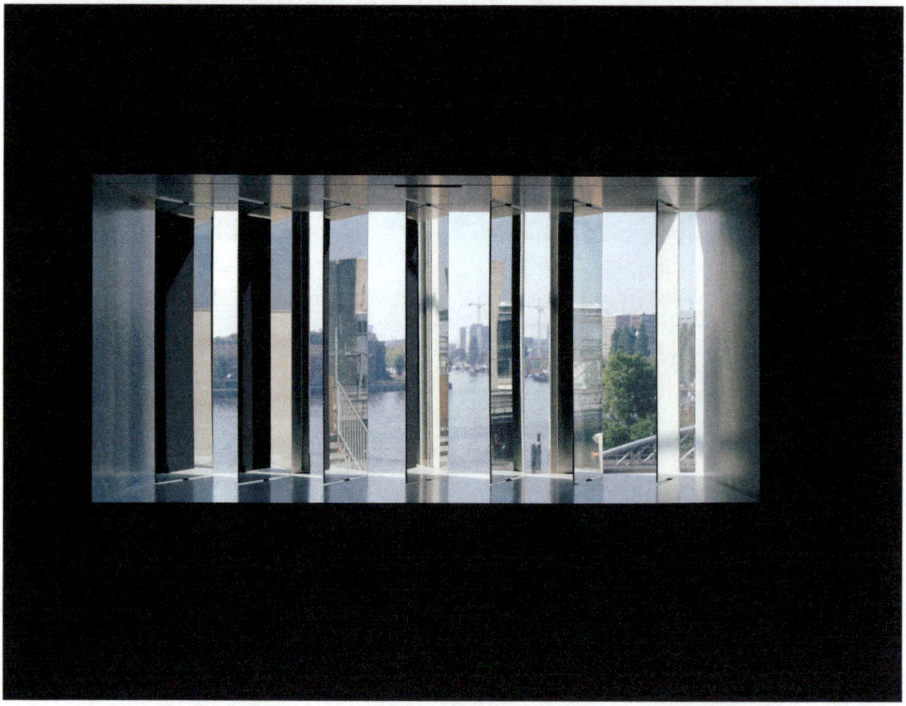

Germaine Kruip
*Daytime*, 2004–2009, mirror and steel, site-specific installation, c. 100 × 200 cm

## GERMAINE KRUIP

Germaine Kruip was born in Castricum (NL) in 1970, currently living and working in Amsterdam and Brussels. She won the second prize at Prix de Rome for Theatre and Visual Art whilst studying Theatre and Fine Arts at DasArts (1998–1999), and later attended the Rijksakademie in Amsterdam (2000–2001).

Kruip's practice in and around her *studio* developed from a *performative* and conceptual background which influences her approach to space and architecture, including the manipulation of sound and light. In her interventions the artist observes and de-structures the surroundings in order to create installations capable of connecting the space, the architecture and the viewer. In her artworks, Kruip transforms the viewer into the protagonist of the space by complementing, neglecting or highlighting architectural elements (for example, *Geometry of the Scattering* (2016) in the Oude Kerk in Amsterdam), thus proceeding with a *curatorial perspective*. By synthesising or fragmenting the complexities hidden in the space (either public or private), Kruip's pieces show her capacity for dealing with and understanding architectural constraints, which are brought back to the viewer in geometrical but monumental gestures.

The process of internalising the space, which occurs in the studio, works on both macro and micro levels in her practice as Kruip designed the Jubilee Coin depicting Queen Beatrix (2005). Working on a small scale, the artist developed a representation of Her Majesty from two different perspectives taken simultaneously, pressed onto both sides of the coin and staging the moment in the in-between space. In 2008, Kruip was commissioned by Jil Sander to design the brand concept store in Soho, NYC.

The artist's background in theatre is apparent in one of her recent artworks, *A Possibility of an Abstraction: Square Danc*e (2013), a performance piece consisting of dervish circle dance choreographed to incorporate alternative geometric shapes.

> "Daytime is a rotation of seven mirrors, one side coated black, installed to fit in a window frame. It reflects daylight into the space; one rotation completed every 14 seconds. They produce a reflection that alternately swells then shrinks– a play of light to the rhythm of gentle breathing. ... In stage-like spaces set up with minimal means, the viewer becomes aware of himself and his perception, which becomes a component of the work." (*Global Contemporary*)

## MATT MULLICAN

Matt Mullican was born in Santa Monica (United States of America) in 1951, currently living and working in Berlin. In 1974 he graduated in Fine Arts (bachelor) at California Institute of Arts. His practice is based on the exploration of distancing the ego from the creative self, touching on limits through different media. Mullican's mental atelier is a psychological *laboratory* where his personal artistic creativity becomes the subject of investigation. Art and science merge in his mind, which is his own playground for understanding his creative self. The scientific method used is hypnotisation, adopted by Mullican since the late 1970s. The outcomes of this process are presented through different media: painting, sculpture, installations, video and performance. Hypnotisation per se is often presented as a *performance* piece. Both performance and his *studio* practice, where the studio is a space for personal reflection, have as their outcome the creation of art objects as witnesses of his experimentation.

Paintings on different surfaces which have a strongly graphic and written character, often presenting numbers, grids, words and other strings of language, are the medium through which Glenn–the artist's creative self–communicates with the outer world. The use of pictographic symbols led him to investigate cosmological, biological and epistemological belief systems, as he did in the piece *Cosmology* (2013) at the Böhm Chapel. "Where do I come from?" is just one of the questions at the basis of his scientific and artistic research which creates a bridge between his individual analysis and research into the order of reality. Surrealist frottage and automatic writing are useful tools in the process of visualisation of the subconscious, that became more precise over the years and changing the names of the creative self from That Person to Glenn. Mullican's scientific investigation on his artistic persona is carried out in his mental laboratory following a scientific method that, through a creative process, brings to the beholder the results of his research in the form of artworks.

> "These abstract geometric forms are combined with more representational, repetitive imagery: grids of letters and numbers, transcriptions of song lyrics, and childlike pictures. Mullican has long been interested in the intersection of public sign systems with personal semiotics. ... Meditation on the notion of artistic subjectivity, and on the limits of distancing the ego from the creative self." (*Global Contemporary*)

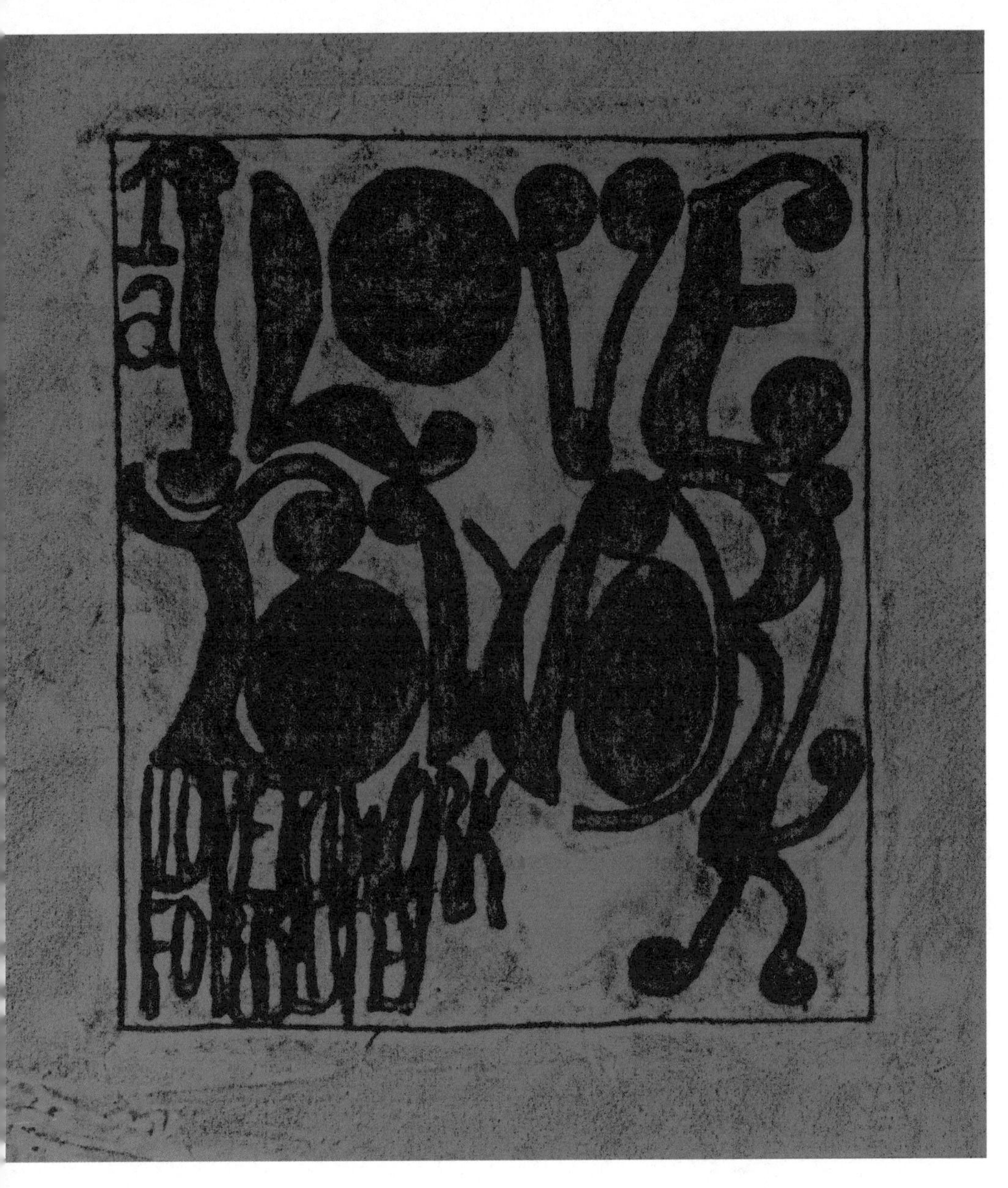


**Matt Mullican**
***Untitled*, 2010, acrylic on canvas, 104.5 × 90.5 cm**

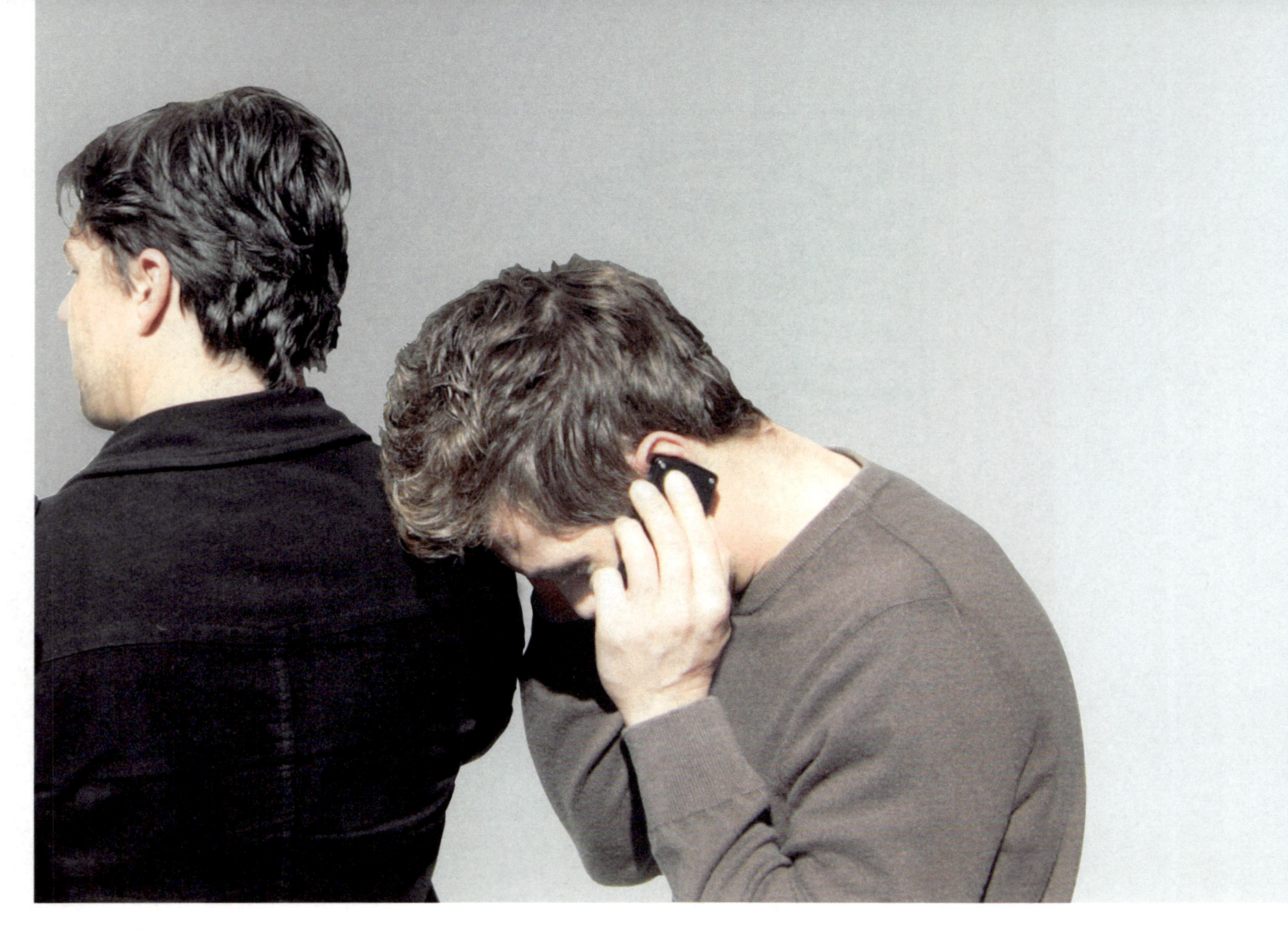

Michelangelo Pistoletto
*Una chiamata (a call)*, 2010, silkscreen on stainless steel mirror, 70 × 100 cm

## MICHELANGELO PISTOLETTO

Michelangelo Pistoletto, born in 1933 in Biella (IT), is a famous protagonist of Arte Povera. Early in his education Pistoletto worked at his father's workshop as a restorer whilst attending a graphic design school for advertising. Painting was the first technique Pistoletto acquired, propelling him to international fame around 1958, the time of *Quadri Specchianti* (mirror paintings) which have been exhibited around the world. This is exemplary of his *studio* practice at that time during his involvement in movements such as Pop Art and Nouveau Realisme.

His participation as an artist in galleries and museums developed during his career in *curatorship*. In 1978 Pistoletto curated *Divisione e Moltiplicazione* and *L'arte assume la religione* (Division and Multiplication of the Mirror and Art Takes On Religion) an exhibition organised in a church in San Sicario, including his own artworks and related publications. His drive towards society and different modalities of organisation deepened his social commitment initiating different activities, including being an *educator* at the Academy of Fine Arts in Vienna as head of the Sculpture Department between 1991 and 1999. Pistoletto started Progetto Arte together with his students, a project aimed at crossing boundaries between different disciplines in order to allow artists to embrace social change.

In 1998 he organised and founded Cittadellarte-Fondazione Pistoletto, a foundation aimed at social engagement through the arts in order to stimulate debate and change in economy, politics, society and art itself, which can be considered the ultimate result of Progetto Arte. Part of this foundation is Università delle Idee, an educative platform hosting seminars and workshops which highlight and combine Pistoletto's interest in education and society. In recent years the artist has launched an incredible number of projects, all complementing or part of his Cittadellarte. To name a few: Terzo Paradiso is an artistic project which underscores this new research direction, comprising an exhibition and a publication which exemplify his activity as a *writer*; Rebirth-Day, is an event occurring every year on December 21st to mark humanity's rebirth and thus remembering the challenges that we are facing; *The Rebirth* (2015) is a *public sculpture* installed in Geneva in front of the Palace of Nations, highlighting Pistoletto's recognition as a *change agent* who is capable of organising social and artistic forces. His advisory role at the Rijksakademie in Amsterdam again brings education at the core of his practice.

> "In the early 1960s Michelangelo Pistoletto made the first *Mirror Paintings*, which directly include the viewer and real time in the work, and open up perspective, reversing the Renaissance perspective. The *Mirror Paintings* are the foundation of his subsequent artistic output and theoretical thought."
> (*Global Contemporary*)

## JAN VAN DER PLOEG

Jan van der Ploeg (1959) was born in Amsterdam where he currently lives and works. He studied at Gerrit Rietveld Academy from 1980 to 1982 then at Croydon College of Art in London and attended the Rijksakademie between 1983 and 1985. During his years at Gerrit Rietveld Academy he moved his studio, together with some friends, out of the school and also used it as exhibition space frequented by his teachers. By taking his studio out of the academy he showed an early interest in creating alternative spaces for his practice where friends and others could participate. Before establishing his own gallery (PS) a decade ago, Van der Ploeg organised different exhibitions in his living room where artworks by international artists were shown. He also hosted the artists themselves in his house, demonstrating his aptitude for connecting people. This very connectedness is at the core of his practice, positioning Van der Ploeg as a *curator* in formal (for example, *Snap in Lyon*) and informal settings. He often participates in collective exhibitions as an artist and a curator, for instance at the Australian Centre for Concrete Art in Fremantle (AU). This practice is rooted in his early travel experience and participation in the Australian and New Zealand cultural life. His Amsterdam gallery PS is, at the same time, a commercial gallery, an artist-run venue and a space for friendship.

*Transferring knowledge* is part of his practice, having been a guest tutor at Goldsmiths College in London and currently a mentor at Mondriaan Fund, allowing him to have a personal relationship with upcoming artists. His interest in cooperating is also expressed in two public artworks for the Rosario Livatino school in Naples on the occasion of the Color Project. There, Van der Ploeg was called to intervene, together with other artists, to change the perception of youngsters within the community of the school as a degenerate place. Collaborations arise mainly outside his private *studio*, within its walls it is a solo practice using all the artist's architectural, environmental and chromatic experiences, investigations and archiving them. His capacity for dealing with space and its manifold complexities led him to create the work *Mobile* (2010) for Mercedes-Benz showroom in Munich: on commission the artist *designed* carpets and floating sculpture, stemming directly from his 'regular' wall painting, which could not be used in that particular space, without either total denunciation or reinvention of the medium painting, as Van der Ploeg did.

> "Jan van der Ploeg's projects always contain an unmistakable element of spatial transformation. They are bound to their context and are directed at the visitor's point of view. Increasingly they seem to have taken on a more figurative formal language. It seems to me that this provides sufficient reason for saying that the old Dutch schism has been sublimated in Van der Ploeg's work–not 'form or fellow', but increasingly 'form and fellow'."
> Rein Wolfs, curator (www.hammer.ucla.edu/exhibitions/2007/hammer-projects-jan-van-der-ploeg/ 27/07/16)

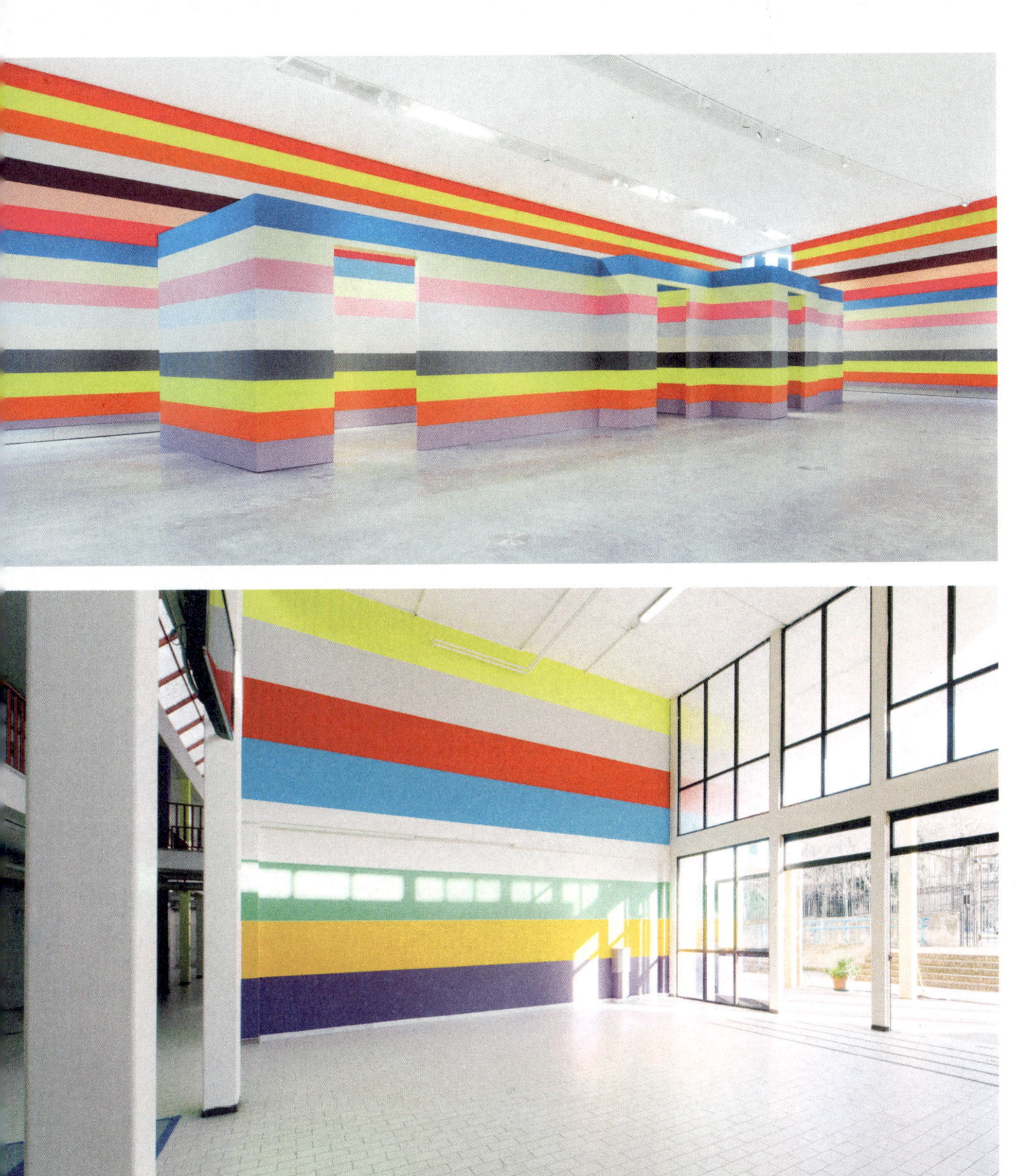

Jan van der Ploeg
*WALL PAINTING No. 379*, 2014, acrylic on wall, 450 × 9000 cm (MOTI, Breda, The Netherlands)
*WALL PAINTING No. 394*, 2014, acrylic on wall, 640 × 2400 cm and 72 columns of 600 cm (I.S.I.S. Rosario Livatino, Naples, Italy)

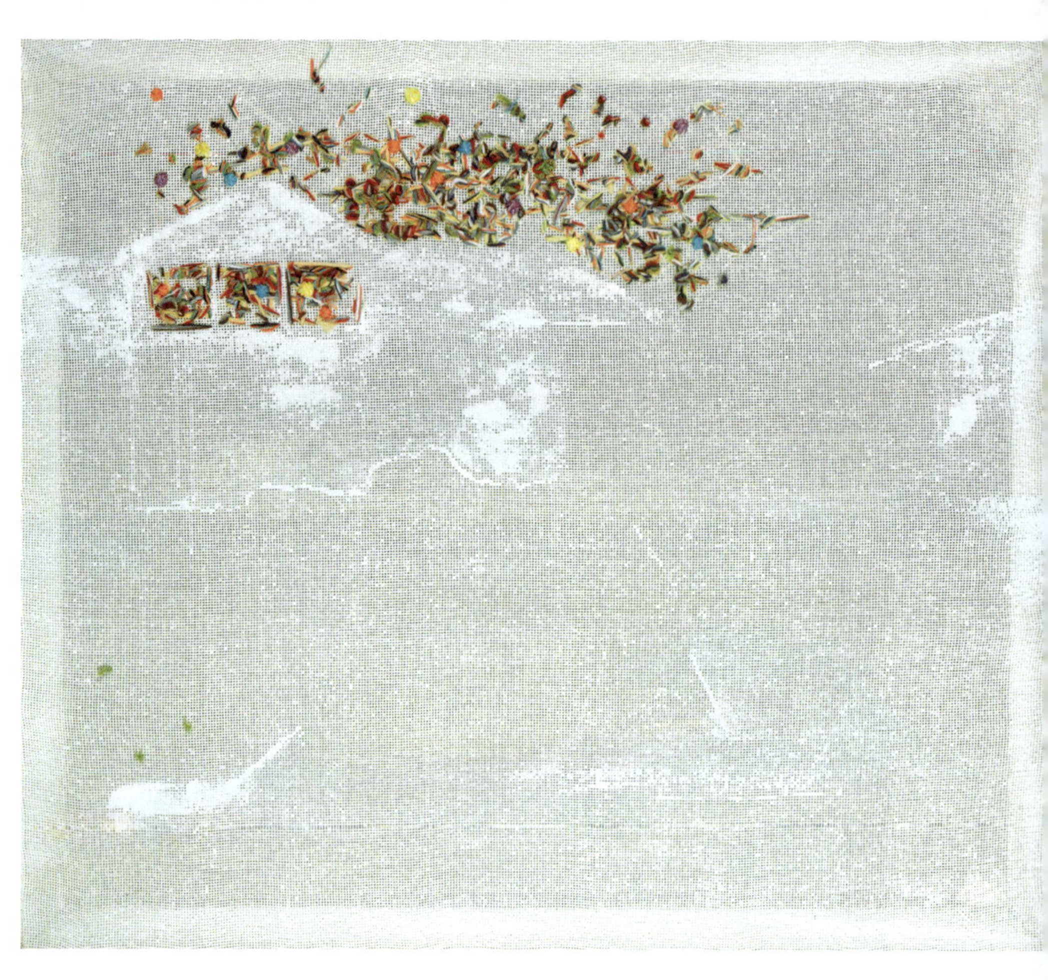

Michael Raedecker
*Shout Out Loud*, 1993, acrylic and embroidery on canvas, 80 × 90 cm

## MICHAEL RAEDECKER

Michael Raedecker was born in Amsterdam (NL) in 1963 and is based in London. He obtained a bachelor's degree in Fashion Design from the Gerrit Rietveld Academy in Amsterdam where he studied from 1985 to 1990; he also became a resident at the Rijksakademie (1993–1994). After two years spent working in Antwerp, he moved to London where he attended Goldsmiths College, between 1996 and 1997.

Michael Raedecker's favourite medium is painting, in which he expresses loneliness and the uneasy feeling of void in contemporary life. The preferred locus for his practice is the *studio*, both as mental and material space, where his creativity unfolds from the perfecting of his craftsmanship. His paintings are characterised by the use of stitches as a final layer on top of many fine layers of paint. The technical skills in stitching are part of his background in fashion design which he brings into his paintings. The studio is the space where the artist is confronted with the tradition of painting and the implications of adopting such a medium, where reflection on its meaning occurs. The studio is also a space for innovation and experimentation, a workshop in which technological limitations are explored.

His feeling for and use of complex materials is expressed in a *designer* position; for example the conception of plans for a coin in aid of fund-raising for several cultural institutions. His work has been recognised and has been receiving awards since the beginning of his professional career–he won the basic prize of Prix de Rome in 1993, was on the jury of the prize in 2005, and was short-listed for the Turner Prize in 2000. He was a jury member for New Contemporaries (2011), thus integrating an *advisory role*, broadening his artist' practice further.

> M.R.: "Embroidery is a craft. It is a hobby, like amateur painting; embroidery doesn't have a status. I had a lot of respect for painting, its history and what had been done by major artists before me. ... Purposely disrespectful and combine 'high'-painting, with 'low'-craft, to create new paintings."
> (*Global Contemporary*)

## JANNIE REGNERUS

Jannie Regnerus, born in 1971 in Oudebildtzijl (NL), lives and works in Haarlem. She was trained as a painter, first at A.B.K in Maastricht (1990–1994) and then a resident at the Rijksakademie (1995–1996), concluding her institutional trajectory at CCA in Kitakyushu (JP) between 2000 and 2001. Two voyages she made between 1998 and 2001 to Far East Asia, earlier in Mongolia and later in Japan, have been fundamental to her practice. Both experiences resulted in novels published under the titles *Full Moon as Best Friend, Two Years in Mongolia* (2005) and *The Sound of Falling Snow, Memories of Japan* (2006). After her debut as a non-fiction author, Regnerus continued writing fiction, including *The Lamb*, her most recent novel nominated for different prizes including Libris Literature Prize. Her activity as a *writer* is not limited to books, but it is also present in her artworks which are predominantly photos and videos of performances; a strong pictorial element is embedded in her artworks, either in a formal capacity in visualizing a subject or as reflection on the pictorial gesture as a performative act or both combined. The visual lyricism of her works is rooted in her Japanese experience that also influenced her choice for paper and written signs as recurrent elements. An example is *Ingredients for a Poem* (2009) exhibited at the Fries Museum in the city of Leeuwarden, a video of a paper comma being washed up by the sea on a beach. The comma is the written sign for breath or break, while the sea is a favourite subject of inspiration for poets and writers.

The living conditions in Mongolia, were such that Regnerus was not equipped with her painting materials, so she started performing her painting activity outside in the open world, as can be seen in *Cloud on a Stick* (1998). By bringing her practice into the world, she opened up her mental atelier to the surroundings which become both a *studio* and a *stage* where the artist performs her stories.

> "When we gaze into a bright light and shut our eyes, yellow dots appear in front of our 'inner-eye'. During the two years that I lived in Mongolia I travelled a lot through ancient landscapes with very few human signs. Often it felt like an inner-landscape, as if I had shut my eyes. In this work, where I place yellow dots in the Mongolian snowscape, I try to melt both worlds together, the one of the inner-eye, the other the actual world."
> (email received on 2 August 2016 from Jannie Regnerus)

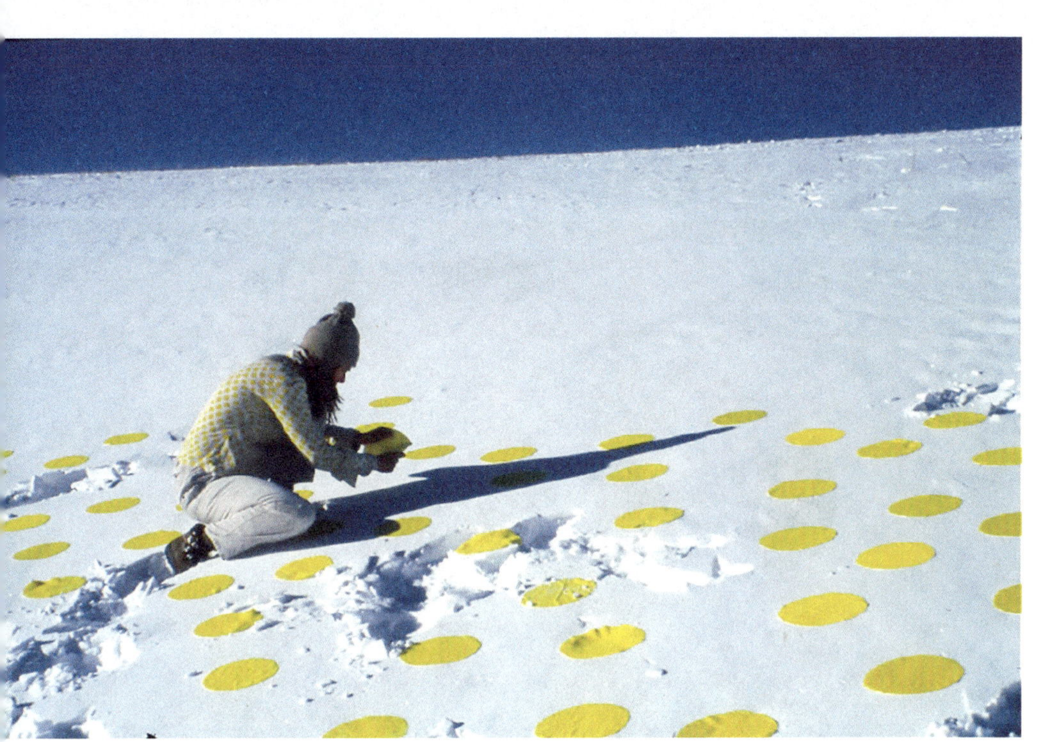

**annie Regnerus**
***ellow Dots*, 1999, c-print on aluminium, 70 × 90 cm**

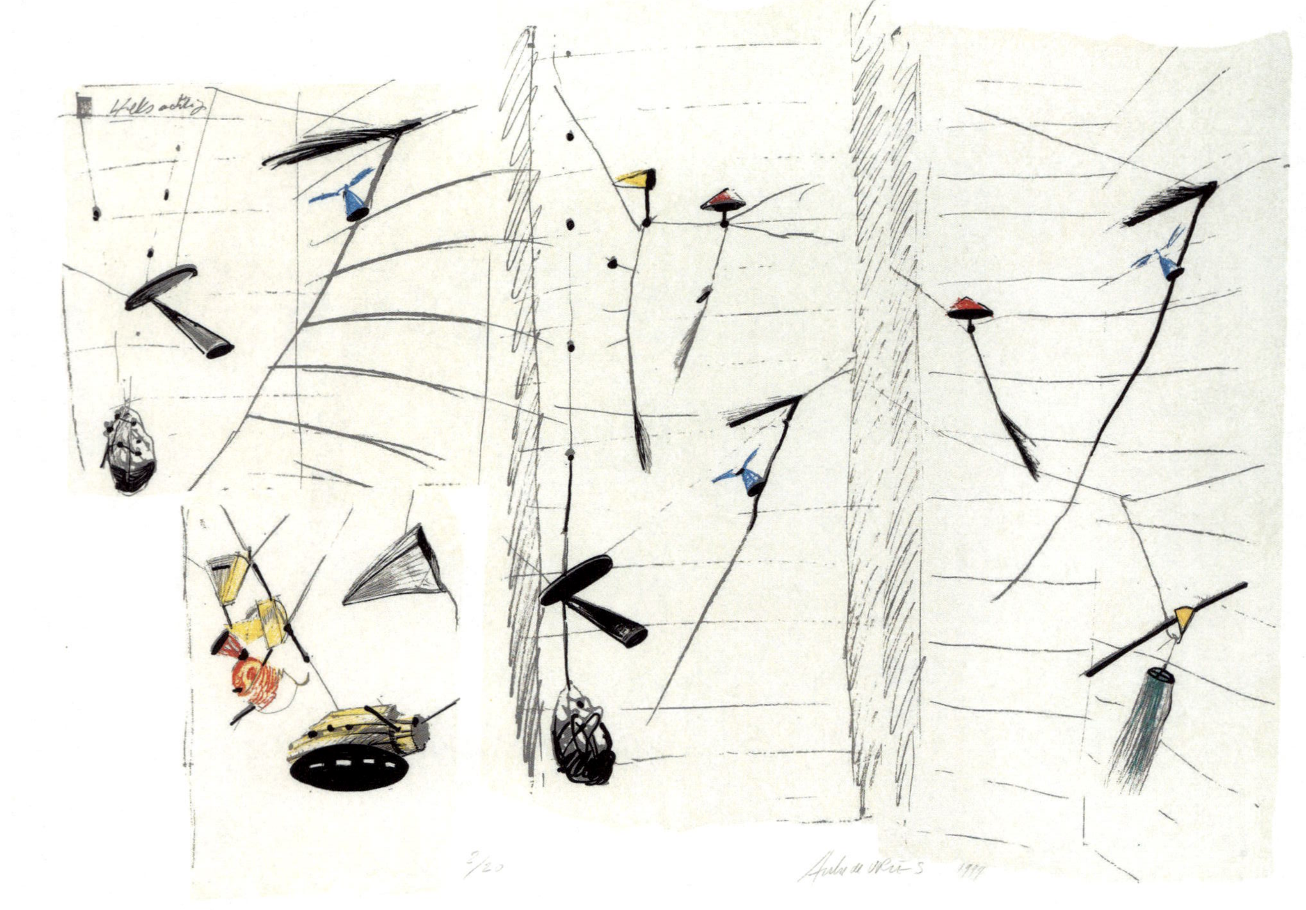

Auke de Vries
*Untitled*, 1999, lithograph, 80 × 110 cm

## AUKE DE VRIES

Auke de Vries, born in 1937 in Bergum, province of Friesland (NL), lives and works in The Hague. He is a self taught artist, creating both paintings and sculpture. One of his first commissions was to *design* and to help realize a shop in the Netherlands. After a short stay in Paris, he continued to produce a large number of drawings and sculptures for *public spaces*. His artistic practice is based in the studio, where the creative process starts with drawing and producing small models almost somewhat reminiscent of bricolage. Originally conceived as supporting material for his graphic art, those small models began to play a central role in his work. Soon they became sculptures and developed later into suspended installations, characterised by tension and engineering like *Maasbeeld* (Meuse Picture), installed at Rotterdam's waterfront in 1986 (composed of a steel wire around 200 metres in length, on which different abstract iron shapes are hung). Initially the municipality of Rotterdam had commissioned De Vries to choose the colour of the new railway bridge over the river in order to visually emphasize it, but de Vries by reacted proposing the *Maasbeeld* sculpture in which all the elements and shapes present in the surroundings are already included. This demonstrates the artist's ability to deal with complexities, both in the sense of internalising the urban space and in organising the technical process. His craftsmanship becomes evident in the studio. He works with a small team, managing all the steps in the process by himself.

This 'solo activity' extends from coping with technicalities of the production process to major architectural interventions, as in the project for restoring an industrial wasteland in Leipzig (DE), which he re-designed in *Slow Speed / Paradise* (1997); or his sculpture in Istanbul on the Galata Bridge, *After the Rain* (2004), through which he questions the architectural contrast between slums and the city centre. His practice is not limited to spatial interventions: he is and has been an educator for different institutions in the Netherlands and adviser at the Rijksakademie between 1986 and 1996.

> "De Vries photographs and makes sketches in natural and urban environments which he transforms into abstract images. ... Where scale and representativity are called for, he reacts with 'drawings' in space; abstract volumes and structures with an unpredictable, quirky presence."
> (*Global Contemporary*)

## GUIDO VAN DER WERVE

Guido van der Werve, born in 1977 in Papendrecht (NL), is currently working and living in Berlin (DE). Before attending art school, he studied classical piano, industrial design, classical archaeology and Russian. He concluded his education at the Rietveld Academy in Amsterdam. From 2006 and 2007 he attended the Rijksakademie in Amsterdam, followed by a year in New York as a resident at the ISCP.

His artistic practice deals with moving images and *performance* in which he aims to obtain and to convey to the audience the directness he appreciates in music. The creative process starts with the perception of an emotion by the artist which is then abstracted into a mood and finally translated into music and images. For this reason his *studio* practice is focused on personal reflection and meditation, during which artistic freedom is found as a result of boredom, being able to undertake action. In his aim for simplicity, Van der Werve has come to focus on everyday gestures that he monumentalises through his performances, in which endurance is a core characteristic stemming from his passion for sports. Both in the earlier works, such as *Nummer acht: Everything is going to be alright* (2007), and recent ones, namely *Nummer zeventien: Killing time attempt one, From the deepest ocean to the highest mountain* (2015), the artist performs impressive physical feats. In the latter he jumps until he reaches the height of Everest and walks in his bathtub to equal the depth of the ocean, in *Nummer acht* he walks in front of an icebreaker travelling through the Gulf of Bothnia (FL).

His work has been acquired by several international museums including MoMA and Stedelijk Museum, and was shown at the Venice Biennale and Performa festival in New York, amongst others. Since 2010, Van der Werve has also *organised* the annual Running to Rachmaninoff Run and other events.

> GvdW: “In a lot of works the landscapes are also just part of the idea of the film; if you want to walk in front of an icebreaker you have to go to an ice sea and if you want to not turn with the world for one day, you have to go to the north pole. ... I usually picture myself quite small, to depersonalise myself. I like to provide my audience with an experience in which they can picture themselves.” (www.artslant.com/ew/artists/rackroom/3004)

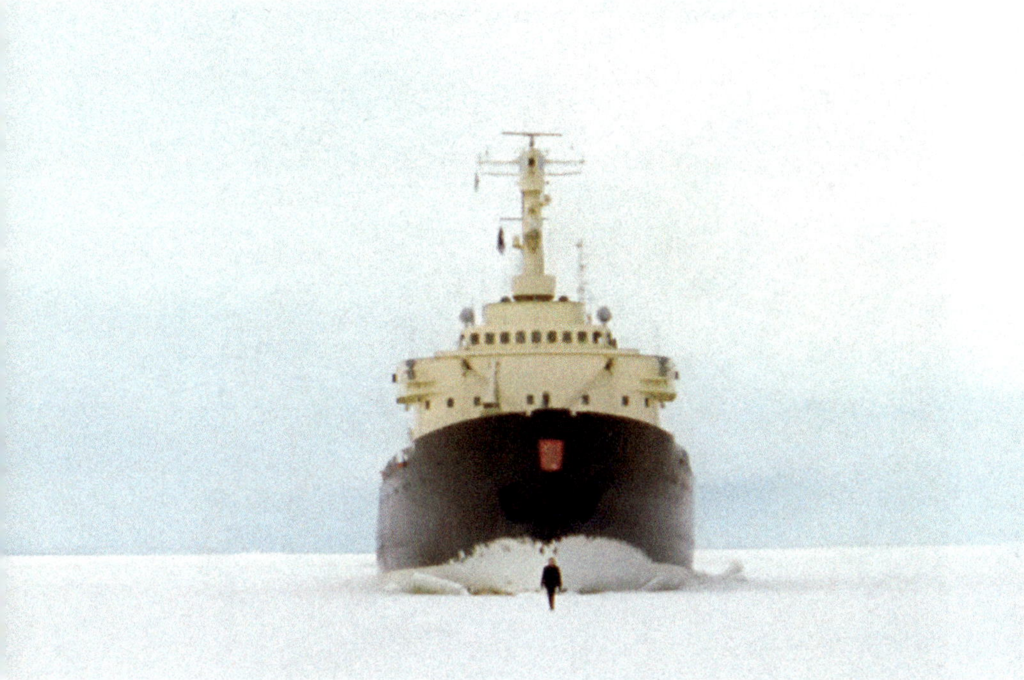

Guido van der Werve
*Nummer acht (Everything is going to be alright)*, 2007, 10'10",
16 mm film to HD, Gulf of Bothnia, FI (courtesy of the artist)

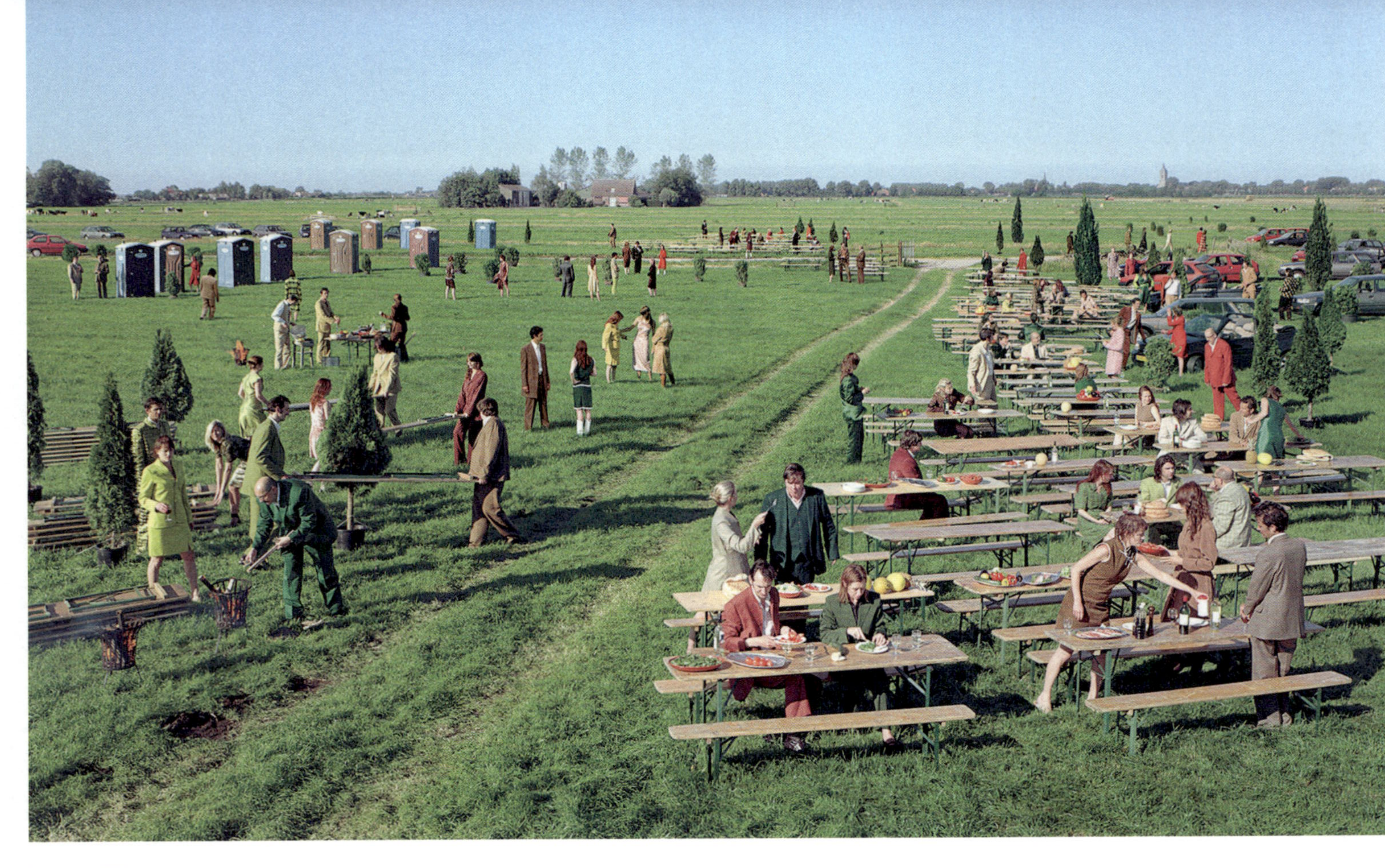

**Sylvie Zijlmans**
**With Hewald Jongenelis, *Ten to One*, 2008, c-print on photo rag, 131 × 215 cm**

## SYLVIE ZIJLMANS

Sylvie Zijlmans is an artist born in Geertruidenberg (NL) in 1964, living and working in Amsterdam. She started at the Academy of Visual Arts in Tilburg (teachers training) and between 1987 and 1989 attended the Rijksakademie in Amsterdam. Her practice deals with different media. Since 1993 she has been collaborating and sharing *studio* space with Hewald Jongenelis though both continue to make independent projects.

Knowledge transfer is at the core of Zijlmans' practice, unfolding through different positions in different environments. Her role as an *educator* is an integral part of her professional activity exemplified by her position at the Gerrit Rietveld Academy's Image and Language department and as a guest lecturer in several institutions namely HKU and DAI in Arnhem, both at MA level. The process of knowledge transfer works both ways within her practice, being an educator by nature. In particular she invites students to participate in her studio practice, which is not only a space for personal reflection but also for cooperation.

Her aptitude for gathering people together and coordinating them instantiates the strong role she plays as *social catalyst*, which is at the basis of two of her recent artworks. In *Magnetic North* (2014) she organises and coordinates, together with Hewald Jongenelis, the inhabitants of Amsterdam Nord (north) in offering them a stage and creating video-recorded performances. This artwork stems from discussions concerning urgent local issues, such as gentrification, between the artists and the neighbourhood community. During the meetings and the performances, knowledge is transferred both from the community to the artist (and vice versa), and within the community itself.

In the *Prison Project* (2016), a commissioned artwork in a Dutch prison, the enclosed institutional environment did not limit the artist's ability to create a reciprocal relationship between the prison staff and herself. This resulted in a social photography project where staff are depicted in a moment of self-understanding and light-hearted collaboration while assembling a bamboo bridge. The final series of photographs was hung in the staff canteen. Zijlmans and Jongenelis catalysed the knowledge transfer between the staff by providing an amicable environment even in such a hierarchical space top-down situation. The pictures show the importance of equality among all staff members.

> "It is not a party. Not simply in the sense that it is an artificial image of a party, but the festivity itself was a celebration. Every aspect of the image received equal attention and the final result is a work full of detail and visual complexity. A relaxed composition with no starring or supporting roles."
> (*Global Contemporary*)

# 3

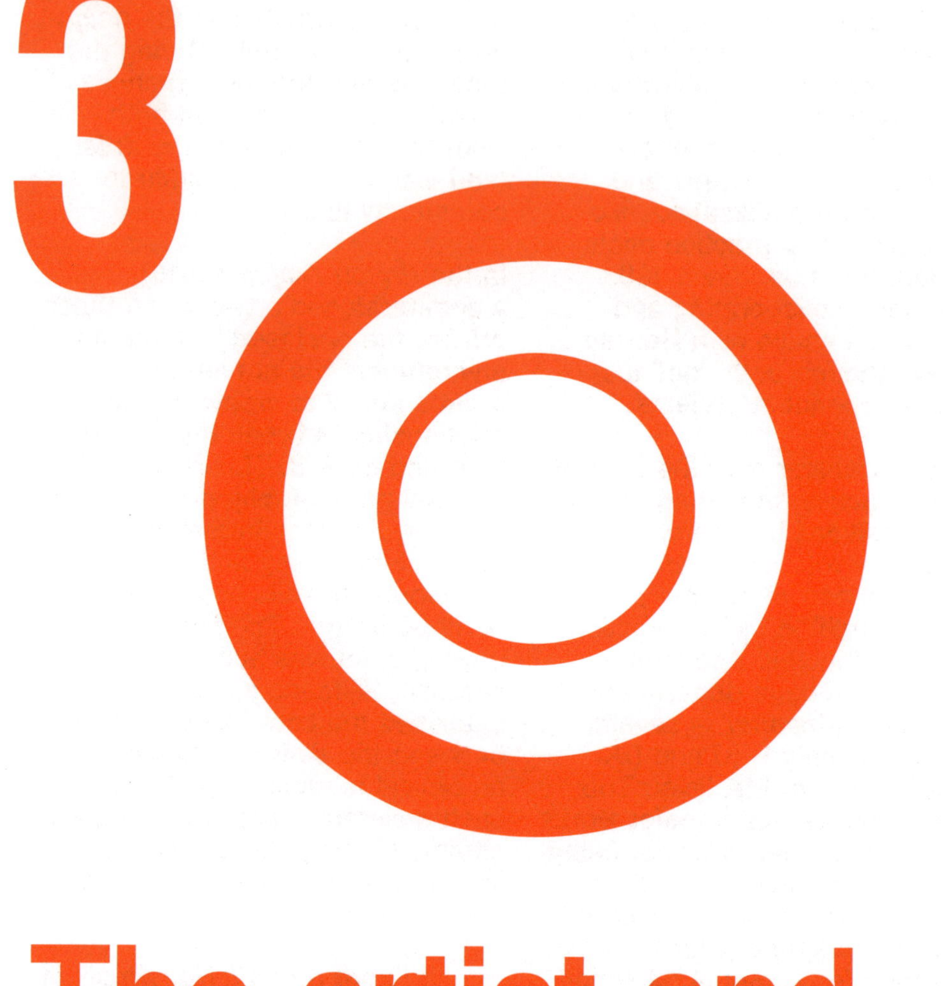

# The artist and his environment, from victim to free spirit

Whereas the previous chapter focused on the inner world with facets and taking a position in the artist's approach to the outside world, this chapter addresses the environment in which the artist operates. In every socio-economic environment, including the art world, we can distinguish between eight force fields. The art market, the artist's potential market, is one. The art market can, in turn, be divided into various market segments, at all events, eleven if you consider the eleven artists' positions discussed in Chapter 2, since the commercial environment changes from one position to another. In 'Artistic practice amid force fields', a closer, bird's eye view is taken of eight social force fields within the art world. After that, we arrive at the above-mentioned eleven market segments within the commercial art market.

Section 'Control variants in the artistic practice' addresses the deployment of collaboration within the art market. The intention here is to reduce feelings of powerlessness and supply tools for diverse situations, for instance for producing work, collaborating with partners such as galleries or other artists when presenting work, as well as better management of dealings with 'clients'. Rather than providing a set 'prescription', we address three basic approaches: how to deal with an externally defined situation that is hard to influence; a situation in which, with dialogue, collaboration on an equal basis can indeed take shape and one in which you yourself direct things, are responsible for almost all aspects of collaboration.

# Artistic practice amid force fields

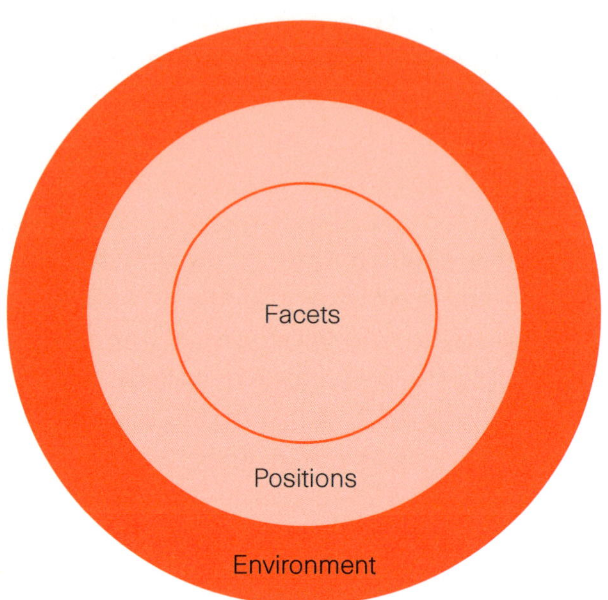


*Figure 10.* (Facets, Positions) Environment

Even though we are, fortunately, not equally aware of it, everyone is to some extent affected every day by the so-called socio-economic force fields surrounding us. By what is or is not permitted according to governmental rules and legislation, by one's own work and that of others in the labour market, and developments in the working population, by national identities and existing and new social outlooks, by what is said and written in the media and the development of the media landscape itself. Everyone acquires goods and knowledge, 'buys'. And everyone offers 'for sale' expertise, capacity in time and attention, and often goods.

### *Playing chess on eight boards, in the art world*

The same eight socio-economic force fields can be differentiated with respect to the artist—of which the art market is the first to be touched on here.

1. Art market 'consumers' of the artists' work, among others museums, collectors, festivals, municipal and other patrons including intermediaries like galleries and agents. This relates to 'sales'. The *market segments* (eleven of them) in the art market are dealt with in 'Positions and the art market'.

There are more force fields:

2. *Acquisition* of knowledge, expertise and materials on the buying market, i.e. the area of suppliers, but centres of expertise/courses as well, plus curators, critics, art historians, philosophers and other academics, and last but not least, fellow artists and artist communities as sources of knowledge, expertise and networks. These are mental and material resources necessary for *developing artistic practice*.
3. The *work* factor. Those who (remunerated or as volunteers) participate in artists' projects in and outside the studio, permanently or temporarily, as well as service providers and friends who help.
4. *Financial resources* to enable investment, for example a bank mortgage, subsidies to start a practice of one's own, for travel and research, projects and the like. This also relates to the reservation of revenue from the sales market for the supply of your 'goods' and services. So, investment resources from the capital market and money set aside for *investments* (being your own bank).
5. *Cultural policy and economic policy* of local, national and international governments regarding art and artists, rules and legislation (including tax laws concerning tax-deductible expenses), incentive measures, location policy (including live/work provisions) as well as funding policies. These are prerequisites for *independent entrepreneurship*, possibilities and constraints which you can encounter.
6. *Press, public opinion* both in the general media and in specialised, professional media, as well as your own channels: websites and social media.

To these six economic force fields relating to the artistic practice, you can add another two factors:

7. Your *own practice* as the focal point, the studio or the artist collective, and its creation, development and maintenance.
8. *Colleagues and competitors*. After all, you are not alone, there are other artists, who, regardless of your dealings as colleagues—whether a lot or a little—are also 'competitors'; the less your kind of work, market segment and working method overlap, the more complementary your work and so the likelihood of getting along as good colleagues.

***Reflection*. What force fields are relevant for you? Make a list of the chief 'actors' around you, in various force fields, also outside the art market, and note each time why a particular actor is or can be of importance for your practice. You can use the following visualisation.**

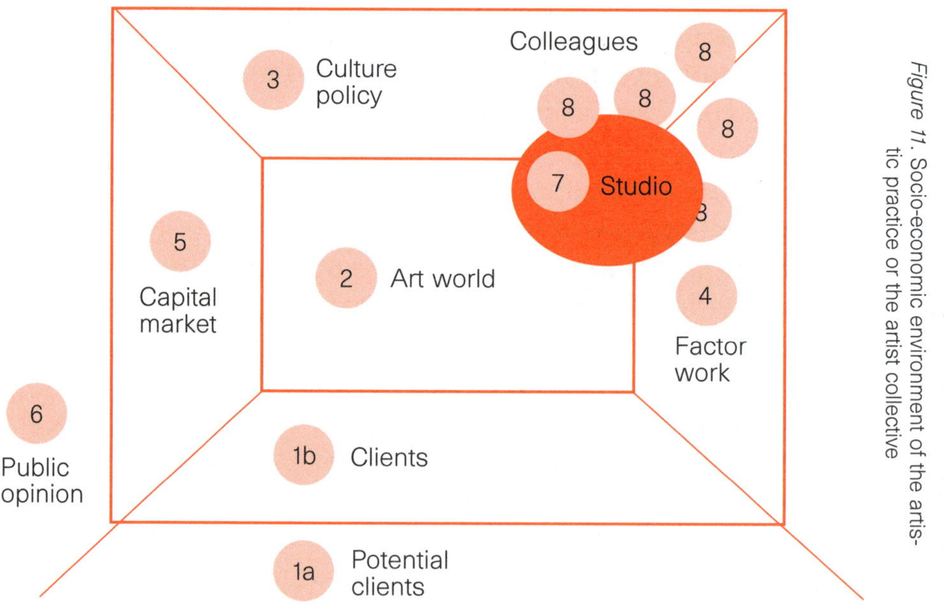


*Figure 11*. Socio-economic environment of the artistic practice or the artist collective

### *Interdependence*

In the art and culture sectors there is a very strong web of interconnections. Many other social sectors contain fewer connections—and as such often better concealed—between socio-economic force fields.* That interconnection or interdependence makes it extra complex for artists and their 'enterprise' to manage their environment, to navigate and act. A selection of cross-connections follows.

– the art world as a buying market, source of knowledge, expertise and materials (2), overlaps the segments of the artist's market (1), because professional buyers, intermediaries and advisers to buyers, are also informers of or sources for artists;
– the art world (2) not only has 'overt', but also 'covert' (well-concealed) contact with civil servants and politicians who are involved in culture policy (3). Lobby connections of this type are not easy to detect;
– politicians, civil servants and other government employees and those working for semi-governmental funds (3) play a big part in funding policy and so can influence the willingness of banks and other financiers (5) in financing the artistic practice and specific projects. Moreover, funding of supply greatly influences prices of art on the art market (1);
– critics, curators and other art professionals often work in public and professional media (6), are a source for 'buying' knowledge and expertise (1), and at the same time personally are 'influencers' (2) of collectors', museums' and patrons' decisions to purchase, in adjudicating, and more extensively when those professionals are deployed as scouts in selecting artists—as with the Prix de Rome, after the Mondriaan Fund had taken over its organisation.

* In the 1960s, Marxist-Leninist student movements (among others) referred to the narrow, nebulous and 'fawning' connection between industry, capital and government as 'the military-industrial complex'; those were the predecessors and perhaps the inspirers of the French economist, Thomas Piketty who, at the start of the twenty-first century, became the symbol of the struggle against economic inequality in capitalist structures.

Acquisition, the interaction of the eight factors makes systematic operation a tough job for artists and their 'undertaking'. I return to management of the environment 145 in 'Control variants in the artistic practice'.

*Positions and the art market*

We are now zooming further into the art market. With the eleven artists' positions we ascertain submarkets or market segments. The commercial fabric varies from one position to another. It comprises presentation platforms as '*showcases*', advisers and opinion makers as *influencers*, intermediaries like galleries as *go-betweens*, and spectators and buyers or patrons as *consumers*. Partners in developing the practice (such as artists' residencies) or producing work, or financers can also be part of that fabric. The following summary provides a brief review for each position. Here, it is more about indicating the mutual differences than giving an in-depth description of each market segment.

– artist 'in the studio', active in the field of museums, biennials, presentation platforms and alternative spaces, art critics and curators, galleries, agents and auction houses, collectors and public at presentation venues, artists' residencies;
– artist 'in public space', in the segments of semi-public buildings, in the street or in digital media, are confronted with juries and committees, politicians, curators, art critics and public media, advisers and mediators between art and government or art and business, technicians, public and private patrons, the public (both voluntary and involuntary audiences); people who are involved positively or negatively: the neighbours, the neighbourhood, the city, tourists and other passers-by, as well as—incidentally—artists' residencies;
– artist 'in the laboratory', in the segment of media and technology institutes, new media festivals and other presentation venues geared to new media, discussion platforms and curators, universities, interested public, technological companies and specific artists' residencies;

– artist 'on the stage', is visually on stage, such as 'stages' like cinema and theatre, art centres and museums focusing on performance art, curators and theatre critics, technicians, public for art and performing arts;
– artist 'as a designer' has various outlets: specific museums and shops, specific critics and curators, specialised galleries, patrons (for instance from industry), media world and private persons, spectators and buyers;
– artist-writer, apart from one of more of the above-mentioned market segments, is also present in the field of libraries, reviewers in the literary world, publishers and book stores, buying and reading public;
– artist 'as a curator', organising exhibitions in a salaried capacity, commissioned or 'in-house': deals with presentation venues and their providers, technical and other assistants, financiers of the presentation, press and art critics, visitors and curator residencies;
– artist 'as an organiser' who creates conditions for other artists, artists' initiatives, providers of space for projects or as living and working accommodation, governments and financiers, participants, visitors and residents in the immediate surroundings;
– artist 'as an adviser', contributing to committees, juries, or independent artists who are selected and/or mentored with their assignments, patrons, technicians and financiers, local population and public media (for art assignments), universities, funds and other organisations (with advice assignments);
– artist 'as an educator' in socio-cultural centres, therapy (occupational) in hospitals, for example, in local communities, for information and educative programmes in museums, as a university staff member, in small-scale configurations, such as providing courses oneself in or outside the studio, in artist talks and as a teacher 'in schools': pupils, students, fellow teachers and all other persons and bodies who call in artists as educators;
– artist 'as a change agent', with interventions in a community, local population, formal bodies, informal communities, key figures, participating artists and other actors.

In Chapter 1 we looked at the source and designation of art works. The sub-markets or market segments described above supply an answer to "where do I want to present my work?" and "for whom do I want to mean something, to be present?". When you take up an artist's position, you automatically define the area in which you operate.

*Public*

The different types of public also make up part of the market. Basically, artists and art students are faced with the choice for an art-public or a non-art public (or both), and the concomitant presentation venues. Throughout all the market segments, the art public consists of people who are 'insiders' to some extent, from professionals to visitors: artists, gallery owners, curators, art critics, collectors, art advisers, festival programmers, specialised shopkeepers, other well-informed parties, including interested visitors to museums and other presentation venues. Sometimes an artist says: "I'm there for everyone, everywhere", but that invariably means "in the first place for myself, because I know what to expect from the public". Non-art public can be subdivided in many different ways, for instance into generations: children, young people, adults and seniors. Into passers-by, 'involuntary audience', people who are not heading for an art space but come into contact with art, possibly in public space; this impartial group is a favourite category for some artists.

Public is not only a 'designation' (in a linear pathway), but regularly also a 'source' (in a circular process). Alongside many forms of social engagement stemming from the artist's own life, exploration of and participation in social processes
37 (see 'Source and designation'), and exchange with artists and other professionals, and alongside presentation in a museum, biennial, art centre, in public space, for many artists their presentation is participatory. The latter amounts to the public no longer being consumers, but participants or co-producers. Fluid transitional areas come about in which the consumer can even be an active partner.

A connection variant with a larger world that tends to be neglected is collaboration of professional artists with enthusiastic amateurs, with no pressure or stimulus from professional platforms. Chloë Neeleman* wrote in her thesis 'The budding of the artist': "At the same time, the unpaid enthusiasm [of amateurs] for the professional is a warm recollection of his own beginnings. Amateurs need professionals to lean on, but similarly, professionals certainly need amateurs. The amateur provides counterweight and so, balance. When the professional associates too much with his own art-loving set, he loses touch with society."

*Three pieces of advice, for when things get complicated*

In such a complex ensemble of force fields, with so many (interwoven) factors, I advise against the writing of a business plan. A business plan is static, by definition—what is today's is yesterday's by tomorrow—and takes up too much 'unsuitable' time. I prefer to advise cogitation on: which presentation venues appeal to you, for whom do you want to be 'present', are new developments taking place that could be important for you, are there opportunities and threats, where and how can you manage things better, do you want to refocus and change your undertaking? There is enough time to analyse management operations in more detail, if necessary, and discuss them with others.

I identify three methods for getting and keeping things under control in complex situations. One follows on naturally from another, i.e. strategy, profiling and control.

1. The rational way, along which all factors are identified and assessed, is no longer sufficient with such complexity (see also 'Decision-making and mixed scanning') and 'muddling through' does not produce the desired result, and has too many elephants in the room. 28
2. You can deploy personal control mechanisms for your own artistic practice. This is dealt with in more detail in 'control variants', the explorer, the colleague, the director. 145 146 149 152

* Chloë Neeleman was the first 'co-reader' of this handbook. In 2015 she wrote in her thesis 'The budding of the artist' at the Royal Academy of Art in The Hague about the relationship between professionals and amateurs.

3. You can create room for manoeuvre using an interface between yourself (in the studio) and the outside world. It gives the outside world something to hold on to and produces more safety and quiet in the studio for you yourself. Think about a 'shield' using your personal profiling.

If you want to formulate that profiling it is wise to return to yourself and your studio. The development of a course of action differs so much from one individual to another that it is hard to give general advice. I suffice with a number of 'profiling concepts', dichotomies and contrasts—always two sides of the same coin.

Here are a few ingredients that are useful for creating an interface of that type:

– *constant and changeable* because your subjects and style remain identifiable, yet surprising because you are experimentally exploring new horizons, for instance in media use;
– *loyal and independent*, but not putting all your eggs in one basket—so not relying on only one or a few people;
– *transparency and diffusion* of the studio. Imagine a studio with a double-glazed wall filled with special gas that reacts when voltage is applied. It has a switch which only the artist can operate: turn it to the left and the wall is completely transparent (you can see everything in the studio), turn it to the right and the wall goes pitch black (and nothing can be seen in the working space), and when the switch is positioned in the centre, the glass becomes hazy, opaque. The latter position is very attractive: an outsider cannot exactly see what is going on in the studio, but can detect movement and assumes energy and activity—protection inside and fascination outside.

Let us now address in more depth the personal strategy for dealing with the art market, like the path to new submarkets.

### *Four market strategies*

An artist can pursue a particular path to a submarket or make new choices, for example by changing his work or entering as yet untapped markets. The individual approach to the market results primarily from the selected network, from the material evaluation with regard to expected income generation, as well as from your character and which personal pattern of interaction you want to resort to. Is your behaviour primarily offensive, defensive or neutral, for instance? There are areas which, however interesting they might be or appear, require behaviour that is not 'you'. When considering taking a new step it is wise to examine repeatedly aspects of the market/submarket, such as:

– saturation of supply (are there already many artists in this segment?);
– volume and nature of demand (are there already many buyers and how well-informed are they about art buying?)
– dynamics (is there movement in the market and are there interesting new possibilities?);
– price level (low, medium, high and very high).

The Russian-American economist Igor Ansoff developed a growth model in 1957 that can be translated for the artistic practice with four forms of market approach. They are addressed below.

This is condensed in a diagram, followed by an explanation:

| PRODUCT \ MARKET | EXISTING MARKET | NEW MARKET |
|---|---|---|
| EXISTING PRODUCT | MARKET PENETRATION | MARKET DEVELOPMENT |
| NEW PRODUCT | PRODUCT DEVELOPMENT | DIVERSIFICATION |

*Figure 12.* Product and market

Work with an existing style, medium and execution is sold to the same kind of consumers: more of the same work for an existing buyers group. When ties with existing contacts are reinforced, we refer to *market penetration*.

Another possibility is that work with an existing style, medium and execution is sold to new consumers whom, as yet, the artist has not yet involved: new markets are explored and approached: *market development*.

For a known, more or less same group of contacts, a new kind of work (a different medium, greatly modified style and/or fundamentally modified execution) is produced and made available. That may be for inner motives or because of (inspiring) signals from this world or that network. Maybe those who have so far purchased existing work will be willing to buy or commission a different kind of work. This strategy is called *product development*.

A striking development in your work plus significance for new groups of buyers can at times go hand in hand: *diversification*.

***Reflection*. Have you experienced, with respect to market strategy, how one thing led to another–for example, a new category of buyer for work that you have been making for some time, or new work, like an artist's book for collectors of your work? Describe the factors that you believe played an important role and outline a plan for a next step in your practice: different work for 'people you know' or already familiar work for 'people you don't know', and how would you go about it?**

### *Expansion of the market position*

Set subjects for discussion in meetings with artists on their professional practice are growth and development. How can you strengthen, consolidate or gradually scale down your current market position; how can you enter different markets, participate in different, new environments which provide more inspiration and satisfaction, and/or how can you develop new methods and make new kinds of work following on from/in line with what you are now doing? I convert the foregoing model into expansion of the artistic practice by translating market approaches into artists' positions.

*Intensification of an existing position*, examples of which are: you carry out projects at the interface of art, science and technology, but you could 'up it' a bit. There are assignments in public space, but there might be a few more. Your performative activities, for instance integrating image and sound, are worth while but too incidental; greater regularity would be welcome. You only occasionally act as a curator—but in that way you accumulate insufficient expertise to intensify the 'connectedness' facet and you want to gain more experience in that field. That is the translation of 'market penetration'.

In this variant, existing client relationships should be nurtured. There is always the lurking risk of market saturation and artist boredom.

*Expansion to another environment.* You could consider, alongside offering your work to an 'art library', selling the same type of work abroad, via an affiliated gallery (if that is required by the partnership agreement). A few more examples: deploy your knowledge and experience in the fields of art, science and technology as an adviser to art committees or businesses, or as a lecturer in art education. In your work in public space there is increased focus on design methods; you would like to encounter high-level design assignments to discover where your strengths lie. Or: your work usually finds its way from the studio to the public by way of a gallery. You had almost forgotten how satisfying it can be to explain art; a part-time lectureship seems worth while. That is the translation of 'market development'.

With this strategic variant, considerable energy must be devoted to looking for and negotiating with different channels There is a lurking risk that there will not be enough time left for creating work.

*Broadening of position, a new position on familiar ground*, for example: you want to find out if your patrons (municipal bodies and members of public participation committees) might also be interested in work you could make in the studio—not prearranged. Or: at the gallery you have suggested curating an exhibition with them, in the gallery or elsewhere. Or: you are working with others in an artist collective on the production and presentation of work, but put out feelers about your setting up and executing educative activities within the collective framework. That is the translation of 'product development'.

When developing a new direction in your work, you are not generating much, if any income, unless it involves an assignment. If your own professional practice does not have the flexibility to cater for what is, as such, a valuable re-orientation, an 'aid' like a working grant or project subsidy can be welcome to tide you over.

*Diversification*. Taking up new positions and, at the same time, breaking fresh ground—which usually amounts to both different work and different buyers—increases risk on both fronts. Not only are there possibilities for market and product development, but, more especially, there are risks with these two market approaches combined. A double undertaking of this type is not necessarily doomed to fail.

Then the diagram will look like this:

| ENVIRONMENT / POSITION | EXISTING MARKET SEGMENT | NEW MARKET SEGMENT |
|---|---|---|
| EXISTING POSITION | INTENSIFICATION | MARKET EXPANSION |
| NEW POSITION | POSITION EXTENSION | DIVERSIFICATION |

*Figure 13*. Position and market environment (free interpretation of Ansoff)

# Control variants

In each of the eleven positions in the eleven sub-markets, situations occur in which artists may feel powerless, because of a lack of recognition of art and artists in society, a lack of self-confidence or the stigma that an inept artist is more authentic than an adept artist. In everyday life, outside of art, artists often find successful solutions for their problems, large or small. While a solution-orientated approach is evidently not considered useful within their own artisthood, as if it is a problematic area, set apart from 'real life', having different rules.

***Reflection*. Look at a relatively complex problem in your private life that you have tackled more or less successfully and perhaps solved. And look at a complex issue you encounter or struggle with in your own artistic practice. Can you learn something from yourself?**

Self-insight into how you approach problems in general should not be underestimated as a key for dealing with many different matters. But, as we have seen, every specific sub-market is complex in itself and moreover, in view of the great
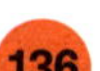

intertwining in the art world, highly susceptible to blunders.

That is why it is a good thing to ponder on forms of social interaction and control mechanisms in particular.

*Control mechanisms in artistic practice*

The term 'directing' is crucial when you operate in one or more aspired-to environments in desired positions, without losing time and attention (a form of energy management). How can you get—and keep—a grip on the forces around you, how can you interact with people and institutions without getting lost? This is also referred to as 'coping': being equal to, a match for, and handling.

There are many different situations in which collaboration, exchange or transactions are the focus, with—to sum up—a number of the points already addressed playing an important part:

- Know where you stand and what you stand for.
- Insight into or a sense of preferred and less preferred situations, not in order to avoid selective choices, but to be somewhat prepared, mentally.
- Know which facets of your artisthood you wish to activate in your practice.
- Know your wishes for the future, what could receive more emphasis and what less. Ambitions and profile of
163 ambitions are dealt with in Chapter 4.
- What is your preferred form of social interaction with others: non-committal, open for a good conversation or taking the lead.

Even if you feel 'powerless', there are possibilities to have and retain influence in your professional career. I differentiate between three patterns of interaction directed at exercising influence. Briefly: (A) A given situation, an existing area in which you operate as an 'explorer', repeatedly choosing whether and how to proceed. Just think of the dune landscape in Chapter 1 dealing with choice, strategy and tactics. (B) An open or 'parity' situation, in which you set up and modify in 'collegial dialogue' with others. (C) A self-defined situation in which you, as a 'director' have considerable influence.

*A. Given situation—the explorer*

There is a given situation over which you have no influence, or perhaps over only minor parts. For example, at a gallery with a professional approach which is successful, has a good reputation and a clear profile. Or: an acclaimed curator who works with or at a leading museum. Or a critic who operates in networks that count and works with respectable media. Or a technician who is considered to be a leading specialist in his field, nationally and internationally.

You cannot make excessive demands with respect to their willingness to meet your wishes: it is your decision, either 'yes' or 'no'. Such power is extreme, even though it might, in the first instance, appear limited. For example: you do not say to a leading, internationally-operating gallery: "I'd get rid of half the artists" or "Wouldn't it be better to relocate the gallery?"

A 'yes' or a 'no' can always be repeated, at every step. In exploratory dealings, when undertaking actual collaboration, when putting the plan into effect, even up to the point of presentation to the outside world and the possible subsequent continuation of collaboration. It occurs more in the theatre than in the visual arts that a performance remains artistically substandard and for the maker/makers its premiere would be out of the question. So, on the evening before the dress rehearsal, two evenings before the premiere, after several try-outs, the decision is taken to call it off. A veritable drama, a horrible choice between a damaged artistic reputation if the performance were to go ahead, and unfulfilled commitments if it is cancelled, damaged friendships, money down the drain, and your reputation as an unreliable wrecker confirmed. Yet perhaps that damage is less than if the performance were to go ahead.

A process had been started that felt like a trap, with no way out. Yet, when it comes to the crunch, that is not the case. It is possible—you can choose between the damage of a 'yes' and the damage of a 'no', even at the last minute—if you dare. However, it is better to avoid a dramatic situation of this type and have that particular step in reserve for the one moment in your career that there is no other alternative. The remedy to prevent a last-minute rift later on is to turn to yourself and ask: "Do I have sufficient confidence in those people and in the proposed plans to take the next step: for an exploratory meeting, when voicing intentions and expectations, when entering into collaboration, when discussing plans, during the process of collaboration? From start to finish, the matter of trust plays an important part, time and again. Only when trust has been achieved can you discuss the preconditions of collaboration in more concrete detail.

Two different perspectives are important if you are planning to do some soul-searching, especially at the initial stage: a '*rational inventory*', a two-dimensional map, and an '*emotional observation*', adding topography to the map, a third dimension.

They both result in the same, integrated rational-emotional assessment, with the head and the heart. Is there sufficient trust for a next step, where are possible doubts and how great and unsolvable are they? And how and when can I check that there won't be too large a problem at the last moment? It is a job for a detective. Let us take the example of collaboration with a gallery: they have taken the initiative or do you consider it fit for you to take the initiative—for instance, through an artist who already works with the gallery. Thanks to the transparency and speed of the Internet it is quite easy to make the rational *inventory* quickly, so no reason to skip it. Which artists are in that 'stable' and what do you think of them? What fringe activities does the gallery have, inside and outside like artists talks, participation in fairs and production of publications, and what do you think of them? Where is the gallery located, what does it look like and what do you think of it? The map is starting to emerge, but is still flat, two dimensional.

Emotional *observation* has long begun, because you keep asking yourself what you think. And it continues, step by step: how does the gallery owner behave, for instance at an opening, vis-à-vis staff, artists connected to the gallery, collectors and public, and are there differences, even tiny ones, in behaviour towards individuals, and how does that feel? To augment your impression of the website and the opening, casually ask if you may pass the reception desk and office to go to the lavatory, and check the atmosphere out, as well as how people are working behind the scenes; that is often a way of sensing the climate.

And the assessments continue. Use both perspectives, the rational and the emotional, inventory and observation, all your *senses*. Take everything in, keep your ears open and see beyond the end of your nose. Because, in such cases, it is permitted to poke your nose in someone's business, after all, it might become your business too. And that should be enough—

repeatedly—to answer the 'yes-or-no' question of trust: will I take the plunge or not? Will I do it unconditionally or do I have reservations, my hesitations that I want to clear up as I go along? This approach increases your possible grip on your own position in a given situation.

***Reflection*. Find examples in your own professional career in which you acted as an explorer and collaboration depended on your 'yes' or 'no'. Are there other examples from your own private life–when you were very young–in which you operated as an explorer? Are there similarities and differences between your private and professional situations?**

### *B. Parity situation—the colleague*

With a more or less *parity situation, a common responsibility* exists. Take, for example, an artist collective with former fellow students, or an experimental project of a young curator, or a new gallery. Then there is a greater chance to operationalise collaboration. Or, if we stay with the gallery example: it will be one managed by peers who have already gained relevant experience, but have not yet 'made it'. Then, you can assume there is a relationship more of equals from the very start, with communication and collaborations between colleagues.

In addition to the inventory and observation using all the senses, it is necessary to be conversant with the other's *vocabulary*, if not, 'collegial' discussion is not possible, you cannot understand each other well. The language of the gallery owner, of the curator, of the critic, of the client, the technical specialist—in short, of everyone with whom you wish to work. You do not need to conform slavishly, but you do need interest and curiosity about collaboration between peers, a genuine dialogue entailing more than just 'yes-or-no' decision-making. The chance that in this way you can get a grip on your contribution to collaboration and perhaps even on the 'new', shared venture, has increased substantially.

An enlightening quote from Jannet Vaessen (the director of Women Inc.): "You will have to convince everyone in their own terminology: with confessional politicians you discuss your proposal as a matter of decency, with liberal political parties you appeal to rational arguments, with populists you use clear language, for neo-liberals you make a business case."* The form changed, but not the content. If you have a command of each other's vocabulary and, in special situations, possibly develop a 'language' yourself, it can be important for getting a grip on the collaborative process.

The following is good example of how to develop your own communication method actively. The artist Helen Verhoeven was commissioned to make a painting for the Netherlands Supreme Court building in The Hague. The painting *The Supreme Court*, measuring 6.47 by 4 metres, was dubbed in the press as 'the new Night Watch'. After its unveiling, she told me about the collaborative process: "In the final stage of the selection process, the Supreme Court approached me through Esther Vonk, an independent visual arts adviser. I met the entire committee, with, apart from Esther, the President, Vice-President, Solicitor General, the Operational Director of the Supreme Court, representatives of the Government Buildings Agency, the contractor and the architects of the new building. We spoke on several occasions, both in the Netherlands and at my studio in Berlin. I made a formal presentation for the approval of subsequent stages, with booklets containing research and sketches to elucidate my ideas, and for one of the booklets I made an outline of parameters."

The location of the bars given in bold indicates the scores, and the variations in width show the margins of the scores, with much or little deviation.

* *De Volkskrant*, 14 September 2015.

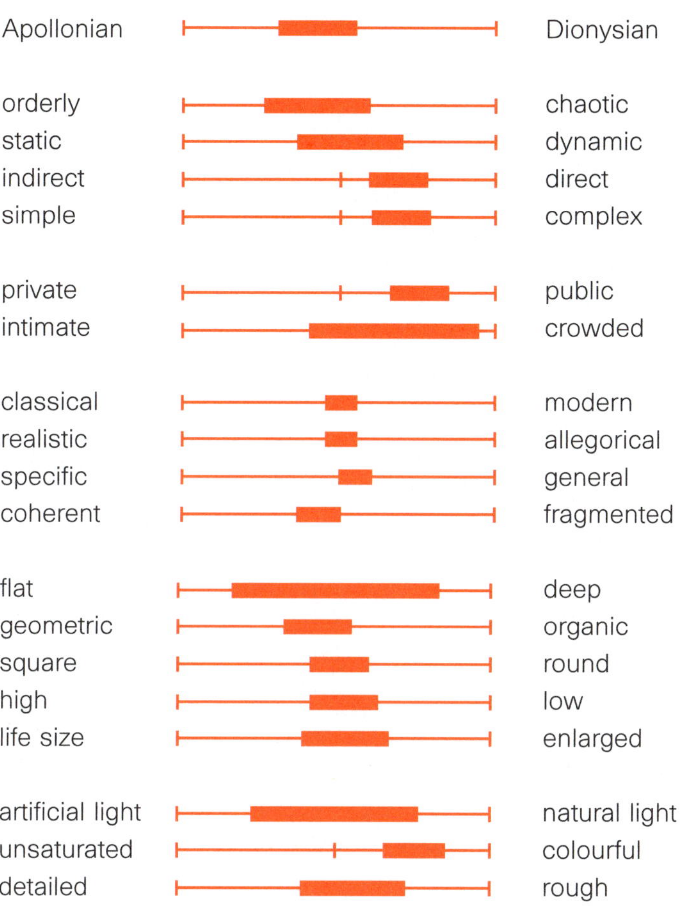


*Figure 14.* Communication mode (Helen Verhoeven)

"… For me, the outline (for the painting) was a way to list the many possibilities within the project, in order to picture them clearly myself and be able to discuss them with the committee in a common language. Since many members of the art committee were not from the art world, I also had a great many photos and art-historical examples to support the various terms. … As an artist, I find it important to continue to see the whole gamut of possibilities. It enables your working method to go on developing. Even though a painter's diagrammatic analysis is not, of course, entirely accurate and actually totally insufficient to describe an art work properly, it is a way to understand and explain your position. That is especially useful when working with others."

***Reflection*. Is that kind of dialogue with a client familiar? When could you take a stance as a 'colleague'? And how did collaboration proceed in a professional setting? Have you ever encountered similar interaction in your private life with important decisions (in a highly simplified form)?**

### *C. Self-defined—the director*

If you initiate activities yourself that entail collaboration, if you have an *open field* that is not fenced in on all sides by a client's prerequisites that cannot be influenced, that can be considered as your own project or temporary collaborative venture with wide-ranging and generous conditions. As an initiator and driving force, you can then be responsible for the direction and the goal. In that case you should indicate how long and how intensively demands will be made on other people's time, what costs could be involved and how you aim to finance the project, which partners (with the allocation of roles and tasks) will be involved. You must be able to identify, select, invite and motivate those partners.

In this case it is again, after rational review, primarily a matter of the *senses, the intuitive* aspect. Here too *empathy and command of the vocabulary* of those with whom you wish to collaborate are necessary. However, there is another essential component, i.e. a compelling idea, call it *vision*. Vision is needed in order to mobilise others, to involve or even captivate them. As an artist, you are a true director in this case, but nothing is worse than someone who claims to direct without having a sense of direction. Someone who wishes to lead without being suitably equipped. The vision of a 'directing' artist is indispensable as a 'pair of spectacles' through which to look critically at influence-able conditions, potential partners in collaboration and, above all, the quality of the outcome of collaboration: the result. In order to make decisions and choices, for now and for later.

***Reflection*. How was collaboration when you were the 'boss' or director? Find examples in your private and professional life. Compare collaboration in which you developed the vision and concept with that when you operated as a 'colleague' or an explorer.**

*Examples of control*

Three examples follow of each of the three control mechanisms, embracing the concept of 'coping' introduced earlier: when collaborating to produce work, collaborating to present work and collaboration between patron and artist as the commissioned party.

*Collaboration for production*. In the production process the three said patterns of interaction can be identified in collaboration between artists. They occur in the relationship between visual artist, for instance with interdisciplinary collaboration between art disciplines. It is possible that one artist *assists* another when creating his or her object. So, as an art professional or handyman, you participate in another's production process. It can be enjoyable, instructive and/or financially attractive. A second variant is *co-production*. In that case, both the ideas and the methods of the two parties should coincide. As is always the case with parity, without hierarchy, it is probably the most difficult position. You can also attend to *coordination yourself* and have another artist assist you in making the work or realising a project requiring an effort from several people.

Collaboration by providing assistance requires confidence in one's own intuition and pursuit of the path of rational inventory and emotional observation. You decide if you want to comply with a given situation. Co-production relates to a form of collaboration among peers and on an equal footing which, in addition, requires affinity with 'the other's' vocabulary. And directing—tying in with the senses and the vocabulary—also demands a 'mobilising' vision in order to motivate others.

*Collaboration for presentation.* Artists can display work at presentation venues such as museums and galleries, as well as organising joint presentations. It may involve an ad hoc collaboration, initiated by one of the parties concerned or by someone else, who invites a number of artists. A long-standing collaboration can also come about which may or may not be specific to a particular venue. There are different motives that can guide artist initiatives of this type. They include the creation of a new distribution and presentation venue of one's own, because access to existing networks is blocked and requires too much, or the wrong kind of energy. Or else a group can be formed where there is so much mutual trust that critical opinions can be exchanged about one another's work. The group can be geared to optimising the work of each individual without seeking to find a common denominator; or actually geared to formulating pictorially—and also often in the spoken and written word—a common standpoint.

With artist collaborations three positions are once more possible: look around for an existing group or an initiative which is being set up, and *join* it. Develop with a group of colleagues/friends *joint activities* and, if all goes well, continue them. Or take the initiative yourself, based on specific ideas, and act as a director when forming the group.

Decision-making on entering into or continuing collaboration in this example relates to the approach with the scout with his 'yes/no' resource based on intuition, the power of collegial dialogue using—and understanding—each other's language, and the persuasiveness of a director with a mission.

*Collaboration with the patron.* Finally, we return once more to the three coping situations, but now with reference to an assignment. In a *given situation* the artist must be able to comprehend and understand what a patron proposes. Wide-ranging freedom is in saying 'yes' or 'no' to him, on a basis of trust. It is often a matter of balancing between financial enticement and the good feeling that someone is paying you attention on the one hand, and, on the other hand, the inner motives and choices concerning the kind of situations in which you would like to wind up. So positioning. A 'yes-no' choice will mainly occur in set, 'closed' assignment situations, when there is little opportunity—if any—for discussion. Incidentally, in that situation, the artist should also reformulate the patron's request in his own terms and conditions. As we have already seen, a good patron withdraws if the artist merely says "OK, I'll do what you want".

In a *situation of more parity* the artist will seek to influence the content and conditions of the assignment, in consultation with a patron who is more 'open' and who inspires confidence So he or she must not only comprehend and understand, but also speak the patron's language. That makes demands on your attitude and experience.

In an *open assignment situation*, the artist will introduce and largely seek to define content and conditions himself, having first decided he has sufficient confidence in collaboration. Accordingly, that not only requires relevant intuition, language and attitude, but considerable conceptual content. The artist must have something worth saying to a patron who is geared to experiment, in order to engage him in the collaboration process.

Back to Helen Verhoeven and the Supreme Court. The initial contact between the committee and Verhoeven brought about a basis for trust for the 'exploration'. A common vocabulary was developed which was accessible for those who were not art experts, and accordingly a parity situation was created for 'collegial dialogue'. In addition, thanks to the power of her vision on the position and history of the Supreme Court, the assignment conditions were enlarged and there was even scope for directing. The commissioned artist supported the client in the pursuit of collaboration geared to experiment. In this case it was because Verhoeven was hospitable, inviting them into her studio to observe her working process by way of sketches and diagrams to analyse the painting. This made things clearer for the committee. When I asked whether artistic freedom might not be less with an assignment of this type compared with one in the 'white cube', Verhoeven answered: "No, rather the opposite."

Whenever I talk about control patterns during my workshops in art education, I give the following exercise. "Turn to a fellow student beside, behind or in front of you, but preferably not someone you know well, and exchange with him/her some of your frustrating experiences regarding collaboration." After some initial hesitation, they just cannot stop! Evidently the sharing of bad experiences is inspiring and amusing. You can organise that yourself.

***Reflection*. Occasionally invite a friend to come for coffee at your home, your studio, at a pavement café, or go for a walk together. Discuss your collaboration experiences. Answer the following questions: what was your worst experience with it, how could you have gone about it better, what did you learn from it?**

People's attitudes not only differ depending on whether they are an explorer, colleague or director, but also depending on their character—for example, cautious or enterprising. They also differ within one individual and vary over time, depending on one's experience with and knowledge of the situation, and probably on one's mood.

*Sometimes an explorer, often a colleague and incidentally a director. With intuition, language and ideas you can go far, even in tricky market situations.*

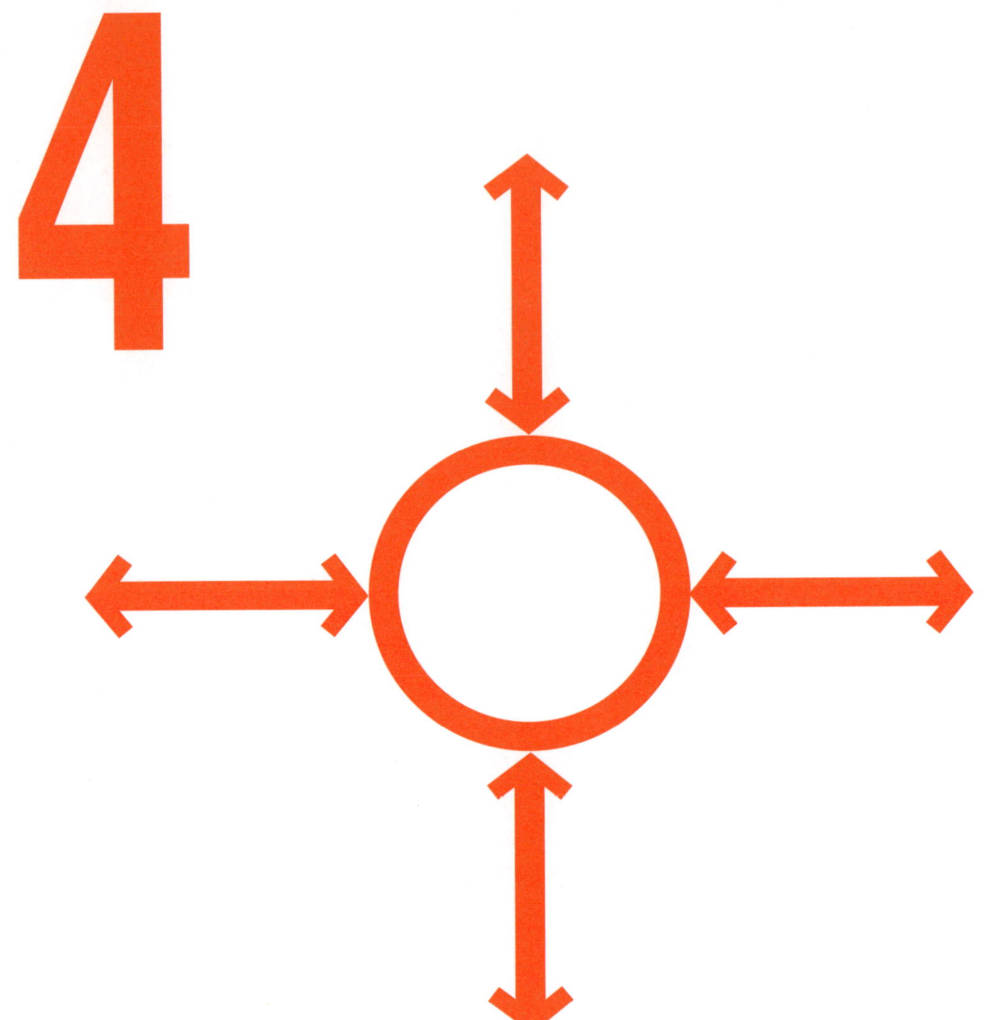

# Dynamic artist-hood, growth and mobility

Regardless of whether we are dealing with priorities within one or more artists' positions, priorities in everyday practice concerning investment of time, attention and money, with collaborations or a specific 'programmatic' choice to pursue further studies, a post-academic institute, a PhD programme or a working period in an artist residency, it is always crucial to know and mobilise your *personal development ambitions*. That is not only relevant for the completion of your studies and the start of your professional career, but also throughout the rest of your career and life.

Apart from concentration on yourself, as reflected in the studio, four interactive dimensions can be identified, so communication with others. Possibly more, but I shall address four. These dimensions form the parameters needed to establish your ambition profile and determine where you want to go. They relate to 'honing' where you stand, artistically, expanding your technical scope, accelerating your professional career and enlarging awareness of your social position as an artist. I do not provide a theoretical analysis of 'dimensions of personal development', but a practical model for your personal use, distilled from the artistic practice. This chapter briefly examines the arrangement of the studio and collaborations between artists, bearing in mind the said dimensions. The origin and importance of this model are explained below, in 'Building for artists: the power of metaphors'.

Growth of artisthood, so the development of the artistic practice, requires mobility and immobility. Travel is a physical form of mobility, 'motion' in many different forms. Travel with art education and research projects or artist residencies as its destination requires careful exploration to facilitate your choice, as well as your actual acceptance. The model in question, enhanced with the instrument of 'learning modes', is a useful aid in the hunt for institutional destinations and a good 'match' between artist and institute. This will be dealt with in 'Matching qualities'.

# Deconstructing the studio into four panels

Every artist has a studio, a physical or mental space, or both, irrespective of the positions in the studio, the laboratory, public space, on the stage, as a designer, artist-writer, curator, organiser, adviser, educator or change agent. This chapter begins in the studio, where you are alone or together with others.

I deconstruct the studio into four components, based on my observations. In this model, the studio is a space containing a table, a work bench, a shelf on the wall, and the door. This deconstruction into components has tremendous metaphorical power. A 'model' developed in this way is instrumental (enlightening, stimulating and applicable) in charting individual ambitions for the development of artistic practice and artisthood. It is also useful for the development of organisations of and for artists, offers common ground when 'matching artists and institutes', as well as when creating built space for artists. But let us start with the model for developing the artistic practice.

The studio contains:

– a *work bench*, with tools, equipment and materials;
– a *table* where the artist can talk, eat and drink with other artists. And with guests from the art world whom he has allowed in;
– a *shelf* with books and precious mementoes. Apart from Internet in the studio, the artist also has access to collections, documentation and other sources of inspiration, from the past and the present. Art, architecture, philosophy, sociology, the natural sciences, as well as travel, politics and economics. In other words, facets of society;
– the studio *door*, which only the artist can open, to other artists, guests, professionals from the art market, if welcome in his/her studio.

### *Dimensions of personal development*

The components (work bench, table, shelf and door) are both concrete and conceptual. They are interactive and concern relationships with the people around you. Accordingly, everything that was said in the last chapter about interaction, directing and control patterns in artistic practice is relevant. One aspect is being on your own, in the physical or mental studio, in the centre of things.

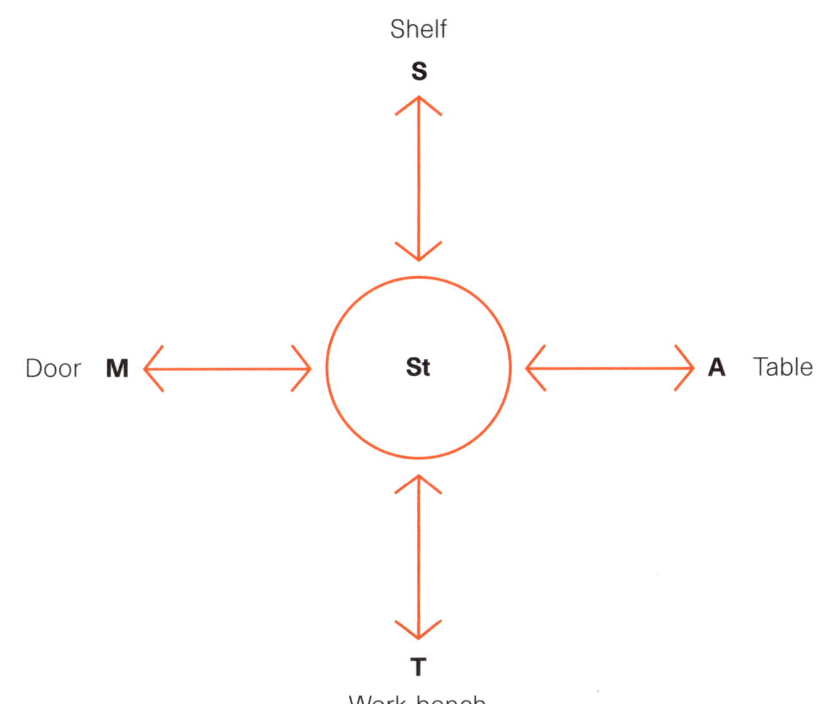


*Figure 15a.* Dimensions and components

The letters A, T, M and S stand for the Artistic dimension, the Technical dimension, the Market dimension and the Society dimension—the table, work bench, door and shelf, respectively. Let me explain.

1. The artistic dimension is, among other things, about authenticity, inner need, power of your ideas and concepts, awareness of your strengths and weaknesses, and your possible uniqueness. With this dimension, development is geared to *honing your artistic place*. Interaction is primarily geared to exchange with other artists, with peers and 'masters' from the artist community, alongside contact with critics and curators.
A. *the table*.

2. The technical dimension covers interest in the 'making' process, discovering what best matches your philosophy and skills, the ability to visualise ideas in a professional way, to be the 'master' of the material rather than the other way round. Attention, time and energy are directed at technical matters, including exchanges and collaboration with technical people. This dimension is geared to increasing your tools, *expanding technical expertise*.
T. *the work bench*.

3. Links with the art market, where money can be made, mainly relates to networking, attention to commercial links. We have seen which parties with whom you have dealings in the eleven art market segments, and how you can get, and keep, a grip on those links by way of three control patterns. *Development objective: acceleration of the professional career*.
M. *the door.*

4. Art history, sociology, philosophy, economics and the like help a little in positioning yourself as an artist in society. Here again—as with the preceding dimensions—you learn most from experiencing things in a variety of situations and positions in society itself, as well as exchanges with others on social themes. The development objective in this dimension is to *deepen awareness and knowledge of the social position of artists*.
S. *the shelf*

In addition, there is the moment of solitude, with no communication with others, when you must fend for yourself when looking for your own 'voice'. *Investigating*, one may refer to theories, the other not. Alone, back again in the physical or mental studio after an exchange and collaboration with artists, technicians and actors in the market and in society, *reflecting* on your artistic place, your technical scope, your professional career, your ambitions in society.

Together, the first two dimensions (A/T) are referred to in art education as the 'artistic-technical domain' and the second two (M/S) as the 'professional-social domain' of artisthood. That is theoretically correct policy terminology, but in workshops, coaching and counselling, I find I am better off with a more expressive 'peg', and notice that metaphors stick better in your mind. The diagram is an important guide and aid for the career path, both for tomorrow or for a period of three to five years, or even much farther off. It can help you choose or relocate premises, or pursue subsequent training, to choose a post-academic institution, an artist residency. These are questions that are relevant and urgent for artists with an advanced career, but also art students and budding artists.

## Personal ambition profile

The model is appropriate as an individual exercise, enabling you to examine priorities in time, energy and attention which now extend to the four interactive dimensions and what, in the future, should—in your perception—occupy a place of greater or lesser importance. An exercise of this type is not only potentially enlightening for the actual choices. It can be equally enlightening in providing greater awareness of freedom of choice and focusing your own strengths.

# Exercise: An ambition profile in five steps

First draw the four dimensions on a piece of paper. Give them plenty of space, because with each step in this diagram something is added.

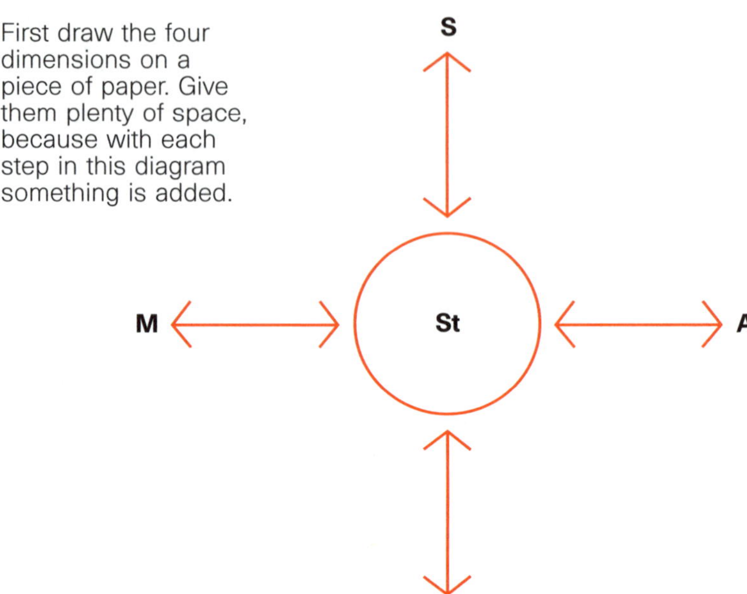


*Figure 15b.* Dimensions (interactive)

Second step. Consider carefully, reflect on your *present* circumstances (a sociologist would call that 'defining the situation') and place a point between 'withdrawal alone' and 'participation together' at each of the four axes.

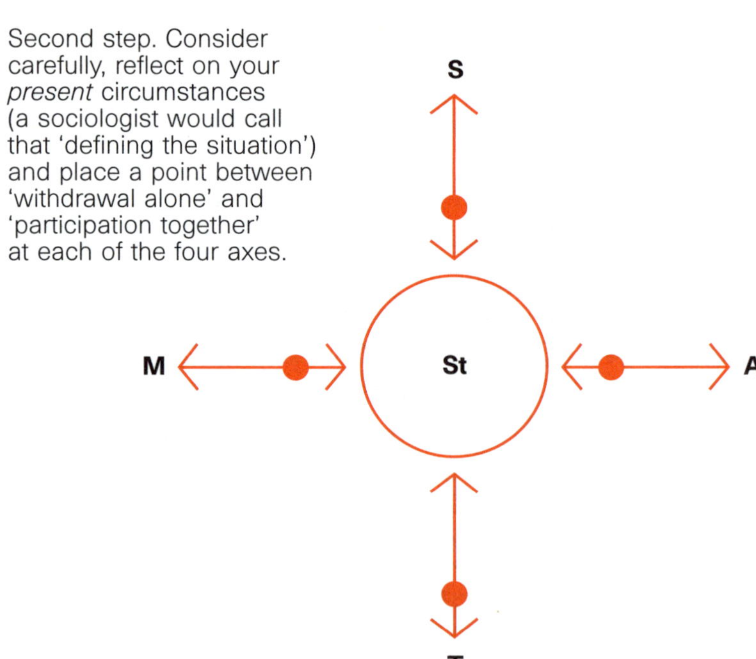


*Figure 15c.* Present positions

So the time, attention and energy you devote to contact with other artists (A), to technology (T), the market (M) and society (S).

Much communication goes to the outside, less attention and more reflection retreat to the centre, the studio.

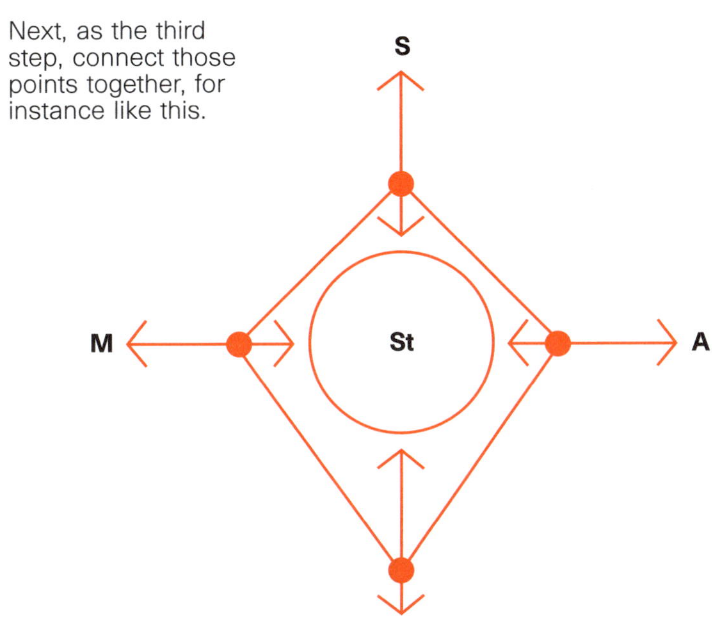


*Figure 15d.* Present profile

Again, consider carefully about experiences, fascination, about plans (tomorrow or in three to five years) and dreams (between dreaming and waking, upon waking or as you fall asleep; in the 'twilight' when a dream is no longer a dream and a plan has no planning as yet).

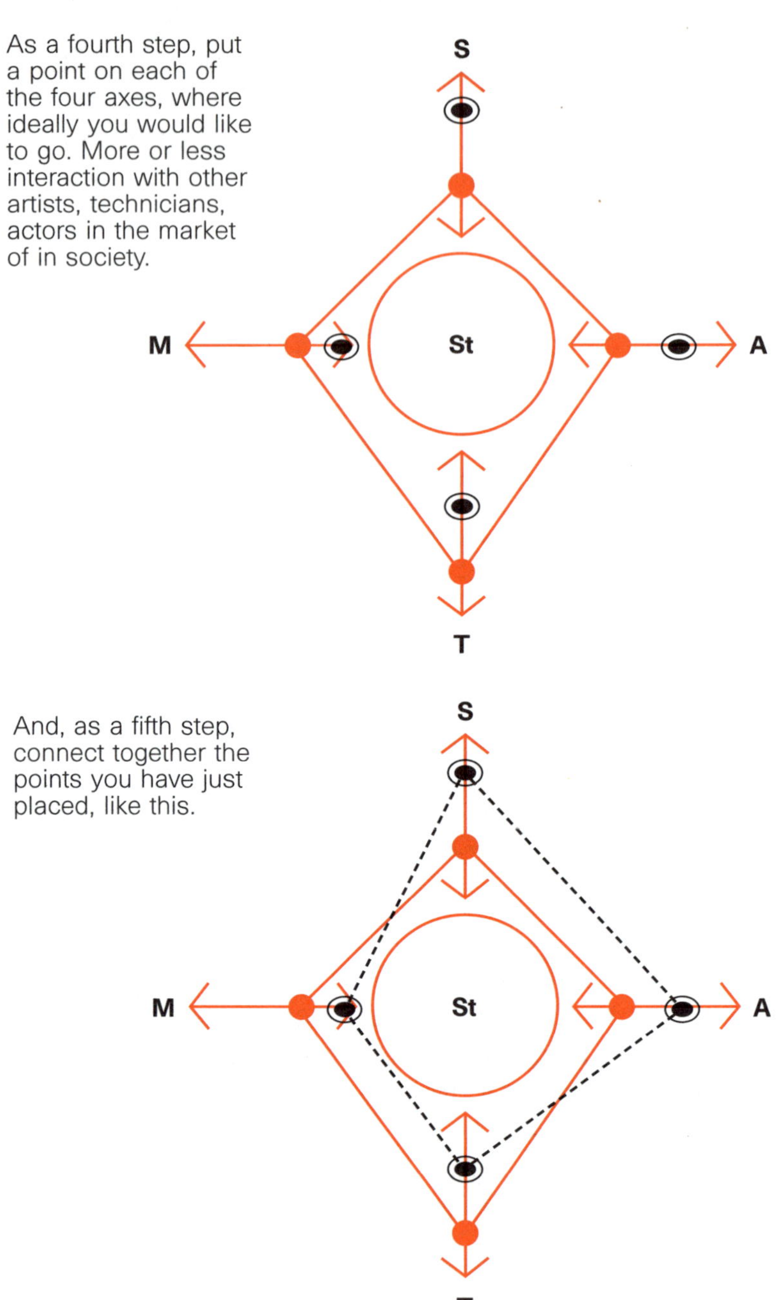


*Figure 15e.* Ambitions

*Figure 15f.* Ambition profile (I)

More contact with other artists, unchanged for technology, less focus on the market and more on your position in society. With this profile you could better not go to a one-person residency on a mountain summit, but to ruangrupa in Jakarta, a group of artists who make interventions in the socio-urban fabric.

Or like this.

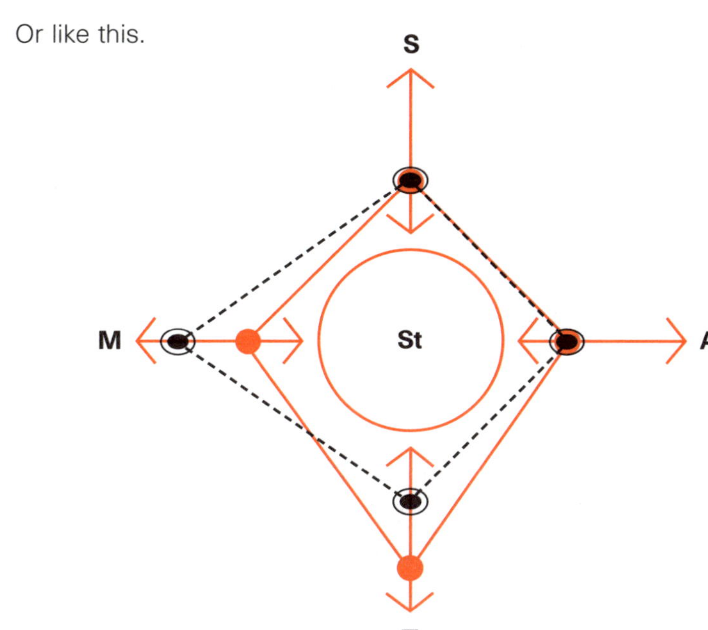


Figure 15g. Ambition profile (II)



With the adjoining profile (fewer artists, more market) it is better to go to a market-orientated residency in New York or another centre in the international art market where curators, critics and collectors pop in.

Low and behold: a profile where you stand and to which, at this point in time, you think you want to head. Put it in a 'drawer' in your mind. Think about it, when necessary, when making practical choices in everyday practice, when opting for further studies, a post-academic institute, a PhD programme or an artist residency. It is by definition a dynamic model that is constantly changing—think of mixed scanning on the trip to the lighthouse. It helps when deciding "on what will I spend time, attention and money?" Or, in other words: how can you—without completely avoiding constructive side-roads—not spend too much time and attention on something that is not much use to you, now and in the future.

## Application of the model when setting up and developing artistic practice

As we have already seen, the dimensions or components of artisthood can be used in several areas: individually, with respect to fitting out the studio, as well as for personal relocation and travel. The model can also be used for analysing collaborations, and it is even helpful for creating built space for artists.

*Fitting out the studio*

What is the primary focus when you sketch your artistic practice and, specifically, fitting out your studio? If you are aiming at meeting and exchange: a good *table*. Or at technical research and production: a first-class *work bench*. Or at presentation and publicity: the open *door*. Or at acquisition of knowledge on art, humankind and society in books, films and Internet: a large *shelf*, in a well-lit space (preferably roomy). Or at combinations of *space*, table, work bench, shelf and door, in your order of priority. Decisions concerning investment for fitting out the artist's studio with use of these dimensions are
203 dealt with in Part II, 'Building blocks'.

*Collaborative ventures between artists*

When artists collaborate in a 'joint venture' (artists' initiatives, events or complex art projects) as well as with curators, gallery owners, technicians and others, they can use the provided dimensions to identify priorities within that collaboration. For instance: is collaboration about discourse focusing on *artistic positioning* (the table); or *joint production or technological research* (work bench); is *presentation in the art market* (the door) paramount; is the joint effort geared to social intervention (the shelf) or is collaboration geared to the feasibility of achieving a studio complex in which each *individual artist has his his/her own studio*.

206 Collaboration among artists reappears in 'A new initiative'.

### *Travelling to institutional destinations*

'You live and learn' is a nice expression when it comes to choosing and improvising, experiencing and reflecting in practice. For many artists—today, but in the past too—travel is an essential part of their experiences. Travel for exhibitions and assignments, travel to form impressions for exploration and research, or travel to institutional destinations such as courses and artist residencies. For all these types of travel, the artistic, technical, commercial and social dimensions are particularly useful in one's search for suitable destinations. They are 'measuring instruments', especially when the dimensions are supplemented with types of learning. This subject is dealt with in more detail in 'Modes of learning' and 'Matching qualities'. 171 174

### *Building for artists: the power of metaphors*

In a structural design for an institute of art education or an artist residency the four dimensions model can also be of use. It can be projected as an example for the programming and renovation of the Rijksakademie Research residency in the late 1980s–early 1990s. From then on it was housed in Amsterdam's former Cavalry Barracks (1863), located between the city centre and a canal. The old stables with the studios on the floor above, around a courtyard with a newly-built tower in the middle.

- *the work bench*, technical Workshops in former stables
- *the table* for conversations, eating and drinking: the Cantina beside the water
- *the shelf* with books and precious mementoes: Library and Collections in the central building, link between indoors and outdoors, and
- *the door* of the studio, which only the artist can open. In a building that is somewhat turned away from the street and belongs to artists 360 days a year. For five days a year the institute is 'taken over' and hospitably welcoming: RijksakademieOPEN.

The model not only steered the building plans, but also, with its metaphorical power, forced breakthroughs.*

# Housed somewhere else for a while

*Development by mobility: it never stands still*

The foremost development of all facets of your artisthood, with positions and differing contexts, takes place by way of 'learning by doing', and that will be addressed in more detail in this chapter. For some artists it is sufficient to work in and around their 'permanent' studio; they have no further desire for relocation or mobility. If they do want to travel, they do so mentally. Some stay close to home of necessity or by volition, on account of supplementary income or to be able to pay more attention to their children. Others want to travel, to destinations or just to be en route.

The travelling artist has always existed. Some residencies give the impression that artists only started going out and about when in recent decades residencies started springing up. Travel to a location of that type is just one form of mobility. There are various reasons for and types of 'travel'.

One kind of mobility stems from a 'run-of-the-mill' or *going-concern practice*, so within the framework of assignments and presentations, close to home or far away, with or without payment of travel expenses, and hospitality from the bodies or persons who invited the artist.

Travel grants, scholarships or project subsidies for Research and Development abroad from funds or educational institutions (in the framework of promoting expertise by artist-lecturers) or other institutes encourage international mobility. Such support for *individual pathways/endeavours and institutional routes*, for instance Master's studies, PhD research, artist residencies and studios abroad from funds like the Mondriaan Fund in the Netherlands, gives extra stimulus to international mobility.

* The post-academic Rijksakademie proved hard to classify for civil servants and also difficult to fit into regulations and standards for government buildings. It is after all, neither a museum, nor an art education institute, office, archive or prison. Limiting guidelines for new-build needed to be 'unfrozen' and ritual procedures relating to detailing down the square millimetre scrapped. What did help–better than detailed arguments–was the real-life image of the artist's studio with simple, appealing pictures of the work bench, the table and the shelf. With metaphors you develop a 'language' that can extend beyond regimes.

*Private trips* to interesting places, including to friends as a couch surfer, or sometimes to a place of one's own, are probably the chief form of mobility. Many artists have places they like to return to regularly.

All these situations entail choice processes. Choices become even more complicated when *institutional destinations* are involved which present themselves alluringly to artists, sometimes even accompanied by money, as is the case with some studios or artist residencies abroad.

The key questions are:

1. What do you find there, does it tie in with your ambitions for development: honing of artistic position, extension of technical palette, acceleration of professional career, clarification of position in society, the four panels.
2. How do people respond to one another there, what forms of interaction or learning geared to your personal development are deployed there? They will be discussed below.
3. What is important for 'matching' of institutional supply and artists' individual ambitions and expectations. This is dealt with in 'Regarding quality and matching'. 177

A trip to an institutional destination, to spend time elsewhere can occur throughout a person's career.

*Modes of learning*

When you opt for an institutional destination, the second approach enquires about behaviour and interaction patterns, for an additional parameter providing clarity about relations with others and, especially, type of learning. That is important in answering the follow questions: can you be there *alone*; who are the *others* and what can you learn from their backgrounds, knowledge and experience and what have you to offer them, are there *experts*, and in what field, from whom you can ask advice and who will indeed give advice. And what are the *working conditions* and living conditions for you and, if a longer period is involved, for your partner, children, the cat.

In health- and geriatric care, the sector where I worked from 1975 to 1982, they referred to self-care, informal care and professional care. In the learning context, I distinguish between four comparable types: self-learning, peer-learning, expert-learning plus 'supportive facilities', and explain them further.

With *self-learning*, you could think of the *individual* reflecting and developing further. Is there time and space to scrutinise the 'baggage' of knowledge, experience and ideas, to pursue—or deviate from—a selected path, incorporate personal history. This means that an institutional destination should have a stimulating, hospitable climate enabling artists or students to reflect in relative seclusion on their own artistic position, their own technical expertise, their personal commercial ambitions and their 'mission' as an artist in society. The ability to spend time alone is an important attribute for self-learning during your art studies. In addition you can put it to good use at post-academic institutes and residencies and, equally, for subsequent professional practice when solitude is a great effort and a major strength. You might say, like self-care as the prime aspect in healthcare, that self-learning is the basis of all learning.

*Peer-learning* relates to the exchange among the artist- or student-population, to the *population make-up*: is everyone of the same age or are there different generations, can they continue to combine criticism and friendship in the discussion on artistic standpoints, do they endorse contrasting views on style or do they all appear to have been made in one uniform mould, do they bring varying types of technical expertise with them, are they from the region, the entire country, from Europe or all continents, from different social and cultural backgrounds? Do they bring with them divergent artists' positions and networks from their countries of origin? Peer-learning constitutes a valuable addition to self-learning, and, with a little imagination can be compared with informal care in healthcare—i.e. a voluntary, informal and warm-hearted exchange based on curiosity and friendship. It is not uncommitted and is often a necessity.

*Expert-learning* with affiliated *experts*, like teachers, mentors or advisers and technical specialists, can play an important part with interaction. Ideally, expert-learning ties in with self-learning and peer-learning. A 'multiplier effect' results: self-learning is intensified, peer-learning is reinforced, and ideas, experiences, knowledge and connections with experts fall in that fertile soil. This input adds considerable value by way of exchange and engagement. Expert-learning is important, but not the be all and end all of knowledge acquisition—that is self-learning.

*Facilitative conditions* are worth mentioning in this context, since they help to determine the different dimensions. I already specified all the *facilities*, such as space to eat and drink with others (the table), workshop space and items for technical research and production (the work bench) and space for presenting yourself, to peers, and possibly also to people in the art world, and to people from the community who are curious about your work (the door). The use of and engagement with facilities of this type supplies a wealth of learning experiences, because technical experiments indirectly enable you to test and hone personal concepts, you realise which technical media give you a platform. The use of studio space demonstrates how important/unimportant that is, and which are the worthwhile specifications of the studio.

As an artist, you can use the information in this chapter together with the dimensions of your personal development (ambitions) and types of learning (interaction) to draw up a list of questions regarding the nature of the institute and what it has to offer, including:

A. Is there time and space for individual reflection, research, experiment and production. For personal exploration of technical possibilities and restrictions. For considering your attitude vis-à-vis the market and for experiencing and studying social contexts on your own (self).
B. Do the fellow artists/students introduce differing views and ideas on art, on production methods, on setting up and maintaining the artistic practice and supply experiences from disparate social, religious and political backgrounds. Do they enlarge or reduce reference frameworks (peer).
C. Are there expert discussion partners who are willing to share generously their knowledge and ideas and reveal to you their position in the art world and society, and the road they took to get there, and who are critical and 'collegial' (expert).
D. What kind of facilities exist, for study, research and production, and do they contribute to honing the artistic position, enlarging the technical reach, accelerating the professional career and awareness of artists' positions in society.

Time and again, the descriptions above reflect—with individual (self), together (peer), feedback (experts) and facilities—the metaphorical dimensions in the studio space: table, work bench, door and shelf.

## Matching qualities

With the dynamic personal profile of your development and ambition under your belt, you can tread the career path to further studies, a post-academic institute or an artist residency—armed with greater self-awareness. Once you have arrived, it is not certain if the 'searching' artist and the 'sought-after' institute go together, if they will interconnect. The matching of qualities decides whether you will be invited to get better acquainted, after which admission follows. We now know approximately what the artist is looking for. What the institute expects requires elucidation and illustration. Then you will know what you can encounter—and here again, the dimensions are of help. I draw from twenty-five years of observing selection juries at the Rijksakademie.

Many thoughts cross the minds of the jury members—mostly artists in the capacity of 'adviser'—they look and listen, asking the artist essential questions like "where do you stand and what do you stand for?" or, in view of future collaboration, think "what do you believe in and do we believe you?". The main purpose is not an objective evaluation of quality, but 'matching'—to answer the question whether the opportunities offered by the institute match the candidate's wishes and expectations, thus meaning there is a chance of added value during a work period. The dimensions in the model also feature, not explicitly, systematically or in a formalised way, but as an intuitive substructure.

*Fictive inner dialogues*

Members of a selection jury want to discover if there is enough scope between what the institute supplies and the artist demands. They are well enough acquainted with what, in this case, the Rijksakademie can offer and effect, so (and here they are again!) the four panels: contact with other artists (A), individual technical research and production (T), personal positioning as regards the market (M) and connections with society (S), as opposed to the artist's concentration on his own studio. If you bear that in mind, you can imagine the following fictive 'inner dialogues' on the various dimensions:

Artistic: A
"Do you look forward to contact with other artists in the studios?" "Yes, I consider that to be of paramount importance, alongside spending time together. I'm not all that interested in the workshops or the library, or in fact being alone in a studio." The jury members will think: "OMG, this candidate will miss out on much of what is on offer here."

Technical: T
With another candidate, another question from the jury: "Will you work in the technical workshops?" "Yes, that's what I've come for. I've been focusing on ceramics for the last ten years and want to do that exclusively for the next two." A silent thought: "OMG, there's so much else apart from the workshop. He'll miss out on a lot here and could better attend a ceramics workshop."

Market: M
Another candidate. Question: "Do you want to interrelate with the art market, discover how to get a grasp of it yourself?" "Yes, I'd like to get networks and tips as to how to take part next year in a gallery at the Frieze in London, that's most important for me. There'll be my own presentations here and there, but I'll also be present at international art fairs." "OMG, he'll miss out on a lot of what is worth while here. Particularly the opportunity to explore market mechanisms in a relative safe haven with protection, and play around with them."

Society: S
And another: "Do you want to discover what, as an artist, you can contribute to society?" "Yes, I'll almost always work in neighbourhoods with refugees, outside the Rijksakademie." "OMG, interesting, but he will miss out on a lot here. Is this an artist or actually a journalist or activist?"

In the studio: St
Lastly: "Are you looking forward to working in your own studio?" "Yes, I'm mainly looking for a studio where I can reflect and work. I'm not particularly interested in contact with other artists, working on presentation, reading in the library or talking about current developments." "OMG, he's missing out on a lot. What will he be reflecting on in that studio?"

These fictive interviews lead us past dimensions and conditions for development. All are simple, stereotype statements that can provide insight: much or little interaction with other artists, isolation? Much or little use of workshops and collaboration with technical specialists: emphasis on conceptualising, avoiding materialisation? Much or little attention for taking control and conforming to market-orientated behaviour: aversion to professionalisation? Much or little orientation on artisthood in society: concentration on 'self' and individualisation? Much or little desire to be alone in one's own studio.

### *Regarding quality and matching*

Matching as described relates to the connection between supply and demand. The factors that are decisive when an institute must choose to invite or admit someone are the natural fascination and curiosity of the individual jury members, assessment of work and individual, and their quality. To conclude this chapter, I shall address briefly the relationship between matching, selection and quality.

Early in October 2012 I attended the 'The Myth of Talent' session in Castrum Peregrini in Amsterdam, in the series of salon evenings for 'Best of Graduates Gerrit Rietveld Academy'. I was there as an 'expert from the audience'. The moderator was Fons Hof, the director of Art Rotterdam, with, as panel members Xander Karskens, curator and currently director of Cobra Museum in Amstelveen and Monika Kackovic, research associate, and meanwhile having obtained her doctorate at the University of Amsterdam. The question was asked: what is quality? My answer was that I couldn't give an answer, since I didn't know the intended context of quality assessment in that case. In the framework of this publication, we can ask whether it relates to one of the contexts of artists' positions, for example in the world outside the studio, like the museum. And what kind and standard of art work is involved: one of a quality appropriate for museum presentation? If so, what kind of museum does that mean, at what level, with what mission, which audience, and what do they in fact offer the artist if he takes part?

In other words, you can only talk about quality of art in relation to targeted matching between two entities, with which I would definitely want to know what the artist is offered before considering whether if that artist does in fact 'fit' there and make a contribution. After all, matching means 'forming a good combination', 'finding something that goes well with something else'—so, two-way traffic.

***Reflection*. Look on line at two artist residencies or Master's programmes, one in which, at first sight, you would fit well and another where you would definitely not feel at home. Why do these residencies suit you, or not?**

After a 'match' has been found between the artist and the targeted destination or pending plan, new situations come about, in different environments and with people who are unknown to start with.

*The table, the work bench*
*The door and the shelf*
*Four panels that have reinforced*
*your sense of direction.*

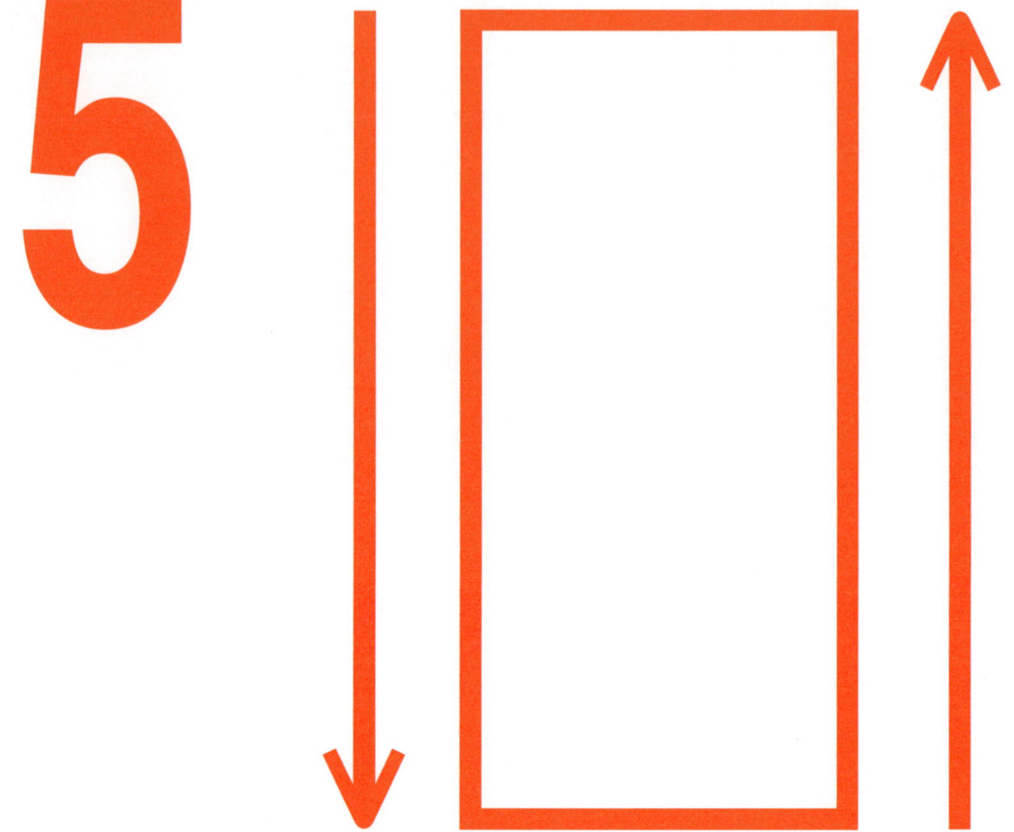


# Fabric of knowledge exchange, collaboration and friendship

So far the artist has been addressed as a solitary individual, going it alone, and doing pretty well as long as he is equipped with self-awareness, personal resources and perseverance. You do encounter prejudices about the social significance of artists, and other forms of opposition, but in the preceding chapters that aspect has been treated only indirectly. The issues dealt with so far, were, in a nutshell:

The first part of this publication, relating to terminology and reflections, started with choice processes. The mantra "where do I stand and what do I stand for?" was introduced. Positioning is something every individual artist must do if he/she is to chart a course, strategy, planning and playing, towards enticing goals on the horizon, but not missing out on the opportunities that occur unexpectedly along the way. An important factor when you develop a personal strategy is to determine the breadth of your own artistic practice (Chapter 1). We entered the studio and in that interior space we encountered sources of inspiration and fascinations, or facets as I have called them, which materialise in artists' positions when the artist presents himself outside his own practice (Chapter 2). The artist tries to 'read' his environment, and the art market in particular, and get a grip on it, for instance with a firm footing in collaborative ventures (Chapter 3). Your practice does not stand still and grows thanks to learning experiences in training and practice, for example by relocation (Chapter 4).

You can largely tackle stereotyping and blockades yourself, using your own voice and armed with arguments. However, if you wish to temper entrenched perceptions of artisthood and defend shared interests, it is important to combine forces, to work together and make use of collective platforms. Since 2010 I have been using the umbrella concept 'fabric of knowledge exchange, collaboration and friendship' to express both small-scale 'coalitions' of individual artists as they come about in collaborative projects, and larger, sometimes institutional coalitions–and their importance. In that context, alumni networks are among the most specific and illustrative of artists' coalitions.

## "How strong is the lonely cyclist?"

The artist as a 'lonely cyclist'* runs up against ignorance at a wide variety of levels; despite opposition of that type he continues on his way, in search of recognition. Below I discuss a number of situations inside and outside the art world in which, as an individual, you can go far by fighting prejudices, anticipating stumbling blocks which you can better address in conjunction with or via others.

### *Are they in fact all artists?*

In the art world, you can clear away a lot of obstacles yourself as you work. People with whom you work directly usually find out soon enough what you do and stand for, as an artist. You can play an active role, as described in the example of Helen Verhoeven (in the section on control mechanisms 145 in Chapter 3). Yet even experts at some distance regularly have entrenched opinions or blind spots. Curators, critics, teachers and others 'in the know', when they look at the artists' positions uncovered in this publication, may wonder "are they in fact all artists?" If art were just a visual object, it would not take long to make up your mind, because artisthood in that case stops about halfway down the list in Figure 16—somewhere between 'designer' and 'curator', at 'writer'. In this model we see a widening of social impact with every higher step, and a withdrawal from the codes in the white cube—as still recognised as a dominant parameter for 'true art'. The point of critical attention, for example with the artist's position as a change agent, is the moment when the visual aspect is of secondary importance, and the visual quality cannot or may not be challenged any more. For instance, when the artist has become primarily an activist, participating in movements for change, or a journalist, observing movements for change in order to report on them, and he no longer wishes to be called to account for his artistic work.

* This reference is to a song (1973) recorded by the Dutch singer/songwriter, Boudewijn de Groot (lyrics by Ruud Engelander. "How strong is the lonely cyclist, hunched over the handlebars, making his way against the headwinds?"

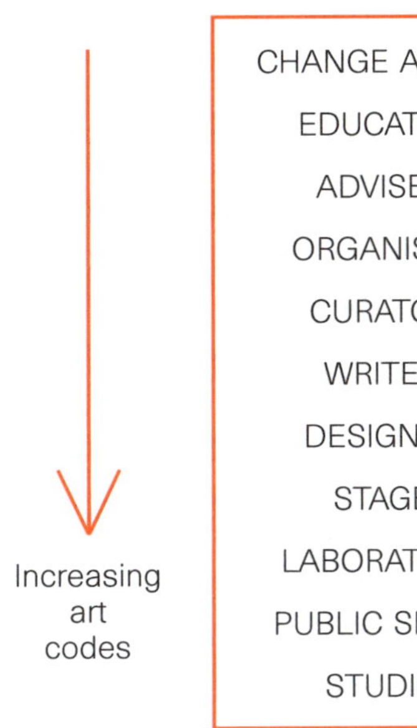


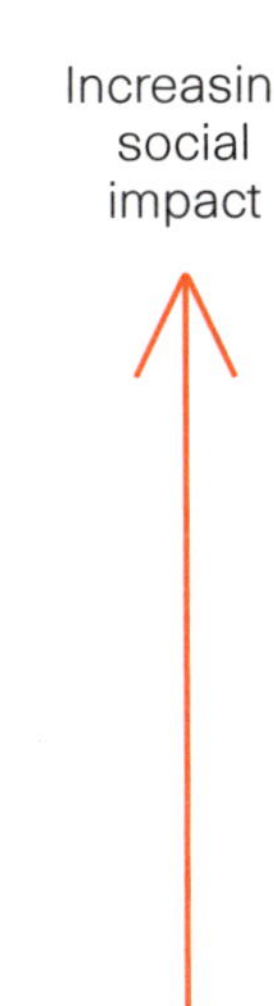


*Figure 16.* Art codes–social impact

The first 'barrier' when artisthood becomes broader (the lack of a visual product) is overcome when motion, sound and words are accepted alongside images. Are performances and artist talks art? Artists are the ones who execute them and determine the quality. Here, I do not define *quality* as an 177
objective standard. It relates to the assessment or resonance in the surroundings in which it takes place, in a similar way to the artist as a change agent in the context of the community in which social intervention takes place. So, what is the *effect* of unravelling the meaning?

When the artistic 'level' is discussed or if artisthood exists (still), the 'specialism for meanings' which was described earlier, is pivotal: the discovery, 'reading' and uncovering of meaning 37
(which is often hidden); internalisation or 'appropriation', with autonomous thinking, rational and intuitive reflection and the finding of unusual, unexpected and revealing solutions. After which they are presented as a 'communicative message'. If we use this definition, the activist or journalist can also be an artist if he defines himself as such and if he is believed by his audience.

### *Discussions with and between experts*

Knowing where you stand and what you stand for is also reflected in your discussion with experts or insiders, as well as in the responsibility you take in your stance (together with other artists) vis-à-vis the public. Your overestimation of experts as well as of the public can produce tremendous 'flops'.

Interaction with experts is quite often based on the premise that 'they' know and understand what it is about, but frequently your work and standpoints need to be accompanied by an explanation. There is an example from the Prix de Rome Urban Design and Landscape Architecture. A young finalist presented his analysis and designs to the international jury of 'heavyweights'.* He drew attention to his carefully thought-out, systematic and complex presentation, but gave no explanation, saying instead: "just take a look". The jury's assessment did not sufficiently appreciate the importance of his multiple analyses, various intervention options and his positions; he was awarded what is called a basic prize. A week later he gave a crystal-clear explanation to interested (though not expert) sponsors. His overestimation and admiration had short-changed the jury. It is worth making the effort to 'commit to your work' and communicate about it. In that way all those involved get an idea about your work and scope to appreciate it, also you contribute to your positioning as an artist.

You should not only be willing to explain your work in interaction with experts, but as an individual artist you also have a responsibility to your public. Many an interested art-lover feels like a fish out of water at art presentations with a substantial theoretical content, when sound knowledge and professional urgency are called for. It would be a good idea if there were to be a sign at the entrance to such presentations saying 'insiders only'. Because they are not for everyone and that reinforces the stigmatisation of so-called elitist art. The aim at a broad-based, large audience in a 'get-together for the in-crowd' causes bad feeling and more harm than good. Who on earth would think of throwing open a dialogue between two leading scientists at a meeting of nuclear physicists to a

* Kees Christiaanse, Sébastien Marot, Branimir Medic, Maarten Schmitt, Maike van Stiphout and Janwillem Schrofer (chairman, without the right to vote).

public that, at best, reads the science section of a newspaper or 'consumes' a popular scientific medium? Exclusive meetings—so ones that exclude—are important, necessary, indispensable. In my board membership of charitable trusts for culture I frequently supported 'hermetic', small-scale get-togethers for specialists, even when I did not entirely understand what they were about. My motto being "I might not be all that keen on them, but they're necessary". I did so out of respect for and confidence in the initiators and a belief in the relevance, even though in the first instance the meetings were for a very small vanguard.

Not only is the curator or organiser of such presentations responsible for defining the targeted public. The participating artist will also have to be involved with the extent of 'inclusivity' and therefore exclusivity of the presentation or event, to avoid disappointment for himself, the organisers and the visitors. Farther away from, rather than closer to 'the general public'. And, more importantly, don't use a blunderbuss approach, but aim well.

*Stereotyping the artist*

Furthermore, the individual artist has contacts outside the art world in which annoying stereotyping can play a part. The stereotyping of artists was touched upon briefly in 'Artists' positions', where the main perception of artistic practice is shaped by the artist 'in the studio'. And that perception largely overshadows the many facets of artisthood, entailing the many professional options, appreciation for the artist and what all this can mean in the art world and society at large. The idea of the artist as a specialist in discovering meanings—in many different ways and by many different means—and returning those meanings trenchantly, continues to be unconvincing. As long as the idea of the lazy, drowsy nincompoop drinking coffee at the kitchen table is not eradicated, there will be no change in public perception of the artist. And closer to home, that idea may be more prevalent than you think, among friends and family for instance. As an artist you can adjust that image yourself, by reciting your 'daily schedule' time and again, to your contacts, so family and friends as well.

An example: "this morning got up at 7.15 am, fortunately my partner is taking the children to school today, 8.20 am appointment at a building site with the architect and the builder, 9.45 am visit to builders' merchants and inspection of building materials (I'm my own buyer), 11.30 am back to the studio, develop working drawings on the computer (I'm my own draughtsman) and reply to urgent mails (I'm my own secretary), 1 pm lunch is a small bistro with a financial adviser (I'm my own bookkeeper), 2 pm at last a couple of hours to work in the studio on a painting and a drawing, 5.30 pm collect the children from child care and shop for the evening meal that I'll cook for a curator from Germany who will eat with us at home—hope that exhibition in Berlin will work out. It was enjoyable, the children are of an age that they don't want to sit at the table but want to serve—for a surreptitious look at what's going on, at 10 pm pretty exhausted, but still a visit to the corner pub, where it was pleasant but I left after three-quarters of an hour because I must be up early tomorrow. Once home I don't feel like sleeping, but check a few things on the Internet (I'm my own Research & Development department). Then toss and turn for a bit and finally a fitful dream. Short night, because ... up early again, for a day teaching at the art academy."

***Reflection*. How do you deal with artist stereotyping in your family or circle of friends? Is your emancipation tactic to explain, as in the foregoing text, everything you do in the course of a day? Or do you do it differently?**

**Take two different days: a very busy one with a succession of detailed activities plus the times, and a day when it doesn't seem as if you do much, but having rested, looked and thought about things, it turns out later that you have done a lot. You can tell others that on one day you resemble a super-manager and on another day a top-ranking academic in deep concentration, and that this (with a degree of self-mockery) is not what you had expected from artisthood.**

*"You make art, of what use is it to us?"*

Now and then you get into situations when you wonder: what am I supposed to do about this? A passer-by who asks you about art. Questions that are hard to answer anyway, since there is no common language and since you do not know if it is interest or an opening gambit for an insoluble debate.

It is worth taking texts that appeal to you a step further, without simplifying them into words of one syllable. Two quotes, one relating to art as a useful personal aid (by the actress and theatre director Lineke Rijxman in the *de Volkskrant* newspaper, 5 September 2015): "Art gives you a useful aid for living life in a way that is more than a succession of coincidences. Art teaches you to make associations, increases your sense of beauty, and makes you more accessible to what takes place between people and what makes them tick. I remember that even as a young child music could affect me in a way that had nothing to do with real life at home. At such times, or during a good play, I could understand the 'universe' better than in everyday reality. It gave me a tremendously rich feeling."

Another quote about art as 'the best remedy for tunnel vision' at a social level comes from the scientist Robbert Dijkgraaf (*NRC Handelsblad* newspaper, 29/30 August 2015) "In this fundamental role of eye-opener, art and science are profoundly public matters. The long-term benefits cannot be isolated and ultimately return to the whole of society. They make the world bigger and richer for everyone. They deposit themselves invisibly in the capillaries of life."

***Reflection*. In a dialogue of this type do you sometimes come up with something unexpected? Do you enter into a conversation? What do you say? See if you can apply the above quotes to someone–child or adult–visiting a museum for the first time or to a chatty possibly interested taxi driver.**

# Combined forces

It is possible to organise the theoretical discussion about art and artists and talks about artistic practice on a small scale, in informal groups, but as soon as a political dimension is involved, such as in institutional settings, forces must inevitably be combined. In this publication the emphasis is on the micro-level, on the individual artist, managing his own practice, participating in 'joint undertakings' and intervening in and supporting organisations in which he is involved directly. I conclude this final chapter of Part II with pulling together and standing up for shared interests.

## *Artists are pioneers*

The emancipation of artists on a social scale cannot be achieved individually. It is important for policy-makers and influencers, and politicians in particular, to be fully aware of the position of artists as role models in contemporary society.

Artists, with their independent profession (in all its multiplicity) are pioneers and examples for an ever-greater part of the working population in a changing society. Let me explain, using the theme 'the artist as a trendsetter and prototype of changing labour utilisation and relations'. This is a frequent topic of discussion in varying circles, and is well illustrated in the discussions conducted by the German artist and professor, Hermann Pitz, at various levels. On the one hand with students (and myself), but he also takes his discussion, by way of the Akademie der Bildenden Künste in Munich, at an organisational or meso-level, to a political forum in Bavaria* (macro-level). The jottings below cover that exchange.

Until far into the twentieth century artists were often minor players and exceptions—not to their displeasure—with regard to prevailing social codes, with—to their displeasure—marginal incomes. At the start of the twenty-first century, they proved to be examples in the ever-greater sector of freelancers

* At the end of 2011 the Alliance 90/The Greens party submitted an interpellation in the parliament of the Free State of Bavaria concerning the position of artists in Germany and in Bavaria in particular, based on a memorandum from the Munich Academy of Fine Arts. It was drawn up by the artist and professor of sculpture, Hermann Pitz, the vice-president of the Academy and also involved in the Rijksakadmie as an adviser (personal contact since 1987).

with their far-reaching self-organisation, unconventional use of time (outside office hours), nomadic residence patterns and a combination of working for themselves and part-time or temporary employment. That ties in with Richard Florida's creative class, in which artists with their multi-faceted artistic practice, working in undefined as well as defined situations, are at the forefront with their work, compared with more career-orientated professions within the creative sector. To my mind, artists form the 'sublimated' top or the focal point of the pyramid of creative professions, rather than dangling somewhere in the expanding freelance sector. In that sense the artist is more of a fundamental researcher than an applied researcher.

In my opinion, artists are not, or insufficiently aware of that forefront position today, as pioneers of tomorrow. Admittedly if they ride on the current, economically determined (neo-liberal) wave of the creative class there will be practical advantages, such as 'breeding grounds' with living + working facilities in every self-respecting city. But alongside the danger that the artist will fit purely pragmatically into a demarcated, restricted position, there is the risk that the relative advantages will be endangered as soon as policy ideas about the creative sector change.

And so the artist has evolved from an exception, as a minor player or 'economic alien', to a prototype of new labour relations, including their positive side, such as opportunity to determine for himself his use of time and energy, as well as the negative aspects such as vulnerability and insecurity.

### *The power of solidarity*

Apart from erasing stereotypes about artisthood, we need political channels, think tanks and the like if new definitions are to be offered and accepted at a macro-level. In addition to traditional institutes (which have long existed in many countries) like Academies of Arts and Sciences, after the Second World War, interests were combined institutionally in Europe, and certainly in the Netherlands, in artists associations to serve as partners in discussions with the government. In recent decades these platforms have become eroded. It is striking that with new initiatives for shaping and elaborating the debate with important actors in the area of culture, including governments, the artists themselves are the prime movers in adding vitality. A good Dutch example is Platform BK (Platform for Visual Arts, www.platformbk.nl) that examines the role of art in society and represents artists, designers and other cultural producers. It describes itself as a link between the art sector, interest groups, politics and media. They seek to conduct a debate on the importance of art for society with the various 'voices' from the arts sector—in the language of the writer, the designer and the artist. The managers and organisers within with the body are makers and other producing, programming or teaching professionals.

At an organisational or meso-level there are more tactile intervention options for artists which have a potentially enhancing effect. Think of examples in which artists and artists institutes, such as residencies, educational institutes or presentation organisations, undertake joint action for maintaining culturally valuable mainstays. When the continued existence of the place where they worked, studied or presented is under threat. For example, the Rijksakademie received many statements from alumni when there was a drastic retrenchment in 2004. And when, seven years later, the Ministry of Cultural Affairs was planning to completely stop the subsidy and close the institute, hundreds of testimonials poured in, as well as a petition from artists and other professionals from the entire art world signed by 7,000 people from all continents. In the ensemble of interested parties or stakeholders, the alumni, with their contribution, form a special, significant category.

## SECRET SOCIETY

**Let me explain the importance of alumni with an example. Artists as advisers attached to the Rijksakademie proposed that I should organise a fund-raising auction with donations from artists for an Endowment Fund. As a third financial 'mainstay', apart from government and private money, funded entirely by the artists involved.* Highly significant in a material sense, but far, far greater, symbolically.**

**The visible and invisible power of alumni–think of them as a kind of secret society–is illustrated nicely in a metaphor relating to an American fungus "The largest organism in the world lives in the Malheur National Park in Oregon. It is a sombre 'honey mushroom' (*Armillaria ostoyae*). This specimen is at least 2,400 years old and covers an area of more than 890 hectares. There are no spectacular photographs of this gigantic being. Most of it, indeed, more than ninety per cent, lives underground, out of sight. Just the odd bunch of brown stalks with obtuse, chocolate-coloured caps, protrude above the ground, a spot on the radar that betrays this enourmous mycelium under the layer of humus."****

* Over 170 artists donated, and work by 120 artists was included in Sotheby's fund-raising auction. The proceeds of more than one million euros benefited the Rijksakademie Endowment Fund (RAEF), from which working budgets are made available to working residents of the Rijksakademie for the coming decades.

** Excerpt from interview with the author by Edo Dijksterhuis in *Global Contemporary, Artists for Artists* (catalogue charity auction Sotheby's, 2010).

# Fabric of knowledge exchange, collaboration and friendship

During my directorship of the Rijksakademie, I became increasingly convinced of the enormous importance of the alumni, and promoted it. Firstly, as a fabric of informal, interpersonal exchange of knowledge in which collaborations take place that are sometimes not apparent to the outside world, and long, profound friendships grow. Secondly, as regards an institute with which they feel they have a bond, there is more obvious expression, as:

– recruiters of new applicants, whom they also regularly support with their applications;
– advisers or sometimes even assistants of the artist during his period of work or study;
– ambassadors and ‘channels’ of introduction to cultural institutions and governments at home and abroad;
– experts or advisers regarding the institute’s policy and activities, but also as
– financial mainstays, with material contributions.

Often—as in the case of the Rijksakademie—ownership falls to them. I am convinced that an institute of this type does not belong to the art market, or to the subsidising government, or to the sponsors and private financiers, or to the management or the board, or to the residents or the students, but to the alumni—the mental owners. They form the powerhouse for transformation, innovation and continuity of art institutes.

Although at first it might seem less obvious, alumni also deploy their resources for providing material support.

# Part II.

# Buildin
# Blocks

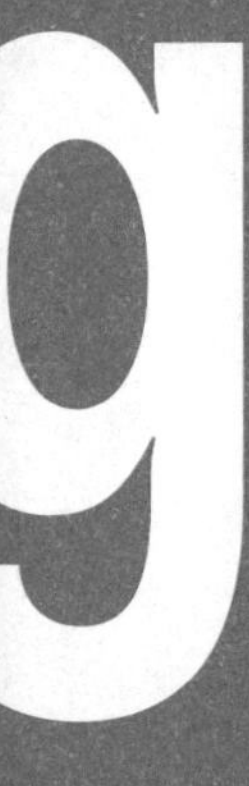

# Part II.

In the following chapters the terminology and reflections from Part I are elaborated on. Concrete tools are supplied for the further development of the artistic practice, including financial aspects and ways to draw up a CV.

The first building block examines plan development and the incongruence between dream and realistic possibilities and obstacles. The reflections in Part I were mainly retrospective, focused on the past and the present. In Part II they are more constructive and prospective: considerations focusing on the future.

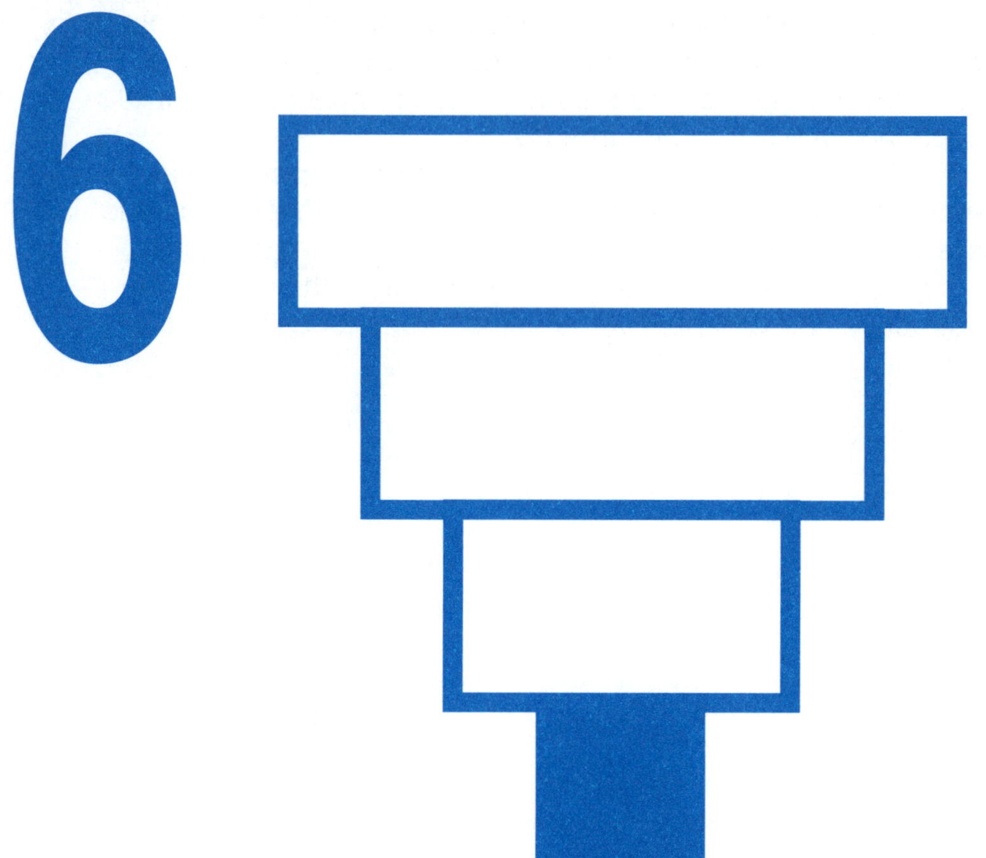

# 6 Building block: Realisation between dream and deed

**With a good sense of direction and flexible improvisation, great ambitions can be fulfilled, if you are also prepared to look for the least vulnerable form–generally small-sized. The set-up and organisation of the studio, or set-up and methods of a new initiative, requires tools with which to operationalise demands and wishes. They will be based on individual priorities, which can sometimes be combined and shared with others if it concerns collaborative action.**

# Constriction

At a later stage, the sense of wonderment you felt before embarking on your 'schooling' and professionalisation as a visual artist, will become narrower. Generally, at the start and during one's art studies, often round the age of twenty, one's personal history tends to recede and 'artistic life' begins, with a clean slate or *tabula rasa*. Some of the important points of departure for individual artisthood and one's own artistic practice that are lost sight of, are:

— parents, brothers and sisters, grandparents and other family members with their professions, fascinations, belief or unbelief, character traits, jokes and disabilities, or a lack of family, being alone;
— own activities as a child, juvenile, adolescent, adult: playing music, cooking, drawing, arranging, organising, building tree houses, working together, daydreaming, reading, documenting, reflecting, telling stories, taking photographs, contradicting, designing the ideal house and travelling, not only in your mind or in books, but also literally. Sometimes already seriously focusing on an artistic discipline, perhaps rudimentary and diverse: music, the stage, dance, writing, visual arts.
— friends around you in a village or a town, at school, often several schools, teachers, examples and role models, correspondence and long conversations.

Before the person in question embarks on his studies and considers the options for the future, the path starts to unfold. Sometimes along one track ("I always wanted to be an artist"), sometimes there are still a few alternatives ("music or anthropology"), and sometimes that person arrives at an art academy by trial and error, as one of the one, two or three options for study, or even a fourth, unexpected, possibility.

Euphoria about freedom and the transition from parental home to 'something else' are often accompanied by a feeling of constriction. Constriction because of the fixation on the art work and its quality, on artisthood, with the emphasis on the ‘real studio artist’, on success in the art market, on ‘dos and don’ts’ in the art world. There is little time for extracurricular, extramural activities that you have to undertake on your own and if you do invest in them, they will rarely be dealt with during your studies; that could be described as a ‘narrow tunnel’. Rarely—unless there is a serious mental crisis—will the personal background be raised as a matter of value for further development. It is as if there were no ‘history’ prior to the start at the academy—that could be described as a ‘short runway’.

It is not unusual for the ‘constriction’ of artisthood to be felt later on—‘mid-career and up’. Again, there will often be a period of intensive re-orientation, after success and disappointment, after commotion and calm. But again, a ‘narrowing’ takes place, i.e. fixation on one track: the artist in the studio with a presence in galleries and museums. The burgeoning wealth of experience, life with partner/partners, child/children, relocation for work or travel recede to the background. Pinnacles in private life outside the studio which appear to be a success but are not perceived as such in the career and the work itself. The keys that are hidden there disappear from sight. Vital areas turn grey.

## Goals on the horizon

The challenge is to head for new goals on the horizon, departing from the fullness of one’s personal life, (semi-) professional career experiences, and present and older work. Or else to head for existing, already identified goals, with more pleasure on the way and more efficacy. So less loss of time and energy, knowing “where I stand and what I stand for”. The first building block, reverting back to terminology, examples and reflections from previous chapters, is a list of questions for yourself.

a. Where do you stand now? Take a look at your *life*: place and year of birth, environment, mother and father, brothers and sisters, their work and their involvement in what you are doing as an artist. Do not avoid sensitive details. Look back over your career so far. Look impartially at your website with documentation and *presentation of your work*.

b. What alternative *options for the future* cross your mind? Scan good and bad experiences from the past, and your desires regarding the future.

c. Describe a picture of *around five years hence*, more realistic than a dream and more imaginative than strict planning, a 'hazy image': where do you stand, what are you doing and in what surroundings, what is going on around you, what kind of people can you see around you?

d. And then, what is your secret *dream*, on the horizon? Reassuringly unrealistic, because you'll never actually reach the horizon, it is always moving farther away. Explain the meaning of that dream for your personal life, consequences for work and the working process; what do you have to give up and what do you get in return?

e. Does the hazy image extending over five years exclude the dream on the horizon, or can you in some way–linear or circular with detours–make a *connecting road* between your hazy image and your dream?

f. What *facets of artisthood* can you identify in those pictures–first the dream far away and then the hazy image closer by–making use of the list of eleven facets/positions and reaching back to your own experiences. What remains, what is eliminated, what is reinforced, what is added?

g. What *experiences* do you want to have in *the coming two years*? What do you want to find out in order to better define the hazy image (or completely adjust it), to discover which of the alternative future options (as in b) or another option you have had not yet identified, are worth while and should be prioritised?

# Greatest ambition, smallest size

In the same way as in two-track decision-making, 'mixed scanning' as it is called, you look to the horizon with a distant 28 gaze while reviewing the possibilities and limitations on the way. You proceed between dream and deed, searching for great ideals and, at the same time, their concrete manifestation, for the 'smallest size', the least vulnerable set-up. I illustrate that by way of two situations: the individual artist's studio and the starting of a new initiative together with others.

*Artist's studio*

As we have seen, whatever artist's position/positions you adopt, every artist has a mental atelier providing scope for all facets of artisthood. When that mental atelier, or the physical 160 studio, is fitted out, energy management plays an important part. Consider the amount of time and attention you want to allot to being alone, to contact with fellow-artists, to studying and research for documentation and inspiration, to preparing and executing work technically, and how much time and attention is to be given to intermediaries, buyers and clients in the market. These are the ever-recurring 'dimensions': table with artists, technical work bench, door to the market, shelf with sources in society.

Two parameters are defining in the studio practice when you take the step to materialisation in physical working conditions and decision-making on investments, they are: 'individual' versus 'collective' and 'mobile' versus 'place-bound'.

*Individual or collective*. 'On your own' is individual by definition. You can organise contact with other artists, individually in your own studio, or collectively, together with others. With respect to technical aspects—study and research in society and dealing with the market—you can emphasise a more individual or a more collective approach, or a combination of the two.

*Place-bound or mobile*. Can you easily be on your own, anywhere, or do you need your own fixed, silent place? How flexible are you about it? Can you easily mix with other artists, regardless of where, or do you prefer your own fixed space where you can be the host? Are you dependent on many 'fixed' sources of information, such as books? Do you go out into the world and take your mobile Internet with you wherever you go? Do you need your own technical facilities in your studio, can you connect them up here and there, or do you take drawing and calculating equipment, your computer with you for designing and preparation, wherever you may be? Do people who are interested in buying or collaborating come to you, do you go to them, or do you primarily keep in touch digitally by e-mail or via your website?

If you bear questions like these in mind, you will probably be better able to take investment decisions on money, time, attention relating to quality and costs of physical studio space: rent, furnishings, energy, fixed or moveable appliances. In fact, you have laid the foundations for a programme of requirements. An overall picture with provisional accents is more important than precise, set priorities, as found in a business plan. Think of it as a 'patch plan' in which the 'weight' and detailing of each of the accents or patches can change over time. You can attribute weights to the above accents using pluses and minuses, for example: very important (++), important (+), not certain (+/-), unimportant (-) and not at all an option, also not in the near future (--). Two examples by way of illustration: *artist alone in the studio* and a *mobile interactive artist*.

• In the first case, 'alone in the studio', the artist is the key figure. He considers it important to be alone a lot, in a fixed space, preferably of his own. He does have contact with other artists, particularly elsewhere. If research, study and the like are part of his working process, they mainly take place elsewhere. Technical research and production are important, take time and there are a lot of technical facilities in the studio. Business contacts are maintained only by or via a gallery, outside the studio.

Here, investments are: large, in good studio space for yourself; average, because little hosting, a smallish table; small, because there is no extensive documentation, archives or books, few shelves; large, on account of the considerable technical facilities, the work bench; and average, in view of the few contacts in the studio with the market, the door. See the figure below.

| * | Time and attention | Physical studio | | |
|---|---|---|---|---|
| | | Individual or collective | Place-bound or mobile | Investment pressure |
| Alone | ++ | Individual | Place-bound | Great |
| Contact artists **Table** | + | Individual | Mobile | Average |
| Research **Shelf** | + - | Individual | Mobile | Small |
| Technical **Work-bench** | ++ | Individual | Place-bound | Great |
| Market **Door** | + | Individual | Mobile | Average |

*Figure 17a.* Investment effects (I)

• The second case is that of the mobile, interactive artist who does want a place of his own, but is able to concentrate and withdraw anywhere. Who finds it important to talk, eat and drink with other artists—as a host. Great attention as regards study and research is shared with others in conversations, seminars and so on, and takes place at the table in the studio as well as at other locations. Technical realisation of work can theoretically take place anywhere, depending on the assignment—from a client, upon a curator's invitation or on your own initiative. There is a fair amount of attention for 'business' contacts, usually taking place on location.

Investments are, successively, average, because studio space is modest, great because of a hospitable studio with table and kitchen, average because much research takes place outside the studio (the shelf), small because there are no extensive technical facilities, no work bench and if facilities are needed they can be organised outside the studio, and: small, in view of the business contacts outside the studio (the door). Illustrated in the following figure:

| * | Time and attention | Physical studio | | |
|---|---|---|---|---|
| | | Individual or collective | Place-bound or mobile | Investment pressure |
| Alone | + | Individual | Mobile | Average |
| Contact artists **Table** | ++ | Collective | Place-bound | Great |
| Research **Shelf** | ++ | Collective | Mobile | Average |
| Technical **Work-bench** | + | Collective | Mobile | Small |
| Market **Door** | + - | Individual | Mobile | Small |

*Figure 17b.* Investment effects (II)

In theory you could look further at which positions and which environments are worked in, and at the combination of facets of artisthood, from the point of view of desirable working conditions. But when you enter new territory, there is enough time to discover quite quickly, by trial and error, what is needed and what investments it entails. The mixed-scanning approach (improvising on the way towards a goal—see also
28 Chapter 1) offers a helping hand.

*A new initiative*

There have always been artists' initiatives, with periods of greater or lesser success. The artist's initiative also serves a purpose when mapping the achievement of goals; it forms a contrast with individual artistic practices. After all, with a joint 'venture', incorrect dimensioning has greater consequences. They not only affect one or more initiators, but also those who become involved as participants for a longer or shorter period. Moreover, the public can also be affected.

Various goals can be identified for artists' initiatives. For example, meeting and exchange between artists, observation and intervention in society, sharing of production facilities, joint presentation of work and also the realisation of good, individual work spaces/studios thanks to joint efforts.

An ideal is evidently sometimes translated into a complex constellation, with an array of activities with differing functions and various public groups, and apparently with a solid, formal organisation structure on top. Ambitions go hand in hand with numbers, the desire to do a great deal at the same time or to carry out very big projects and arrange everything well, and in detail. I shall first outline the pitfalls that must be avoided. It is a plan that illustrates well the potential risks if the undertaking is *over-sized*. I also give suggestions for an approach entailing fewer risks. Followed by an example of what is, from the start, a more promising approach close to home.

During his working period at the Rijksakademie (2011/2012), U.O.-I., an artist from Nigeria, developed a plan he wanted to introduce after his return home.* There was considerable interest in his well thought-out plan, and he even had the prospect of financing from funds and other bodies. The plan comprised some five components: an art study programme, a children's programme, a community outreach project, a library, and artist residency focusing on photography, and possibly more. His plan had one huge problem, namely, if he were to receive funds for the proposal and all the concomitant functions, he would be visited every week by a delegation from Europe (policy officials, funding officers, politicians) who had to be entertained, shown round the city and surroundings, and accompanied into the depths of the red light districts. Once every six months, a policy update would be required, taking a few weeks of work. He would have hardly any time in his own studio. After three years, he might hear: "This is possibly the most attractive project we have ever supported, but there has

* 'Anonymous identification': the initials indicate that the examples are not fictitious, but the names are not recognisable for people who do not know the artists.

now been a change in policy, and we're stopping." In a case like that, the artist's artisthood has not only drained away during those three years, but his first, so promising project has collapsed. To the distress of all who contributed to it and had become fond of it.

A less vulnerable approach would be:

1. Which external function (art study programme, children's programme, community outreach project, library, artist's residency) is closest to your heart, and would, under great pressure, continues to be most treasured and important for you, and forms the core?
2. How can you reach that core in the most simple way deploying your own resources: what does your partner do, is he/she willing to work with you; is there an available house where you can live and in which part can be used on behalf of that core; is there, for instance, an organisation with which you can and want to collaborate?
3. See how the balance between that 'undertaking' and time and space for your own artisthood works out. Is there still enough space, also in the longer term?
4. When you have reached the core, consider the following step: one of the other functions, also treasured, also an important ambition, but not the most important. Re-examine costs and added value for yourself as an artist. Search for preconditions, for minimal dependence, vulnerability. Rack your brains, prepare yourself, test and consult.
5. Take the next step, if you still want to:
– the second step succeeds: good;
– if not: no problem, the core is still there and you have had an interesting, instructive failure. That is a valuable learning moment, particularly if you describe and take a critical look at the hurdles during the process.

This kind of growth strategy can be presented as an inverted pyramid, with 'the smallest size' forming the essential basis.

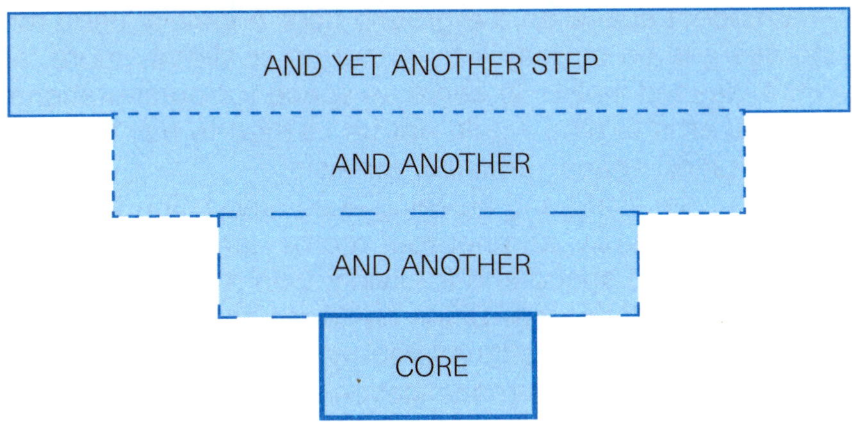

*Figure 18.* New initiative



And now another example, with a view to financial underpinning of 'the greatest ambition with the *smallest size*'. Over a two-day period in 2012, I gave a series of talks at OCAT (OCT Contemporary Art Terminal) in Shenzhen, China, near Hong Kong. The most successful part was the closing afternoon with 'speed-dating'. During one of the speed dates, a case had to be solved. The objective being to find a realistic 'size' for a great personal ambition. I summarise our elaboration of the case to help better understand the 'everyday character' of a possible solution by reducing it to common-or-garden dimensions.

The initial proposition was: "I am a Chinese curator, my husband is an artist and comes from America, there are three of us—my daughter is now one year old. I want to set up a national artist residency in Wuhan, for the city itself, and with international connections."

We drew up a brief inventory of several factors, such as the size and character of the city, the existing artist population, and together arrived in old neighbourhoods with large, unoccupied houses which might still be standing ten years hence now the building frenzy is abating. The option that unfolded was, first of all, to propose to the local authorities to boost culture in the city without financial support from them, but with their permission to make use of a large old house, free of charge. It would be good for the city and its standing, and certainly for the neighbourhood where the house is situated. We then walked together through the house, in our imagination, and rapidly began fitting it out:

— a modest space on the ground floor originally used for storage and so on, say 4 by 4 metres or slightly more, and white-washed walls. To serve as space for presentations by *local* artists, who would not be obliged to pay for the presentation space—unusual, for Asia;
— apart from living and sleeping accommodation for the artist's own family, another four rooms, large enough to be used as studio space and for living, with a bedroom alcove. Where four artists from China could reside, for periods of three to six months: cultural variety is great, the (written) language facilitates communication and their expectations are realistic. That would produce a *national* artist residency.
— We also found a spacious room in 'our' house, large enough for a double bed and a child's bed. For artist friends from abroad (including America) who visit and stay over. We went a step farther: you are sitting at the table with your husband and daughter, a local artist is in the middle of mounting an exhibition in the presentation space with four Chinese residents and the guest, an artist from abroad. Altogether there are eight to ten people present. The cook (whom you have quickly found) is cooking; you eat. One of the residents says to the guest, the *international* artist: "I'd like to show you my work in the studio upstairs, would you like to see it?" and the guest goes with him. Another resident would like that too, the guest suggests doing so the next day. Before you know where you are, the guest from abroad stays for two or three days and asks if he or she may come back one more time. Whereupon you, the hostess, organiser of the residency, say "of course, when you're in the area, you'll be very welcome."

And so we arrived, in a planning 'game', at an artist residency which can become locally 'embedded' in the city's artistic community, a national residency with international connections via the visiting artist, who acts informally as an adviser for the resident in the studio, with no expenses for emolument and travel, no red tape with visas. So local, national and international ramifications, with limited dependency and vulnerability.

The core of these two examples (Nigeria and China) is that you venture into what, for you personally, is most essential, is crucial. Look for the smallest size. And only enlarge your plan if larger is inevitable or absolutely necessary. Minimise your loss, strive for balance between expenses and income—that is what you would call 'break-even'.

If income is insufficient to realise your greatest, most precious ambition (with the smallest size), compensate the deficit with a somewhat less 'favourite' yet stimulating activity that makes money. It might be something you were doing already and that went quite well, made money and could be continued 'in moderation', without reluctance. As far as the curator in the previous case was concerned: she had a paid commission for an exhibition, her husband sold work and would have a studio for free in the big old house. And if that were not enough, there would be a slice of income to serve as a basis for the 'core'. With every concession (assuming one has to be made) there should be a better rate in order to maximise profit from that activity—you could call it payment with a little 'compensation'. In Figure 19, in which the core may gradually increase, obviously involving growing costs and risks, we now see the other side of the same coin: the material underpinning of the 'core'. The dream and the deed.



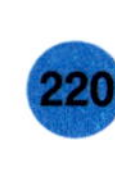


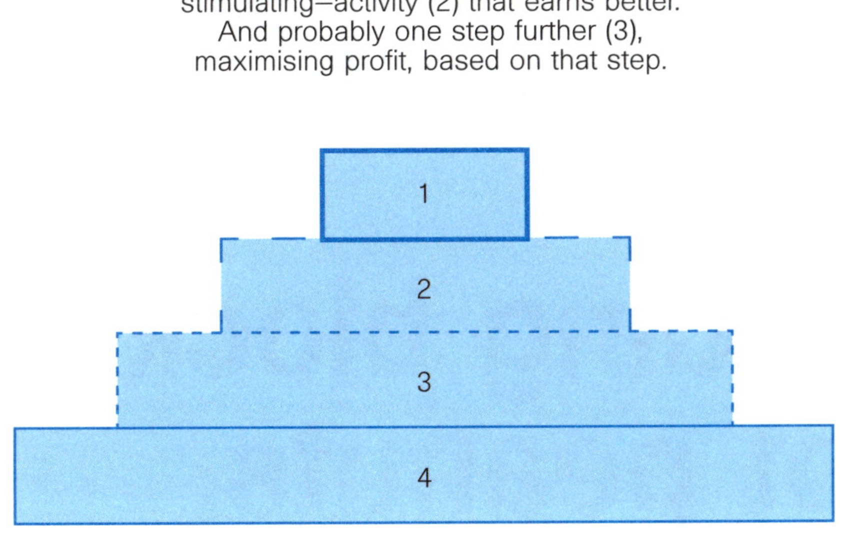


*Figure 19.* Reinforcing basis

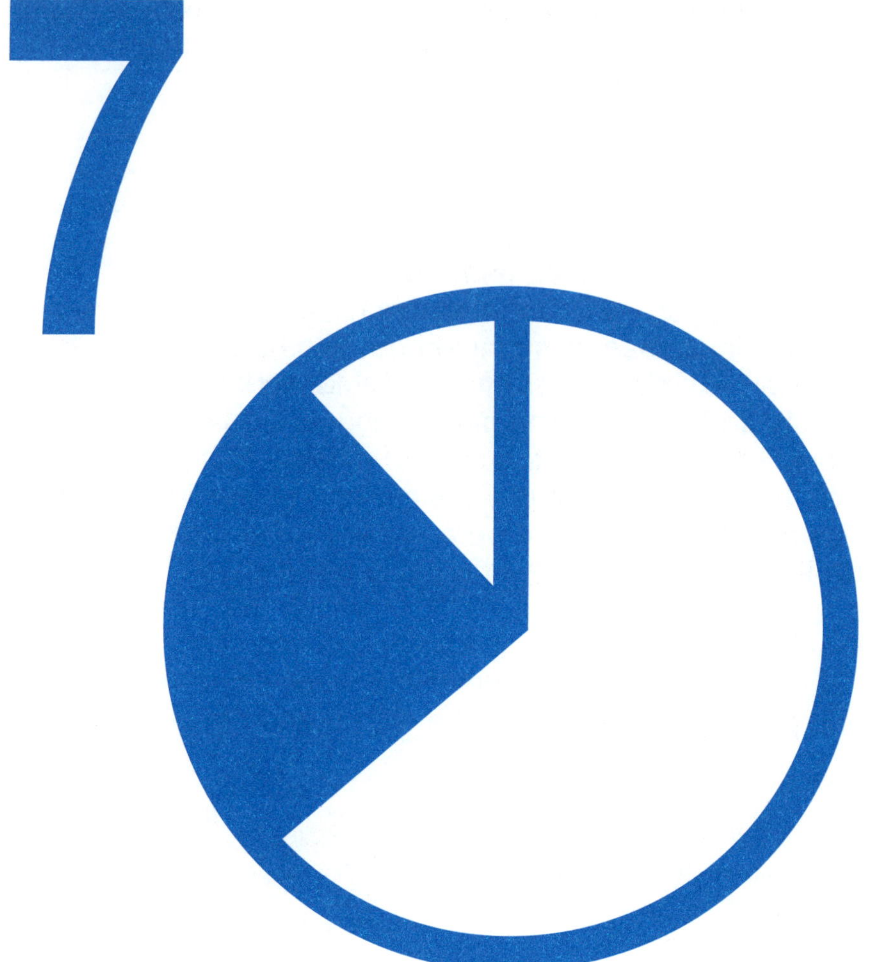

# Building block: Not peanuts, but payment

A budget says much about plans, wishes and demands, it is a programmatic representation. For instance, in the section 'Creative process and money; Integral project budgeting' effectively reflects the connection between figures and the creation process. Not as a bookkeeping exercise, but as an approach that brings about awareness of investments, enhances self-respect, contributes to personal profiling, helps in the acquisition of financial resources, also stimulates the social reassessment of artists. Even though in 'Financial components' we take a closer look at practical matters like needs, income and expenditure, it is again a matter of considering essentials in depth, before going on to apply them to the artistic practice. The sections 'Pricing art works' and 'Transfer of work' establish a connection between the significance of the work for the artist and the prerequisites concerning (the moment of) its transfer to the buyer or person who commissioned it. The actual pricing is dealt with briefly and seen in the context of informative models, which, incidentally, only apply until market forces (be they positive or negative) put their relevance into perspective.

# Creative process and money

One of the most moving parts of *Uncle Tom's Cabin* (1852, Harriet Beecher Stowe) is when Eliza, clutching her baby Harry to her breast, leaps from one block of ice to another and, exhausted, eventually reaches the other side of the Ohio river. The final step after a long journey. That kind of leap forward is not the worst survival strategy, but it is impossible to keep on repeating a solution like that. Time and again, many an artist fails (or manages at the last minute) to realise a project, by always working with short-term perspectives (happy that he is 'allowed' to be an artist). "If I can just get financing for the final step, the project is finished." As such there is little wrong with incrementalising (step-by-step) financing models, like incidental crowd-funding, but with recurring, largish-scale projects it will not work, partly because willingness to invest in the same artist diminishes.

An example from a studio at the Rijksakademie: a resident artist approached me with an urgent question: I need € 6,000 for my project, I've got 2,000, but how can I secure the remaining 4,000?" My question: "Have you got a few hours to spare? I want, must, know all about your project and how it came about." We got to work, and a summary (partly fictionalised) of our conversation follows.

— How did the plan for the art project originate, was the idea directly related to prior activities and acquired expertise?
— When was that? Four years ago. Did you immediately start working on it, a lot? A few hours a week perhaps? When did that increase, for example to a day a week? And in your studio before coming to the Rijksakademie for two years, one day a week—say, 80 days in two years, so 640 hours in that period. And this last year, three days a week, so another 120 days. Altogether 960 hours.
— That residency in Japan—was that also defined by this project, was it part of your research? And I gather that the Mondriaan Fund's contribution to your travel expenses was intended for developing networks focusing on the

presentation of this project abroad after its completion.
— Please show some documentation on the project. Did that prototype a few months back really cost € 500 in materials? What technical specialists advised and supervised you, did they spend a lot of time on it? And lucky you—that a friend was able to help you for an entire week.
— So this year you spent about 50% of the resources and infrastructure provided here at the Rijksakademie Research Residency on this project?
— You will be investing € 2,000 of your own resources and are still looking for another € 4,000. Correct?

Have I properly understood everything you have told me? OK, we'll make a fresh estimate, content-based and integral, not just one marginal component, not just the end.

*Integral project budgeting*

Briefly, in seven steps:

| | |
|---|---|
| 1. Expertise acquired in previous projects, instrumental for this project. | p.m. |
| 2. Development of idea (4 years ago) | p.m. |
| 3. Exploration, research, models and design (640 hours and 960 hours) 1,600 hours (3 and 2 years previously) at € 25 | € 40,000 |
| 4. Residency in Japan (cost of participation, accommodation, residency and travel paid for by a fund) | € 12,000 |
| 5. Travel allowance (network development for presentation) | € 2,000 |

| 6. Prototype | |
|---|---|
| — material via Rijksakademie (see 7) | p.m. |
| — advice and supervision, artistic and technical, Rijksakademie (see 7) | p.m. |
| — assistance from friend (40 hours at € 25) | € 1,000 |
| | |
| 7. Rijksakademie: studio including energy, infrastructure (library, collections, Cantina, etc.), technical advice and supervision, research and production material, accommodation, grant, of which 50% used this year for this project | € 33,000 |
| | |
| 8. Still to invest: | |
| — from own means | € 2,000 |
| — from experiments fund | € 1,000 |
| — required (external) liquidity/ additional resources | € 3,000 |

If we review the origin and history of this protect, the turnaround time and time spent, all expenses for research, everything—apart from very marginal items (which you include, pro memoria, because they would otherwise thwart the project)—you capitalise 'everything'. Including all the residencies and grants financed by others, help from friends, we arrive at a total investment (regardless of where financing came from) of € 94,000 and not € 6,000 for a final 'ice floe'. And I immediately promised help, as it was a good project.

Now he could approach a financier, fund or maecenas with head held high and say: "This project costs altogether € 94,000; I have already been instrumental in investing € 90,000. I was looking for € 4,000, but the director of the Rijksakademie has just promised me € 1,000 from the experiments kitty. So I still have only € 3,000 to go." Many a financier will be favourably disposed to make a modest contribution to the success of a great project with such an impressive track record of personal input.

An approach like this has several benefits or values, in which I identify three levels:

– At the personal (micro) level you increase awareness of what you have already managed to do, how many people and resources you have succeeded in mobilising and the scope of your investment. It increases your self-respect and can contribute to your personal profiling in the art world.
– At a tactical-organisational (meso) level, this approach increases your chance of ultimate financing considerably.
– At a social (macro) level an approach of this type contributes to the emancipation of artists, to a social reappraisal thanks to greater awareness of 'everything it entails'.

The essence of this account is that you are not 'out in the cold' with your work. Everything that is visible and less visible is collected, you have acquired it thanks to your individual qualities: your work, your personality, your reputation, your approach to a complex project, your dealings with professionals and friends, and, last but not least, your ability and willingness to speak the language your financier understands. You obtained or mobilised contributions that you went on to invest in a project: a residency in Japan for which you had been invited, assistance from friends who made an effort for you personally, you acquired a place at the Rijksakademie on account of your potential for development, et cetera. The artist is not out in the cold, but is a central figure who takes a decision to earn and a decision to invest. 149

*Artist subsidises the community*

Many of the items in integral project budgeting actually relate to virtual flows of funds. No tangible cash is involved and so misunderstandings can occur. I'll give another example in which self-awareness, the acquisition of support and the realisation of an artist's significance for society are reflected insufficiently. To paraphrase an old socialist emancipatory pronouncement, 'workers do not have the hands of beggars' thus stressing their social value and significance, and so you could say 'artists do not have the hands of beggars'.

The executive councillor for culture of a big city had

spoken out, very positively, on the realisation of more live/work accommodation for artists and other creative people, co-financed by the municipality. Saying to an artist that five years after the project was started up, those spaces should become available for new cohorts—by then the municipality would have given enough support out of public funds. The artist explained to me that correct calculation would reveal that an artist contributes to the community with lectures, guest lessons free of charge or for a minimum fee, presentations with little, if any, recompense, defrays the cost of the development stage himself, makes art works available at non-commercial rates, and contributes to events that are important in economic, political, urban planning, social and cultural terms, without an allowance for expenses. Even with monumental projects, the artist invariably pays the final financing out of his own pocket. It then becomes clear that not the artist but the community is the gross earner.

## Financial components

Having reflected on “where do I stand, financially”, as addressed in the section on integral budgeting as a kind of wake-up call, it is now time to look at a few commercial approaches. Let us start with the professional practice with respect to needs and required expenditure on the one hand, and income to cover it, on the other hand. One of the expenses experienced in the practice relates to the ‘personal income’ item—work-related pay—which forms the basis of personal housekeeping. Income required to cover the artist’s private needs (and those of his or her dependents). The economics of the personal household and the professional practice, the ‘business’, are interwoven.

### *Professional practice*

The facets of artisthood that you activate in your practice influence income and expenditure alike. Positions in the studio, in the laboratory, with commissions, on the stage and as a designer require means of investment (see 'Artist's studio', investment pressure). With the professional positions of curator, organiser and adviser, the additional costs may be more favourable than expected and as the physical studio starts to play a more modest part, the pressure on expenditure for the studio also decreases. As an educator (if you are employed somewhere as a teacher) additional costs for that professional position are limited, perhaps travel expenses are not adequately met and you have to make up the difference yourself, and you also have some extra expenses for reading matter for study. If your studio also serves as teaching space, it might require a little more expenditure to make it suitable. 204

*Expenditure mix in artistic practice*

When you start up the business operations for a professional practice, it is worth consulting a financial adviser in order to obtain a tailor-made 'model' appropriate for your individual situation and one that is manageable for you. Obviously it is important for your artistic purposes, like being able to create work, being able to make headway with it and continue your own development. Here, a suggestion with a few main themes relating to the connection between professional and private expenditure.

| Studio turnover | the outcome of your income mix |
|---|---|
| *Deduct* | practice costs: your own 'labour' costs, office costs (telephone, subscriptions, administration etc.), housing costs (energy, rent/mortgage for the studio), depreciation (fittings and fixtures and, possibly studio building) |
| *Gross operating result* | gross profit or loss |

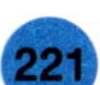

| | |
|---|---|
| *Deduct* | tax allocation for investments in Research & Development like study, travel, research, etc. in the framework of practising your profession which are not offset by income, for example contributions from funds. |
| *Net result* | if available, to be used to pay off debts, develop new projects and/or increase your own income for personal circumstances, for example changes in balance of mutual position of breadwinner. |

*Income mix artistic practice*

211 First let us examine Figure 19 'Reinforcing basis', in which, with your priorities, in mind, you keep going a step further with 'additional income' to achieve your main goal, to realise the core facets. In the following questions the numbers refer to Figure 20. Which facet/facets of artisthood is/are among your highest priorities (1)? What facets are not primary, but are still part of your artistic domain (2)? And so on, depending on each individual definition (broad or narrow) of artisthood. What income is not covered but is still important on account of inspiration, relaxation, social contact, independence (3)? And what income is necessary if and when there is an 'emergency' (4)?

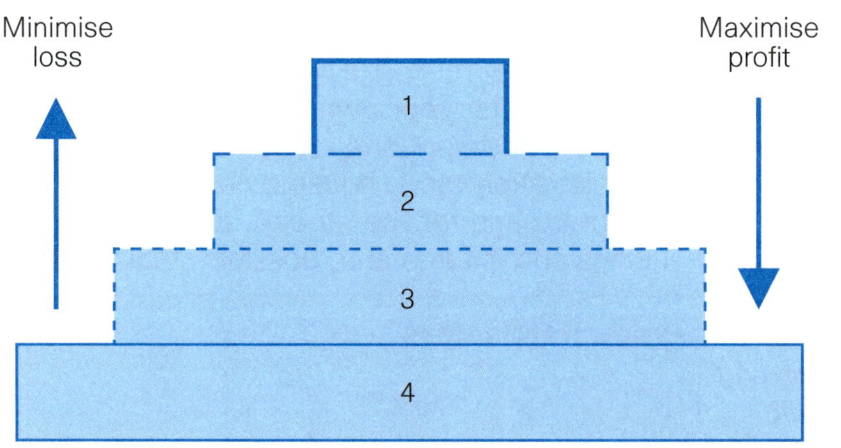


*Figure 20.* Priorities

Below there is a list of 7 income categories:

— *Income from the (art) market*. Sale of one-off—unique—work; sale of work in editions (multiples, artist's books); representation fees and art library fee; copyright (of visual material); remuneration for assignments and projects.
— *Other income from art*, if your practice is defined broadly, is grouped under 1 and, narrowly, under 2 or even 3. design assignments; payment for curatorship; fee for an organisational job; remuneration with committees, juries and company advice; income from teaching (art), socio-cultural work, museum education, occupational therapy; also earnings from seminars, lectures and publications, or your own activities in the studio or at home; income from a community project.
— *Sidelines*, not related to art, but relating substantively to your personal and/or professional life.
— *Income resulting from economic necessity*, if and as long as inevitable: casual/odd jobs, social benefits and other forms of income.
— *Support programmes* for art projects and artists: starting-, project-, travel-, production grants, and over 20 examples of income components: presentation subsidies, study and research grants, cost of living allowances, loans, contributions of materials; prizes artist residencies or studio programmes.
— *Income from capital* or 'past work': interest and dividend on investments; State pension or pension from the Artists Pension Trust, and sickness benefits.
— *Private and miscellaneous* support: from partner, family, maecenas; from subletting living space when temporarily absent; subletting studio when temporarily absent or 'needs must'.

*Personal circumstances*

What do you need and what do you already have? It is wise to make two or three 'needs' scenarios: optimum and minimum, and possibly an ideal situation. It is more about awareness of what is or can be important than exact, statistical data. Here too, I advise a (serious) approach. Are you alone, are there two of you, are there children—if so, how many, how old? Are you the breadwinner, or you a 'double-income' couple, or is your partner the breadwinner? Is there some social benefit? Do you have possessions, is there a likelihood that you will inherit something from the family at some stage and, if necessary, can you already lay claim to it? What about housing? Do you like what you have, do you share accommodation with others, do you rent or own it, with or without a mortgage or loan from the family? What are the fixed costs for energy, insurance and so on, and the variable costs, the housekeeping budget? Do you, or should you, set aside something for deferred income in illness or old-age?

There are two possible outcomes as regards needs. One is a worst-case scenario: under very high pressure of circumstances, with the material minimum required for your survival on your own or as a family. Another scenario is characterised by a reasonable balance between expenditure and income. When conducting an exercise like this you will discover what you already have and what you might get. The result of the exercise produces an indication of your private needs from income generated by work.

Your own costs from day-to-day operations contribute to three types of costs in your private situation:

— income (1) from work required to cover your needs in accordance with the minimum or optimum scenario, and in favourable circumstances;
— investments (2) in hobbies and your further personal development through study geared to your own interests, unlike R&D costs of the artistic practice and in even more favourable circumstances;
— extra redemptions (3) and allocations for future, unexpected expenditure from personal housekeeping. Ideally, pension contributions are included in the first category

Two examples:

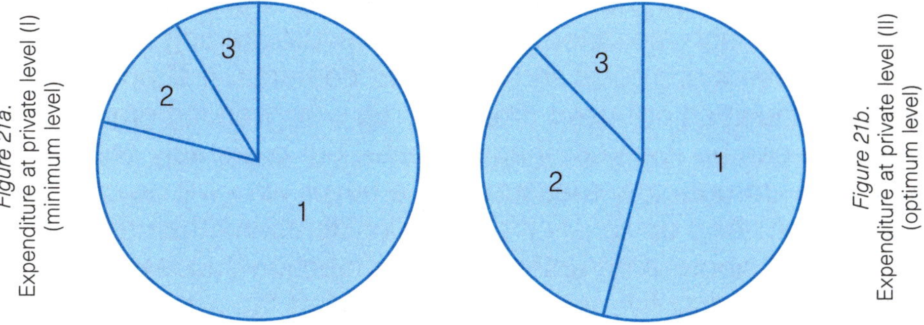


*Figure 21a.* Expenditure at private level (I) (minimum level)

*Figure 21b.* Expenditure at private level (II) (optimum level)

In the left-hand diagram almost all income is needed to cover primary necessities of life (1), little is left for your own development (2) and there is hardly any scope to achieve a healthier financial structure with only a minimal buffer to provide for contingencies (3). The right-hand diagram presents a more positive picture, i.e. there is more income and, as a consequence, greater leeway for hobbies and personal development (2) and slightly more scope for unexpected 'incidents'(3).

## Pricing art works

The subject of pricing is somewhat shrouded in secrecy: evidently it is 'not done' to say much about it. You often hear artists say to one another: "'Just' decide on a price." As a budding artist you won't get far with that. Of course there are no hard and fast rules, of course you should ask around, deliberate and, above all, do not switch off your emotions when determining a price. A few pieces of advice follow.

### *Price calculation*

When prices are calculated, the following elements play a part: wage/hours invested, materials, rent, energy and studio maintenance, and miscellaneous costs.

Factors relating to reduction or increase in price can also be taken into account: stage of development; use of supporting artists' amenities; vulnerability and life span of work; expectations when sale is postponed, and also—tentatively–the extent of the buyer's enthusiasm and respect for the work. It can be important to reduce the price, because it is sometimes a good thing not to charge too much, so when your career is just starting and when the purchasers are good and important contacts. If supporting artists' amenities are used (like a starter's or working grant), the price can be lowered, if appropriate, but preferably only as a tactical 'introductory measure' for a buyer who will be of future importance. And obviously if other considerations than the purely commercial apply. If an artist proves to function successfully in the market, say five years after he has left the art academy, he can raise the price—assuming the market permits. It can of course be sooner or later.

There are several approaches to the subject of pricing: "don't talk about it, better to keep silent". Or "trust the people with whom you do business, and leave it to them". That will be the gallery owner, collector or patron. Or "make sure you build up a good relationship of trust with your business partners and discuss prices openly, as good colleagues, familiarising
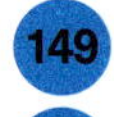
149 yourself with the material and the vocabulary—as we saw earlier."
148 In the latter case it is worth first finding out (rational inventory) whether you and your business partner have enough of a common basis (emotional observation), and also to study some reference material. Three approaches to calculation follow, stemming from the United States, the Netherlands and Germany.

*Models*

The first source is a quantitative model from the Working Artists and the Greater Economy (W.A.G.E.) in New York, founded in 2008 as an activist pressure group, the aim being: to regulate the payment of artist fees by non-profit organisations. They use a 'fee calculator' comprising fourteen price categories (www.wageforwork.com/2/fee-calculator), namely: solo exhibition, solo project, two-person exhibition, group exhibition, 3–5 artists, group exhibition, 6+ artists, performance of existing work, performance, commission of new work, solo screening, event with multiple participants, artist talk or reading, lecture/seminar/workshop, existing text for publication, commissioned text for publication, day rate for performers.

The Netherlands developed the artists' fees Guideline, following discussions and negotiations between representatives of artists and presentation bodies, and possibly also fuelled by the W.A.G.E. fee calculator. It became effective on 1 January 2017 for 'non-selling' exhibitions at the participating institutes in the Netherlands. The complete guideline, checklist and calculator, in both Dutch and English, can be found at www.kunstenaarshonorarium.nl. Without mentioning sums, since they vary over time, it can be summarised as follows. A distinction is made between set remuneration for the production of new work (not counting expense allowance), modification of existing work and usage fee (representation fee) for existing work in an exhibition, including allowance for activities relating to the work, for example its mounting. The table with minimum remunerations also differentiates the allowances according to cases in which more than one artist is the 'supplier'.

The third model addressed here, the Pitz model from Germany, also has a quantitative focus. The artist Hermann Pitz included the Pitz Formula in his compilation *ABC der Klasse Pitz. Dictionnaire raisonné des arts* (2014) consisting of provisional calculations. It is based on five different formulas focusing on two- and three-dimensional 'one-off' pieces, installations, small sculptures in editions and two-dimensional work in editions. It is primarily intended for artists starting out on their professional careers before pricing ceases to be model-based and is 'taken over' by market processes.

### *The force of the market*

The balance between supply and demand, the artist's track record with exhibitions, publications and actual selling prices, and his intersubjective reputation with professionals like inner circles of curators, collectors, patrons, art lovers and buyers, as well as the wider public, have been dealt with directly or
indirectly in this publication, for instance in 'The artist and his 131
environment: from victim to free spirit'.

When an artist arrives in the high-end art market by virtue of such factors, pricing models as described can be put aside and possibly looked back on nostalgically at a later stage as the time "when everything used to be straightforward". The same applies for the artist in the low-end art market, who will occasionally take out the calculating models, looking longingly towards the future: "If only I no longer needed to feel like a beggar, but a worthy interlocutor."

## Transfer of work

*Significance of the work*. The work can, for a wide variety of personal reasons, have such great significance for the artist, that 'ordinary' sale is not appropriate at that stage. There are several possible considerations:

— The work is important now, for this stage in development and "I want to keep it with me for now". You could then say to a buyer: "Please come back another time, then and then" or "You can buy it now, but I'll hand it over in four months or a year, for example, and you can pay the other half of the purchase price then" (delivery time).
— The work forms a turning point in the artist's development; he can conclude that a work like this should be purchased by a special buyer, for example, a museum—thus enhancing his reputation.
— The work is part of the artist's oeuvre that should definitely be kept intact and complete; in that case, it is essential that it remain in his possession for the time being.
— With its content or form, the work plays such a crucial role for the artist himself that he decides either not to sell it or to sell it to a very good personal contact, for instance a friend or good artist-colleague with whom he has a relationship of trust.

Incidentally, it is always worth agreeing on the following *four principles*, and specifying them in a contract of sale:

— The buyer will conserve (and insure) the work properly, in the interests of the work, the buyer and the artist. That may seem unnecessary, but the 'prudent person' principle is not always applied as a matter-of-course.

- The artist can avail himself of his own work for a period of five years after sale, for example, at most once every two years, for a loan for an exhibition, and after that period renegotiation is always possible. This is in the interests of both the artist and the buyer, as presentation in a museum usually increases the work's value and the artist's reputation.
- The artist will be consulted, or at least informed by the owner if the work is presented in public, and under which conditions.
- If the work is resold, the artist will be informed as to the new owner (and preferably the price of transaction). This is the most sensitive point, and quite a few buyers are very much against it.

Arrangements of this type may perhaps reduce the unpleasant feeling of 'loss' when a work is sold. So when selling a work, it is always a good idea to consider: do you really want to sell; when do you want to sell; to whom do you want to sell: friend, important contact, with a view to future career, or also to 'ordinary' buyers? Under which conditions, as regards delivery time and subsequent accessibility of work, and what would that cost.

If sale of this type is considered as an *investment in the artist's personal future*, there are two important aspects, i.e. the visibility of the work and the effect on the artistic practice. There are several interpretations of 'visibility'. The work is:

- permanently kept in private circles;
- on view permanently/for a longer time, because it is a work in public space intended for a large, mixed audience;
- on view irregularly/hardly ever, for a specific audience, because the work is mostly in the storage premises of a museum or collector.

Sales affect the repute of the artist when the work is displayed in interesting places, when one buyer tips off another, and when the work is sold to a collector whose name would not be out of place on the artist's CV. Even without public 'visibility', the work's and the artist's repute can increase when the work features in a respectable public or private collection.

# 8

# Building block: Curriculum Vitae as synthesis

**Curriculum literally means 'course' (of a race) and 'curriculum vitae' (CV) is a way of saying 'the course of (my) life'. The curriculum is also the equivalent of the learning process. The first meaning is retrospective, the second prospective. I will follow a similar approach to the one taken in the preceding chapters and not deal in this 'building block' with the curriculum vitae as something in the pluperfect, but as the synthesis between past and present, a future-orientated action plan. In this chapter the various functions of a CV are examined.**

# Separate worlds: the artistic CV

Artists' CVs often omit background–personal–information, interests and projects during the individual's youth and life beyond the professional. Moreover, the CV covering an artistic career is frequently arranged chronologically, so 'autonomous' work first, followed by less autonomous, such as applied art, and lastly some fringe activities. If several artists' positions are involved they are often not reflected to best advantage. This chapter describes the added value of a more inclusive CV, as a representation of, and, primarily for yourself.

During 'Positioning' workshops at institutes of art education, I ask students to send me a CV in advance. They ask what that CV should look like. My answer is: "I'm not telling you, see for yourself." It is a callous test with a worrying outcome: a CV lacking the place and year of birth, starting on the first day at the art academy, as if nothing had taken place before that; projects, including quite interesting ones in the areas of music or writing outside the course programme, are not mentioned. Jobs, big or small, even when indicating competences which art education proudly note for its accreditation (think of collaboration and communicative skills) are entirely absent.

Nine out of ten artists' CVs have the same omissions, important components which receive too little attention:

— Name, website and e-mail address, as well as 'lives and works in' are usually included, but place and year of birth are quite often omitted. Personal background is very rarely mentioned, past life and family make-up are not referred to, and there is no personal profile.
— Education usually only relates to art education, other (university and higher vocational) studies are omitted, and secondary education is only rarely mentioned. However, residencies are fashionable and are noted.
— Exhibitions take the first place, usually headed by a list of solo exhibitions, followed by group exhibitions, then collections, prizes and grants.

– Assignments follow, lectureships often come as an afterthought, and projects and other activities hardly get a mention. Usually, the artist's own publications and a biography of the artist are not stated.

A CV featuring a ubiquitous hierarchy between 'non-commissioned (so-called autonomous) art' and 'low' art (with less prestige in the art market) is conformist and geared purely to the traditional museum segment of the art market. It is based on the idea of the 'autonomous' artist, waiting in the isolation of his studio, for the 'redeeming' gallery owner or museum curator. An artistic CV of this type barely works, if at all, in such a limited view of artisthood. What does the set, standard line-up of exhibitions tell about the artist? It contains no distinguishing tie-in, giving the reader the feeling of dealing with a format and not a person. A more inclusive CV can actually arouse the reader's curiosity, also about the exhibitions.

But what does it actually matter who in the art market asks the artist for a CV? Is it of consequence?

## Significance, value and content of a CV

As was indicated in Chapter 1, in 'Business know-how and promotion', artists do not by nature take care of their promotion and public relations themselves. You do not sell more with portfolios and CVs, you do not disrupt distorted market relations in which there is a large supply of art and a limited demand. There are exceptions: presentations of graduation work at art academies. In such cases it is worth having visual and verbal material at your disposal. Visitors are particularly keen to have information about artists in whose work they are interested. 30

*Mirror, logbook, database and 'signpost'*

It is sensible to look for a new, strictly personal approach for the CV which tells more than the 'artistic CV' described above. I shall single out five values or functions.

– First of all, the CV is a *mirror, a logbook and a signpost*. A mirror which reflects you, your career and your life, a logbook of events, and a pointer for further, new steps.
– Secondly, the CV forms the *personal database of your network*, an overview of what you have done, where, when and with whom, in your artistic practice. Unlike a list of names in an address directory, your CV adds colour to your network.
– Thirdly, the CV in an integrated, complete form, is a basis for *data management* (e.g. on your own website); in a way, you are guiding what critics, curators, gallery owners, academics and others write or say about you, if only because you take the initiative yourself and do not passively wait and see. It is your move: "This contains information that I think is important, if you would like to know more, please ask me and tell what you make of it and what you want to do with it before making it 'public'."
– Fourthly, the CV is a necessary document when you enrol in a Master's programme, at a post-academic institute, artist's residency or apply for a grant.
– Fifthly–and lastly–the CV is a document that may be of use when you meet someone for the first time and are asked *for more details*. Also, it would not go amiss to have an informative, attractive CV on your website–but not too prominent and not too detailed. It does no harm to let others make an effort to get to know you: arouse curiosity and don't satisfy it too quickly!

*Content, a personal composition*

Obviously, the content of each person's CV is as individual as a fingerprint, but the composition or form also varies from one person to another. I make four divisions. Most require introspection, but it is not an easy matter to reveal personal aspects and relate them to your professional career. 'Interchange'–getting feedback–is important when drawing up a CV of this type. It can be a dialogue with a confidant from among your friends, a mentor or other interlocutor with relevant experience, but some people are able to achieve an approach like this in a dialogue with themselves.

1. *Personal*. Standard data such as place and year of birth, with a brief description of the personal background, as well as a concise link between background and artisthood.
2. *Learning*. Mention all education, not only that relating to art. If it is too complex, summarise to avoid excess of detail. Artist residencies and grants, as well as prizes and awards can be seen as 'learning moments' rather than separate prestigious events. Learning not only entails the acquisition of knowledge, but also passing it on. This section should also contain artist talks, lectures, seminars, written contributions, guest lectureships and teaching posts. If the teaching post is an important part of artisthood, it is more appropriate to mention it in the next section of the CV.
3. *Connecting*. Identify what your most important artist's positions are with respect to connecting your activities to the public. If two or three positions are dominant in the individual artistic practice, you should avoid ranking them hierarchically. So do not put the positions one below the other, but beside one another (in two columns). 237

Then something unexpected takes place: cross connections become more apparent to you: one inspires the other, or one contact generates another. And if there are three important positions, make two columns, for example, that end with a third position underneath, taking up the entire width. Admittedly that position comes after the other two, but is 'upgraded' to an equivalent position as the base for the other two (see example II). 240

The different positions can relate to one another in various ways. You can choose between: noting them separately, or touching with a relationship arising between the two positions, or partially overlapping with the possibility of a third area arising, or fully overlapping. See the following diagram:

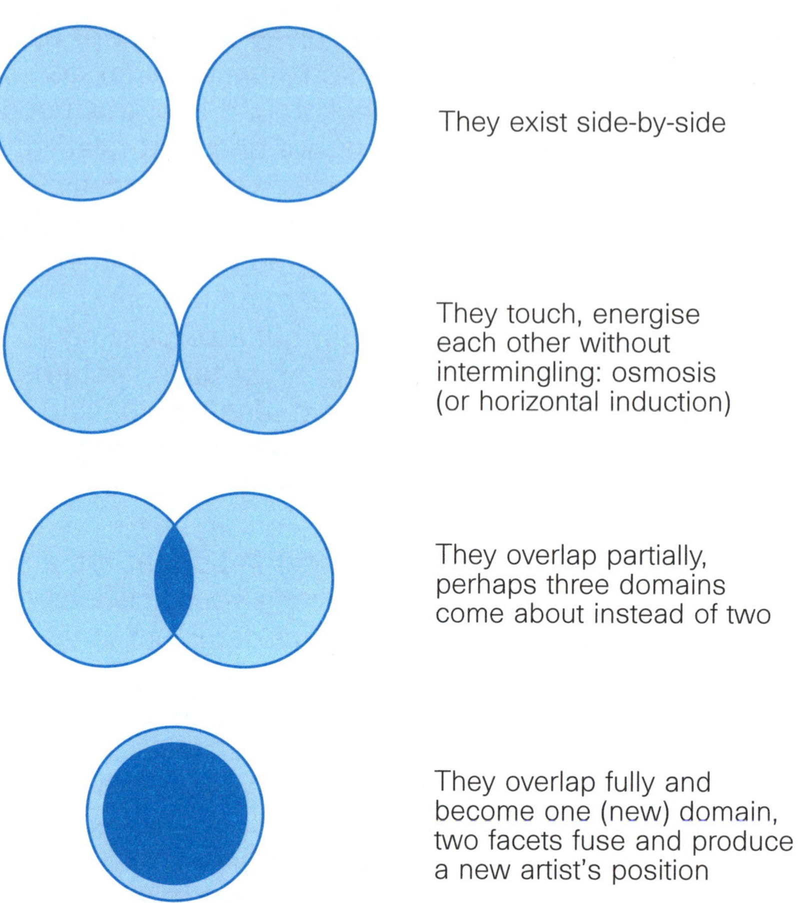


*Figure 22.* Relationship between artists' positions

It is not only important to denote the positions, but also to indicate them in keeping with what they have in common, the core of your artisthood. That core is more likely to relate to the facets of artisthood than to artists' positions within the professional, market-orientated practice. For example, if you think of the 'social dimension of an object' in public space it stimulates thinking of the 'object' in a museum setting. Or: a teaching post energises you as you become acquainted with new, unexpected ideas and confronts you with your studio work, et cetera.

When you single out your professional activities in the art world in general and the art market in particular, there is always some form of collaboration. It is very important to be precise and, more especially, generous. Mention precisely titles, locations and data concerning exhibitions, assignments, lectures and projects. Be generous in indicating who commissioned the work and which other artists participated, which curator played a part, particularly if it is someone your trust and with whom you have worked well. You can play around with the arrangement of that information: details in italics or in a smaller letter size whet the curiosity, and similarly, a modest footnote can have considerable impact.

4. *Remainder*. What happens to the work and the information on the artist and the art work? In this section, collections (including public collections) are listed with their names, and private collections are included anonymously or with just a few names. The same applies for a bibliography (with monographs, articles, reviews, television programmes and so on). Artist's books are more at home in the 'Connecting' section as art works that link up with the public, unless the book has the character of a documentary or catalogue.

## Basic portfolio and biographical notes

The main purpose of a CV as described here, is to document your own 'history', in both professional and personal terms, with a view to the future. This kind of chronicling also entails making and maintaining an image bank, so there is sufficient suitable visual material to draw up an overview of work in the form of a portfolio. It is not a bad idea to make and keep notes recording personal observations, experiences and opinions. Just think of reflecting on the work, the working process, sources that have or have not been used, artist statements and personal recollections that are, or have been of some importance for the work and working process.

In short, there are three kinds of files:

— the CV, as dealt with extensively above;
— the image bank or basic portfolio;
— biographical notes and observations.

These three ingredients are important for:

— compiling personal documentation, for your own use as a mirror, logbook and database;
— enrolling or applying for follow-up studies, artist residency and grants from funds and authorities;
— producing printed information for potential collectors, gallery owners, patrons, critics, curators, interested parties outside the art world. Only supply that information on request. And do not forget the people in your surroundings, your friends and relations, who will be pleased to have this information;
— designing a website—nowadays an indispensable element of every artistic practice; it can also function as a base
43 for Instagram and social media. Not that it is all that profit-
able, but it is considered unprofessional not to have one.

*Personal documentation* can be as extensive as you wish, but at all events includes a CV, biographical notes, records of work and working process, artist statements, as well as anything you think you need for your mirror, logbook etc. and applications or for interested parties.

*Applications* entail more. That aspect is not dealt with in this publication because it is only possible to provide relevant information after careful consideration of selection and matching processes in general and detailed examination (if possible) of the requirements that vary from one case to another, and the procedure in question. The minimum will include a selection of visual material, a CV, specific motivation and information on the plan or art project.

As the artist's career and reputation progress, the importance of the *CV for interested* parties will diminish; by then it is no longer a matter of a tabula rasa arousing curiosity about the beginner. When an artist finishes his studies and embarks on his career, information provided by the CV is at its most important, whereas not much can be said about his artistic achievements. I recommend that a concise information leaflet of two pages at most be drawn up for graduation work, based on the CV. Think of a personal mix of CV, 'quote' from the biography and a selection from the portfolio (the same elements as used for the personal website). A printed leaflet of this type should be unpretentious, generous and informative as such—so not making do with a referral to the artist's website, implying the reader should 'see for himself'.

Following on from 'values' of a CV, one can gauge the difference in communicative intensity in the varying 'temperatures' when the new CV is used: 231

| | |
|---|---|
| — on own initiative, unsolicited; | COLD |
| — through social media, with known recipients; | LUKEWARM |
| — on request, by a gallery owner, collector or when applying for a grant, a course, a residency; | WARM |
| — just for yourself, as mirror, database, 'signpost', etc. | VERY WARM |

## Two examples of a CV, plus information leaflet

Here two different CV approaches that can be pinpointed from the infinite number of variations based on artists' positions. They are 'Artist in the studio and in public space' and 'Studio *and* educator *and* organiser'. Apart from the 'Personal' block, they have unconventional headings: Learning, Connecting and Remainder. The headings are intended only for your own use, and not for third parties—the person reading the CV will not have a clue what such headings stand for.

*I. Example: artist in the studio and artist in public space*

## PERSONAL

Personal background: *interests in the family home (or else developed yourself), father's and mother's work (for example, suggesting an international, nomadic youth), family with siblings (or in fact space for your own world as an only child), social, cultural and/or religious background (and what might, in a nutshell, be of interest for those 'reading' the work or working process), combining and connecting various cultural interests (for example, 'writing of prose and poetry had faded somewhat into the background, but have recently resurfaced alongside visual work'), studies (for example, if erratic: 'broad interest, apparent in a varied palette of programmes, some of which are incomplete')*. Keep it short, but as complete as possible. It makes you 'human'.

*Personal*

— name, website, e-mail address
— place and year of birth
— lives and works in

## LEARNING

— education, including secondary school/schools (and location)
— artist residencies
— prizes, grants
— artist talks, seminars, lectures
— guest lectureships
— own articles (about your own art or that of others), no artist's books, they belong in the next section on work and public (Connecting). No articles and reviews on your work, they belong in the bibliography ( Remainder) and no literary work because that belongs in the next block (as a connecting position).

## CONNECTING

Provide an explanatory introduction to a multifaceted artisthood, as in this example: '*the studio forms the basis for the work on show in a gallery and museum, as well as for work—commissioned—in public space. Erroneously termed 'autonomous' work and more 'applied' work are complementary (sources of inspiration, of energy, widening of technical scope, interaction with varying types in different worlds) and mutually reinforcing (through integration and actually confrontation).*' Consider and choose your words carefully.

*Presentations*
Titles, locations and exhibition dates, solo or groups, supervision/curatorship, etc.

*Commissions and projects*
Titles, locations and dates, patrons, particulars if any (possibly grouping by theme instead of by date).

## REMAINDER

*Collections, bibliography*
Collections, bibliography, etc. If one section takes up too much space: reduce and condense (so not 40 articles), set aside chronology (no list of date to start with), change your angle and go for content: themes, writers, media (in this part you could add dates and, in moderation put them in running text in brackets.)

### *II. Example 2: artist in the studio, as an educator and as an organiser*

**PERSONAL** (see previous example)

**LEARNING**
If the position of educator is one of the two or three chief positions, omit from this section: artist talks, seminars, guest lectureships–include them in the following part (connecting) with lectureships and transfer.

**CONNECTING**
The introductory text links up 'school', 'studio' and 'platform', for example: *'The work is linked to and derives from questions relating to the position of the middle-aged woman, my social involvement is shaped in my lectureship, inside and outside official programmes, namely in the platforms in my studio, in artists' initiatives, in my own publications. My studio work is not concealed in my lectureship, but is not always in the forefront.'* In this way you create cohesion, for yourself and for those who are interested in you.

| *Educatorship/transfer* | *Exhibitions* |
|---|---|
| Where, when, with whom, particulars (special exhibitions, artist's books and so on). | If too 'scant' in scope (compared with lectureships) perhaps add further explanation, (e.g. special themes) etc. |

*Platforms*
If a third position forms an important mainstay alongside lectureships and exhibitions, such as organising meetings, artist residencies or other artist initiatives, the position can also be given a place, namely: self-organised (what, where, when), with others (why, with whom, where, when).

The platforms of 'the artist as an organiser' will 'support' the two columns above, before lectureship and exhibitions.

## REMAINDER

See the previous example. Perhaps say something about 'remainder' from the angles of both lectureship and transfer to future generations of young artists. Document using catalogues, articles and collections based on the 'exhibitions' component, and also define follow-ups you give based on your platforms and the feedback you get. So, specify the 'harvest' of your efforts.

*There is no standard*

If you have an artistic practice that presents itself as an 'organisation', you can, if you like, suffice with a more simple CV for the 'outside world'. In that case, the undertaking is 'displayed in the shop window', the personal details of the artist as the 'shopkeeper' stay inside. Banu Cennetoğlu (Rijksakademie, 2002–2003) makes choices what she reveals and what not. Her 'company' BAS (artist's space, books and artist talks) in Istanbul comes first; her personal life is normally concealed. However, the invitation to make an art project 'book of professions' challenged her to make another, compelling CV, in which she does not hesitate to mention various professional activities and her private life, with no urgent order of preference, in her own words, and in a repetitive style.

| | |
|---|---|
| **2015–2012 / Istanbul** | **mother, freelance artist, editor, director of a non-profit organisation, collector, accountant, organiser, adviser;** |
| **2012–2007 / Istanbul** | **mother, freelance artist, editor, director of a non-profit organisation, collector, accountant, organiser;** |
| **2007–2005 / Istanbul** | **freelance artist, editor, director of a non-profit organisation, collector, accountant, organiser;** |
| **2005–2004 / Amsterdam** | **freelance artist;** |
| **2004–2002 / Amsterdam** | **subsidised artistic practitioner;** |
| **2002–1999 / New York** | **coffee-shop manager who photographs;** |
| **1990–1996 / New York** | **professional photographer, barmaid, coffee-shop barista, coat-checker, babysitter;** |
| **1996–1995 / Paris** | **professional photographer, sales person, translator;** |
| **1995–1994 / Paris** | **photography student, photo darkroom cleaner, sales person;** |
| **1994–1993 / Istanbul** | **psychology student, professional photographer, fashion editor;** |
| **1993–1990 / Istanbul** | **psychology student, photographer's assistant, fashion editor;** |
| **1990–1989 / Istanbul** | **psychology student, tourist guide, translator, trade fair hostess, animator;** |
| **1989–1986 / Istanbul** | **high school student, private tutor.** |

**Source: conceived for www.bookofprofessions.blogspot.com.tr**

*A concise information leaflet*

Divide up your CV in the way suggested: Personal, Learning, Connecting and Remainder. A few tips for fleshing out a scant CV.

PERSONAL. Consider adding a personal quote after having given standard information on where you were born, are currently living and working. For example "the road from the farm (or Protestant village) to the art academy was long and hard" (it tells that you are independent and can stay the course, motivated, strong-willed and courageous). Or "musical family, I opted first for the visual arts, for me music takes second place (tells: cultural background, makes choices for himself, wide interests, dual talent?).

LEARNING. All secondary education, even if only partially completed. Consider adding a sentence to precede 'education': "Because of widespread interests and somewhat unsettled family circumstances, a diversity of schooling prior to the serious focus on visual art and philosophy (or something else with which you have evidently familiarised yourself) during the last five years"(tells: self-assured, no fool, seeks and finds).

CONNECTING. Before listing your professional activities, for example in the relevant columns, provide a professional profile serving to overarch your activities, such as: "In the studio I generally work alone, and organise various activities together with others inside the art world and outside it." You might add a recent photo of yourself with a good likeness accompanying a project in the studio (a reminder for interested parties).

# So now...

If you are satisfied with your new CV approach, a considerable distance has been covered and much has been achieved.

The personal background has been examined and an effort has been made to condense and integrate it in the career path. Personal history and positioning in the art world and society as a whole have been compacted into one or two sentences.

The career has been reviewed. The artistic practice re-balanced by reassessing and interconnecting the individual positions, preceding them with a concise profile that unites those facets or positions. There is now order rather than disorder.

An overall picture is achieved by grouping the 'blocks'. A profile or 'pattern' may emerge that reveals the artist as a researcher, maker, scientist, interventionist, magician, host or hostess, or a helicopter pilot—crossing through the various facets.

This, broadly speaking, is what a different variation on the CV amounts to. The details are a powerful source of information. When names of curators, patrons and others are included, they will be with you for life.

It is a major exercise to draw up a CV like this, but it is worth while. You have:

— a mirror, logbook and signpost;
— a personal database of your network;
— a basis for data management, and
— a document for when the occasion arises,
with application to an institute, or upon request.

# Part III.

# Origins

# Part III.

In Chapter 9 'A slice of life', career patterns—my own and those of artists—are compared and analysed.

'The counselling of artists' gives a peek into what goes on behind closed doors when artists are coached. Three different career patterns are described, based on counselling in coaching sessions and workshops by and for artists. They are also more generally applicable for anyone interested in their own career pattern and that of others. In 'Author's career dissected' it is not I who pestered the artist with questions and analysed the replies—the roles have been reversed and my professional and private career paths are 'dissected', with the addition of some personal 'autobiographical asides'. For each stage of my career and private life, reflections (posed as questions) are included to mirror the reader's professional and private career. To conclude, the findings are reviewed.

This exercise supplies a touchstone for those who are self-employed in small- to medium-sized (creative) enterprises, including artists, and for wage-earners (such as lecturers, curators, staff members, programmers or executives). When their own situation is compared with my background, they get an idea of iteration cycles in charting one's course and improvisation. Essential points in this publication are addressed (once more):

- listening to your own preferences, thus enabling you to better chart your course;
- dealing with what initially are situations that cannot be influenced;
- redefining your own task and position, identifying strengths and weaknesses, and:
- transforming the context in which you work, using core qualities.

This chapter is the concluding part of the central theme: *influencing circumstances to your advantage or finding your way among them so you can make a worthwhile contribution that corresponds to your personal qualities.*

The third section concludes with a description of how this publication came about, in the form of Acknowledgements in Chapter 10.

# 9

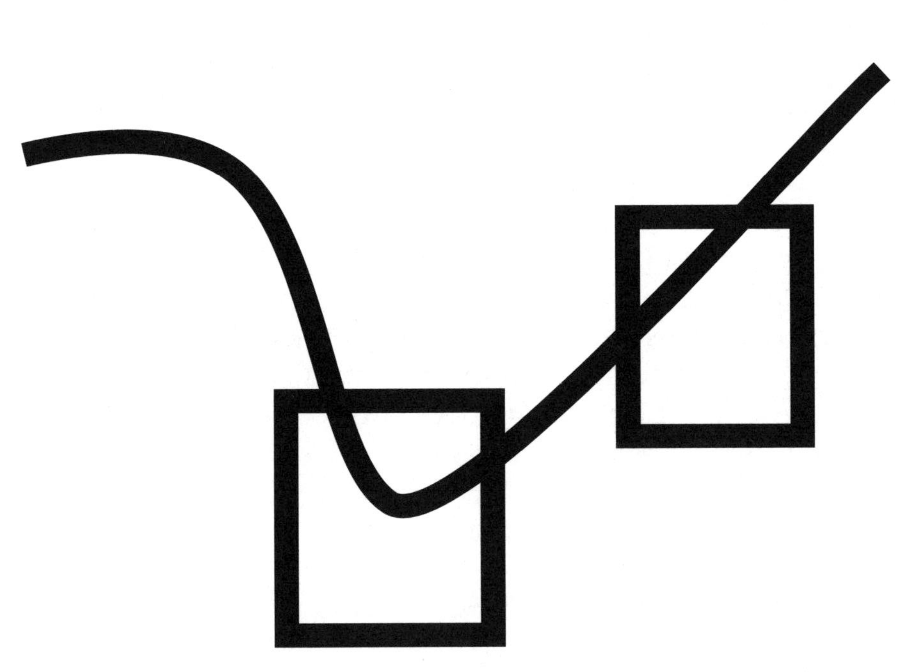

# A slice of life

**This chapter takes a look behind the closed doors of counselling, as well as identifying several career patterns which have also served as a yardstick for my own professional and private career.**

## Counselling of artists: sources of experience

### *Rijksakademie, workshops and coaching*

The interactive exchange with artists and art students is based on contacts at the Rijksakademie and with alumni following their stay in Amsterdam, with artists in coaching sessions and during workshops, with Bachelor and Master students as well as with artists in residencies in the Netherlands and abroad. In the 'Positioning by artists' working groups, which started in the early 1990s, I discussed for the first time terms like artists' strategies, the personal definition of artisthood, artists' typologies and artists' positions. The workshops on positioning in art institutes since 2014 have followed the topics which have been addressed in this publication.

### *Coaching artists*

I will use the coaching sessions I initiated after I left the Rijksakademie as an example of the integral approach to professional positioning, based on pointers in both the professional and private career.

In my case, coaching is always about artists with a 'history': mid-career and up; you then have a basis on which to proceed together. When the artist proves to be interested—and contacts me—we make an appointment. I ask him/her to send me in advance one or several specific questions and a CV, and to bring along documentation of the work on a laptop. I also indicate that we will touch upon personal life, professional career and work (and its presentation). They form the points of the 'triangular map of the day'.

The coaching session is held at my home, in an informal setting. At the start, I give every artist scope to become familiar with the place and the ambience, while I absent myself for a moment to make coffee. The conversation begins informally and proceeds to deal with what the artist has actually come for.

*Personal life*. Bearing the CV in mind, I ask questions about the artist's personal background. These questions often lead to sensitive turning points, major events in his life.

*Career*. I prefer to avoid looking at work at that stage in order to postpone normative affinity (beautiful, ugly, attractive, uninteresting) until my curiosity about the person as a whole has become so great and so strong that a personal opinion on the work is of little consequence. By then the work is no longer an autonomous 'thing', but a gateway to other aspects of the artist's life. When, during the session, we finally arrive at the work, I concentrate among other things on the connection between the work and the personal background. If the distance is so great and, with the best will in the world, no sign of the artist's own history can be detected, the conversation falters. If the work is dominant and sticks literally very closely to the personal history and does not elude self-therapeutic exercise, the whole situation becomes too hot for me to handle. Finally, the CV, which I had skimmed through just before the session, is addressed so we can proceed.

The discussions do not follow a set, linear pattern. I sometimes jump from one subject to another as I feel my way. It serves to loosen people up and stops the 'coachee' from becoming fixated and withdrawn into a self-construct. Throughout the session the main question for coachees is: "where do I stand and what do I stand for?" I challenge them to characterise themselves: "I'm a host, looking for conditions for others. Who are you? An anthropologist? Helicopter pilot? Psychologist? Director? Draughtsman? Journalist or activist?"

The next step is to go through the CV using the problem areas mentioned by the artist in an e-mail. Some of the questions the artist might ask prior to the coaching session include: "I have attractive assignments in public space, but galleries don't want to know"; "My studio is in the Netherlands, I have performance projects in Germany together with other artists, but not in the Netherlands", or "I organise round-table discussions based on themes that I supply, my work is on display in 'alternative' project venues at home and abroad, I'm now working with films, but my lectureship takes up time and energy; I'm looking for focus and set priorities." We touch on the almost inevitable hierarchy between artists' positions, such as the artist in the studio as the ideal, and the other positions.

The pendulum swings back to everyday reality, the material circumstances. What scope do you have? A discussion about expenditure now and in ideal circumstances, income: distribution, volume, vulnerable areas, including the threat of discontinuity. Are you the sole breadwinner or do you share the responsibility with your partner for life? Who is the provider and what does it feel like? Is there some capital, for example a studio or dwelling of your own, or is there the prospect of something else (an inheritance)?

Once we have reached that stage, the die is cast and we can begin construction, if it has not already begun—with confrontational questions from me and reflections from the artist himself. Now we get going with:

– the artist's own plan to set something up or change something, its personal urgency, pointers to achieve it, but primarily clarification of the crux: what is closest to your heart, how can you fulfil your greatest ambition with the least possible activity. This route belongs in Part II and
203 is dealt with in the Building block 'Greatest ambition, smallest size'.
– a revised personal CV as a database and signpost for further career development, a mirror in which connections can be seen between personal and professional life, and work. This route is dealt with extensively in Part II,
228 Chapter 8, Building block 'Curriculum Vitae as synthesis'.

# Career patterns



During discussions with artists and art students personal origins are an important topic. One has travelled a long and bumpy road 'from farm to art academy', another has had a smoother path, with parents who might both be artists (or perhaps grandfather or grandmother painted); in that case, artisthood is passed on from one generation to another. When we look at the work and talk about it another pattern may emerge within the artist's own history, for example: a recurring theme crops up like a common thread 'what happened to me as a child', regardless of the materials and forms used in the work. Perhaps the private and professional career have been capricious, involving trial and error, with at first sight few pointers, but which can, with moments of doubt (moments in-between), can be a useful aid for understanding one's own personal background and mapping further steps.

*Continuity and discontinuity*

Three patterns are looked at: family-related, the common thread and the seeker.

*Family-related.* If, within a personal background (family culture, environment, family tradition) studies or vocation, the first job, the second and third follow on from each other, that can be described as continuity and cohesion. Just think of generations pursuing law studies, or an art academy, or an eldest son going to a seminary. That could be sketched as follows:

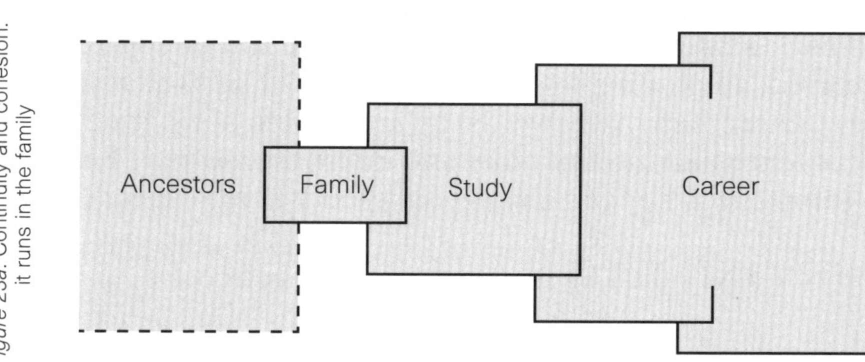


*Figure 23a.* Continuity and cohesion: it runs in the family

An ongoing line need not apply literally if it pertains to identity characteristics, such as 'they're all builders in our family, we're always involved somehow in construction'. You could call it an inter-generational pattern, with continuity and connection or cohesion between generations.

*The common thread*. Apart from continuity in professions or continuity in identity between generations, there may also be a continuous line within one career, a series as found in the history of music: in boyhood singing in a choir, learning a musical instrument with support from father, mother or a maecenas, working as an organist, teaching, composing and, finally, the director of a music school. Or else, also within one career: carpenter, artist, then cabinetmaker's training and then technical specialist assisting artists. Or architecture studies, architect, researcher and writer. Or graphic design studies, teaching and lastly visual artist.

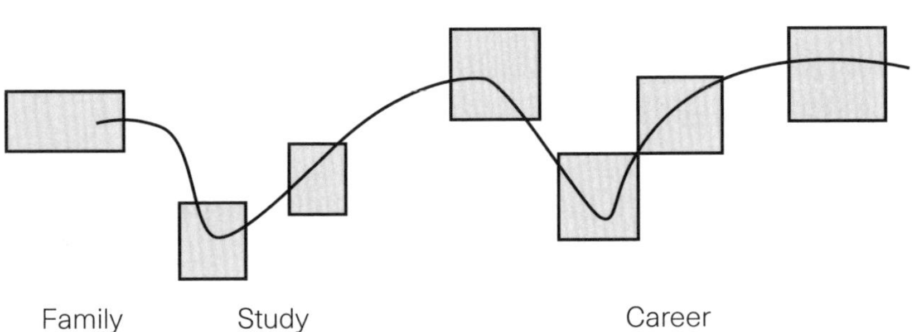


*Figure 23b.* Discontinuity and internal cohesion: the Common Thread

If there is no clear connection—in the first part of the career—it gives an impression of discontinuity. But as soon as you can look back a little longer, a 'common thread' can be sometimes perceived, amounting to internal cohesion. The sketch above gives (better than many words) an impression of a pattern like that of (external) discontinuity and internal cohesion. There is a connection, but you usually only see it in retrospect, after having taken a few steps or in the latter part of your career. That could be called an intra-generational pattern.

***Reflection*. Can you detect in your career, be it short or already longer, an 'anchor' extending through experiences and perhaps providing a pointer for "where do I stand and what I stand for?" Are you, apart from an artist, basically also a helicopter pilot, teacher, host, detective?**

*The seeker*. Initially there may seem to be no rhyme or reason when you consider your entire career, you cannot detect a common thread. Do not be too concerned—try to make a different analysis. So not an integral, more extended (i.e. longitudinal) analysis, but concentrate on shorter 'moments' and the whole combination of circumstances at those moments (i.e. transversal). In other words, seek out turning points or fault lines. In mathematics, in the doctrine of limits, you do not look at a long line, but at the smallest moment where you can detect an alteration of change of course.

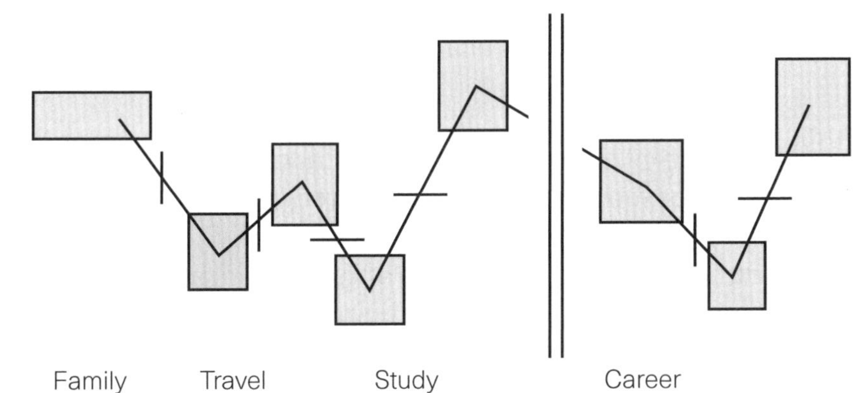


*Figure 23c*. Fracture planes and reorientations: moments in-between

These fracture moments or turning points can be orientational, if you want to discover what motivates you, what might be your inner compass, certainly if the 'great common thread' lets you down. Perhaps you can discover a recurring pattern in the reorientations, a connection. For instance, always 'the challenge', always 'convivial and human', always 'new and unknown', always 'somewhere else on the globe', always 'socially relevant' or always 'a combination of rest and unrest', etc.

***Reflection*. Look at the transitions in the above sketch *between* the jobs, activities, studies, leaving home, travel and so on. The moments between home and studies; one study and another; studies and world tour; world tour and work; work and studies; work and other work. What happened? What was going on? Were there doubts, ambitions, considerations, anxieties, moods, choices that are indicative of subsequent choices?**

More than one pattern will invariably apply for one person:

– an inter-generational pattern, a recurring mainstay for several generations. Symbolic ('repeatedly structural engineers') or according to profession ('repeatedly lawyers');
– an intra-generational pattern, common thread throughout the entire career;
– a fracture plane pattern, moments of reorientation and restarting between projects or jobs.

In each career pattern, choices are unavoidable.

The inter-generational family pattern has several variants, namely either integrate your own career pattern into or allow it to arise from the family background, or fight against that background and enter into confrontation, or dismiss it, distance yourself from and ignore family history. Then you may discover at a later stage that the family pattern persists in your career and life.

The intra-generational, longitudinal pattern, in which you seek the common thread within one career (your own), is usually only recognisable in retrospect, with an advanced stage of the career. Sometimes someone (parents, friends, teachers) 'marks' you, giving you a nickname, early on, but the implications are generally only apparent later as you 'fill up' with experiences.

The third pattern entails an insistent, sometimes rather exhausting problem when choices are made, when key moments occur between projects or jobs. A deeper layer is penetrated as questions are asked about the moments in-between, and their interconnection. For example: is the next step merely a means of escaping an existing situation? Does it entail reflection 'drawing back to make a better jump forward'? Is it the stimulating challenge to break fresh ground?

## Author's career, dissected

Studied in Rotterdam, lived in Noorderhoeve commune in Ursem, and since 1976 in Heemstede. Worked in Amsterdam between 1971 and 2010. During my career I have primarily been employed in salaried positions, alternating with periods of unemployment and reorientation. The interweaving of personal and professional life is described below.

*Amsterdam*

I was born in Amsterdam on 24 May 1945, in a family with an older brother and three older sisters. I was an underweight, scrawny, wartime baby, born just after the winter of famine (1944–1945) and two weeks after the Liberation. That year my parents returned to Kennemerland. It is a coastal region that includes the towns of Haarlem, Zandvoort, Bloemendaal, Heemstede and Aerdenhout.

*Kennemerland*

*Secondary school*, the Jac. P. Thijsse Lyceum in Overveen until 1963. My schooling was not exactly plain sailing. I did not feel at home in the school's elitist setting or with the curriculum, and eventually switched from a science-orientated programme to the liberal arts. I swotted for my exams with friends from the Amsterdam area. The emergency measure to prevent me getting mired down in secondary school proved worth while. The pressure cooker of state exams, subjects that appealed to me and the creation of my own setting with friends heralded a new period. Was the emergency measure a choice, an inner compass or coincidence?

***Reflection*. How did your schooling go? Did you fit in or go your own way? What was your 'salvation'? Did you have to make radical choices? Do you sometimes think back, to the considerations at that time? Are you still learning from it?**

### *Rotterdam*

*Erasmus University (Rotterdam, 1964–1971).*
An inspiring teacher was of inportance. The economics teacher and my father (a designer and manufacturer of steel furniture) made Economics a fairly obvious choice. I had already sampled the charms of Amsterdam. I soon escaped the straitjacket of study and embarked enthusiastically on acting at the Rotterdam theatre company. In the long vacation I fled to my parents' house and celebrated the summer with friends, while studying seriously, writing, making music or rehearsing. We were on the threshold of adulthood, thought we were special and imagined we could make an important contribution in life.

At the end of the first year I failed the exams with terrible marks. I couldn't lose face and dedicated myself to my studies, passing the Economics exam the following year. However, in 1966 I switched to Sociology—another feeling of 'familiarity' comparable with the switch in secondary school. During my Master's studies I opted for Organisational Sociology with Project Organisation in the building sector as my main subject, with Industrial Design as my subsidiary (at Delft University of Technology). I studied and combined my studies with the activities in the student drama society, film club, students union and a busy personal life, day and night. I was then living in my 'own' little house, which served as a welcoming 'port of call': A 'salon' in Rotterdam.

**_Reflection_. When was there some indication of logic or structure between the ages of 16 and around 22? Did you have a 'gap year' for travel or different studies (with which, according to your parents, you could earn some money)? What were 'anchors' in your life? Was it the security of your studies, contact with fellow students, your extracurricular activities, love and friendship? What qualities did you then possess for dealing with problems that you now think back on?**

*Amsterdam*

*Marketing and advertising (Amsterdam, 1972–1975).* After graduation I immediately sent an unsolicited application to many management consultancies in the Netherlands. I was invited by almost all of them for an interview. Their reactions were always identical: "We're interested. You have the 'presence' of a senior, but you still have to learn the business. Could you return later on?" Everything went quiet and I had been without work for six months. Something had to happen.

After a lightning procedure, I started work at Young & Rubicam-Koster as an account executive and developmental executive to "do something about the organisational development". Advertising and marketing were new fields to learn more about. A few weeks after I started, it transpired that new offices were to be built and I suggested that supervision of that building work would be a useful addition to the completely unclear remit of the 'developmental executive'. I plunged into the construction process, as the 'building pastor', until the new-build was completed and occupied in 1975. Again having given no thought to the future, when the project was finished, I was once more unemployed. Building had also become a serious matter in my private life. I had purchased with my partner and five other couples a farmhouse in Ursem, Noord Holland. It functioned again as a 'salon' or sorts. I undertook the coordination of construction and in 1973 we moved in. The development stage was exciting, but the actual living patterns of weekend and permanent use proved incompatible. In 1976 we moved with our baby daughter (born in 1975) to Heemstede.

*Public welfare and health care (Amsterdam, 1975–1980).* After Young & Rubicam-Koster had given me notice, I was on unemployment benefit. There was a child on the way, so far no panic, though the urgency to find a new job increased. After a succession of letters and interviews, and several months, I got two options to choose from: management officer for the conurbation of Zaandstad or 'deputy manager for special projects' at the R.C. Maagdenhuis Foundation, originally an orphanage founded in 1572. The institution was meanwhile involved in child welfare, healthcare and geriatric care operating partially as a support fund. I opted for a sector with which I was least familiar and found most fascinating—a social sector and a Roman Catholic world in which I was unacquainted. My work entailed dealing with requests for donations focusing on innovative developments in mental health care, alternative forms of assistance for the young and spearheading policy for the elderly.

Again, there were unexpected developments. A few months after my appointment, the almost non-existent board of Huize Vredenburgh, a home for elderly women, had approached the management of the Maagdenhuis with a view to finding a new purpose deploying existing capital. I was keen to get involved and became the 'building and organisation coordinator' of what, a few years later, was to be a large development comprising a church, a residential care home and semi-residential services: New Vredenburgh, 'Centre for Local Senior Citizens'. After its delivery and the set-up of the organisation in 1980, my appointment came to an end and once more I was 'on the street'. This time I had a plan to start my own consultancy. Independence seemed appealing, and organisation consulting did too. I had to put food on the table. There were two more daughters by now. Why did I choose to work for the unknown Maagdenhuis project instead of making the (linear) choice for management consultancy in Zaandstad? Was that chance or intuition?

**_Reflection_. Is there an inner compass that you can rely on? One that you must safeguard from jamming devices (magnetic fields)? Do you detect moments in your own experience of quite considerable changes in direction that proved later to have made a contribution?**

*Advisers for policy and organisation (Amsterdam, 1980–1982).* As I was making enquiries about setting up my own consultancy, I got talking to the directors of IKON policy consultants, advisers for strategy and organisation. The advantages of working together with them soon became apparent. There would be a base with professional colleagues, working in teams with special people, critical evaluation and a support framework, and, in addition, excellent terms of employment instead of great financial uncertainty and vulnerability of a 'one-man band'. Again, it was new, certainly in instructive surroundings, with rigorous feedback. I learned about work based on analyses and less purely on willpower. I also learned that especially in critical situations, you must muster the most forceful opposition however unpleasant it may be. The work was a kind of catharsis for me, but my turnover was not great. I did not like the imbalances and after a year and a half, presented the partners with my analysis—consultancy in a highly critical, professional environment was extremely useful, but my strength lay in helping to build, in constructing as well as analysing. And so I wished to end our collaboration eventually. Not long after that, a former contact of mine at the Ministry of Culture, resulted in an unexpected assignment. The challenge was to attempt to make an outline for the future of the highly controversial institute, the Rijksakademie. It came at just the right time. Work to be done and food on the table for the family.

**_Reflection_. Is the realisation that your strength lies elsewhere, for instance 'developing and constructing', up front among other people, rather than at a distance as in the case of an adviser, an undeniable fact? Or is it more mysterious, that you first have to 'clean up' ruthlessly (first throw away the old shoes before getting new ones) to make way for a new assignment.**

*Rijksakademie, post-academic institute for visual arts (Amsterdam 1982–2010).*
In the late 1970s–early1980s, an almost catastrophic disaster struck the traditional Rijksakademie, shut away as it was in its ivory tower. The Ministry of Culture's decision to abolish it was blocked at the very last minute by the Lower House of Parliament. In 1982 I began, at the Ministry's request, as the Rijksakademie's interim director and adviser. Uncertain and with little knowledge of the visual arts. Talks with people in and around the Rijksakademie, and in particular pointers from the artists' studios, were, alongside secondary analysis, an important source of information when I was launching the reorganisation. After the Minister and the Lower House had approved the proposals for reorganisation and the first steps had been taken in the never-ending process for change, I was appointed in January 1985 as the director and professor holding the chair for the 'socio-economic position of the visual artist'. My curiosity about the artists' studios proved to be legitimate. A professor's remit covers three components: research, organisation and education. In my case, organisation entailed the strategic positioning of the institute in a transitional phase between education and professional practice. The aim was to create a new 'border crossing', as well as resources for budding artists by way of funds and as well as what was then post-graduate education (subsequently the Master's degree). After we had moved the Rijksakademie to the Cavalry Barracks and the organisation had stabilised, my educational relationship with the artists took shape in working groups with the title 'Positioning'. I made an in-house handbook which was to be the basis for later workshops and coaching. Many of the topics dealt with in this publications were advanced then.

During my 28-year period at the Rijksakademie I compiled a miscellany of notes concerning organisation; the transformation of a nineteenth-century Academy into the Rijksakademie Residency, a leading international institute. This archive forms a basic source for me. Only the first of the six topics 'Vitalisation, a radical reorganisation process' about the management of change was to be published in the *Handboek Management Kunst en Cultuur* (Bohn Stafleu van Loghum, 1991).

*Heemstede*

*Valtana, own business (Heemstede, 2010 to the present).*
In May 2010 I left the Rijksakademie and founded my one-man business, Valtana Consultancy. Contrary to my expectations, I was not pounced upon as an organisation consultant. That meant an opportunity to reflect and readjust. I visited the studios of artist friends fairly regularly. What initially were casual chats with artists at my home developed further, and one thing led to another. The artist's studio as a source of inspiration and energy, in this case for the current 'palette' of Valtana: coaching at the crossroads of career, personal life and work, counselling through workshops and seminars, as well as exchange of knowledge (since early 2015) in the framework of my Fellowship at the HKU, University of the Arts, Utrecht.

*Career in retrospect*

When I review my own career, there are three combined patterns that strike me.

An *inter-generational pattern*: 'in our family we're all 255
cabinetmakers/builders, or teachers/supervisors, and basically
that is what I am too.' When I was eighteen a friend referred
consistently to me as a 'host', which turned out to be somewhat
prophetic considering the subsequent 'salons' and hospitable
surroundings for others (friends, parents, artists). Initially I paid
little heed to what he said, later 'the penny dropped' and the
*common thread* emerged clearly. And then, lastly, the *'seeking'* 256
*moments in between*. The most profound layer of the three 257
patterns which I shall consider more closely.

The remarkable manoeuvre to switch direction during my secondary education might count as 'drawing back to make a better jump forward'. The change in direction at university, is reminiscent of a 'ditherer'. The first job in an advertising and marketing agency was influenced by force of—financial—circumstances, and curiosity. Another non-linear step followed: not the proposed advisory role but the choice for the unpredictable area of child welfare and geriatric care. The decision to join a strategy and organisation consultancy seemed logical. It was a fairly short venture, but heralded the following step, to the Rijksakademie. That leap into the unknown, with absolutely no certainty and at that stage no personal ambitions for my future, proved in the course of the next twenty-eight years to be 'just the ticket'. Everything coalesced. It took a while before I became what I actually had already been from an early age.

In my case, there were regularly gaps between projects, or jobs. My fixation on the current process, without anticipating what might happen next, produced unwanted moments of 'downtime' after one job was completed. Yet they proved useful for reflection and reorientation. They are valuable moments, not only when you think about the next practical step, but also, chiefly, about what drives you.

*Project-based work*

When you have a hybrid career you need more patience and more observations over a longer period, in order to discover the common thread and your strengths and weaknesses.

I like project-based work. I am fascinated by the combination of rational, structural aspects of project organisation and the emotional dimension of a temporary collaborative venture of this type. Handing over on time the rational structure with an objective (the horizon), steps in a set time frame (planning), financial preconditions (budget) and the people who contribute (staffing) as in a relay race. The emotional side: starting with the kick of the unknown, the tingling uncertainty of fresh ground, drawing on aspects of knowledge and experience of your own and of others, with respect to people who are as yet unfamiliar. Dealing with uncertainties is not one of my good points, but an essential, stimulating source of energy. Even within a long-term context like my directorship of the Rijksakademie, project-based work proved possible if larger issues were chopped up into smaller sections and then addressed as separate projects. In addition, there were new artists coming in each year, each time generating a new world, as it were.

One of the attractive aspects of 'a project' is that it has an end, when it is wound up and handed over: the completed project is returned to the principal, the art work goes to the buyer, generated knowledge to interested parties (through teaching or writing). And the people with whom there was such an intense interaction may perhaps remain tucked away in your heart, but are no longer fulltime partners. A brand-new day dawns, full of uncertainties, questions and people. That is thrilling.

# 10

# Acknowledgements

*From the artist's studio to the studio*

The most important steps that led to this publication follow below, in chronological order. Many people have contributed with critical remarks and encouragement. I owe them a debt of great gratitude; without their input this book would not have been possible.

*1982*
First introduction to the practice of visual artists. Discussions with artists and visits to their studios outside the Rijksakademie, and talks with the students at that time, the aim being to diagnose the situation and develop future perspectives for the institute. In 1983 and 1984 the proposals were approved by the Lower House and the Minister of Culture, as well as by the Rijksakademie community.

*1985*
Appointment as professor-cum-director of the new chair for the 'socio-economic position of the visual artist'.

*1986–*
National and international orientation in artists' studios, art academies and artist residencies in order to fine-tune new policy and the design of the new accommodation (architect Koen van Velsen) Kavallerie Kazerne in Sarphatistraat, Amsterdam, which was occupied in 1992.

*1993*
Working groups 'Positioning by artists' for which I made a handbook. Meetings every year in small groups of 'participants' (later 'residents') in the framework of the socio-economic position of visual artists. Also, starting that year, summer visits to meet with artists in all the individual studios in the Rijksakademie regarding the working process and prospects.

*2007*
Contacts with alumni, (former) advisers and Prix de Rome jury members stepped up, including studio visits in many countries in preparation for the fund-raising auction 'Global Contemporary, Artists for Artists' in June 2010, at my farewell from the Rijksakademie.

*2013*
Start of individual coaching of artists in Heemstede. The in-house handbook that had gone astray was rediscovered twenty years later. In 2014 the first workshops for programmes at ArtEZ Institute of the Arts in Arnhem, Minerva and Frank Mohr Institute in Groningen. Ten years after more were added, at AKI-ArtEZ in Enschede, Royal Academy of Art in The Hague, Rietveld Academy in Amsterdam and Fine Art BA and MA of the HKU University of the Arts Utrecht (to which I was affiliated). Day sessions with dozens of mid-career artists (2013–2017) and over 650 short, frank discussions with art students on their personal backgrounds, dreams and ambitions (2014–2017) supplied a wealth of information and insight.

*2015*
I started re-editing the in-house handbook, with additional presentation materials for the workshops and notes from coaching. Annelie Musters (art academy, active in the field of artist residencies, cultural foundations and art education) and Chloë Neeleman (artist, participant in 'Positioning in the Kabk' workshop in 2015) read through and commented on the initial, rudimentary text.

*2016*
Half-way through writing this publication and sometimes going round in circles, I felt the need to touch base, for broader and more systematic *feedback from the studios* and insight into individual experiences.

Fifty artists were selected from Rijksakademie circles because of their prominence, the feeling that they had varied practices, personal contact and a balanced representation of males and females, and artists from the Netherlands and abroad.

Response was high (33 respondents, 66%), the geographical spread global:

Narda Alvarado, Carlos Amorales, Tiong Ang, Mark Boulos, Olga Chernysheva, Martha Colburn, Sean Dower, Claudia Fontes, Meshac Gaba, Dora Garcia Lopez, Hans van Houwelingen, Paul Klemann, Jean Bernard Koeman, Meiro Koizumi, Cees Krijnen, Germaine Kruip, Alexandra Leykauf, Jacco Olivier, Esther Polak/Ivar van Bekkum, Michael Raedecker, Mathilde Rosier, Mounira Al Solh, Viviane Sassen, Praneet Soi, Berend Strik, Esther Tielemans, Helen Verhoeven, Maria Verstappen/Erwin Driessens, Roy Villevoye, Kan Xuan and Sylvie Zijlmans.

It was possible to trace prototypes of artistic practices and patterns of practice development from the material and the artists' clarifications, as mentioned in 'Exploration: signals from the studio'. There was no need for statistic perfection in a quantitative sense, but if a—qualitatively—valid picture were to emerge and the tentatively developed artists' positions could be verified, all the better. A few convincing profiles tell more about reality than mountains of numbers.

A six-month *traineeship project* was undertaken by Amelie de Haan and Leonardo Dellanoce of MA studies World Art Studies at the University of Leiden (Professor Kitty Zijlmans). Amelie provided substantive input and co-organised a specially set-up reading group in the HKU, moderated by Bart van Rosmalen, lector of Art and Professionalisation. In three sessions he developed special types of discussion, i.e. Contemplative Dialogue, Critical Response Process and Polyphonic Reading. A select group of artists, lecturers, critics, scientists, programmers and managers took part in one or more of the meetings and discussed material from the manuscript: Paul Adriaanse, Nirav Christophe, Edo Dijksterhuis, Carolien Hermans, Jean Bernard Koeman, Annelie Musters, Myrthe Nagtzaam, Carolien Oostveen, Maya Rasker, Jules van de Vijver, Annemiek Vera and Maria Verstappen.

Leonardo concentrated on 22 artists' biographies and we visited studios, talked to artists and submitted the texts to the artists. In that way twenty-two 'snapshots' came about, of the integrated practices of Carlos Amorales, David Bade, Driessens & Verstappen, Marlene Dumas, Claudia Fontes, Alicia Framis, Meschac Gaba, Ryan Gander, Antony Gormley, Hama Goro, Sigurdur Gudmundsson, Hans van Houwelingen, Joan Jonas, Germaine Kruip, Matt Mullican, Michelangelo Pistoletto, Jan van der Ploeg, Michael Raedecker, Jannie Regnerus, Auke de Vries, Guido van der Werve and Sylvie Zijlmans.

*2017*

After extensive investigations into potential publishers and informative discussions, in the autumn of 2016 the collaboration with Valiz Publishers' Astrid Vorstermans got underway. A thorough editorial process with Noor Mertens lasting three months was followed by a round of equally thorough final editing by Els Brinkman. The English translation was tackled by Wendy van Os-Thompson, graphic design by Laura Pappa. In the final year, the material was also discussed during working visits to Ivan Grubanov in Belgrade and Hermann Pitz in Munich. During the final stages, testimonials were given by Maria Barnas, Annelie Musters, Kitty Zijlmans and others.

At the same time as the content of the manuscript was being finalised, a 'friends-funding' campaign was conducted together with Valiz and my daughter Hester. Consultations with art institutes and fund raising by Valiz resulted in the commitment of some foundations and organisations to support the project.

I am deeply happy with so much encouragement, loyalty and belief and want to thank everybody wholeheartedly.

Janwillem Schrofer, April 2018

# Friends and funding



The following friends generously helped to make this publication possible:

Maarten Asscher
Rob Defares
Linda Dekker-Klein Essink
Yvonne van Eekelen
Susan Gloudemans
Ilse Hughan
Wjm. Kok
José de Lange
Martin Lenikus
Anton Meester & Helga Kos
Marieke & Pieter Sanders
Annemarie Schrofer
Kea Schrofer
Willem Sijthoff & Machteld Vos
Arthur Sonnen
Harry Swaak
Academie Minerva/Dorothea van der Meulen, Groningen
HKU University of the Arts/Jules van de Vijver, Utrecht
Rietveld Academie/Ben Zegers, Amsterdam
Rijksakademie/Marietta Dirker, Amsterdam
Robben Stichting

FUNDING
This publication has been generously supported by
Mondriaan Fund
Gravin van Bylandt Stichting
De Gijselaar-Hintzenfonds
Stichting Stokroos
and other organisations and individuals.

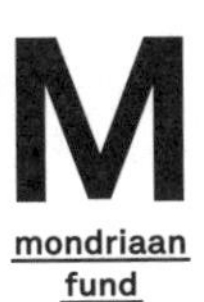


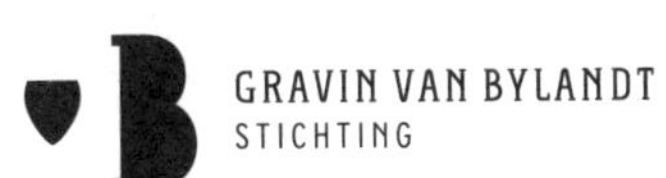


De Gijselaar-Hintzenfonds

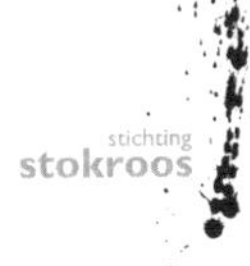

# Index of terms

# Index of names

# Index of organisations

# Colophon

Author:
Janwillem Schrofer

Artists' descriptions
assistance (pp. 86–129):
Leonardo Dellanoce

Structural editing:
Noor Mertens

Translation Dutch-English:
Wendy van Os-Thompson

Copy-editing/proofreading:
Els Brinkman

Index:
Nic de Jong, Elke Stevens

Design:
Laura Pappa

Typefaces:
Neue Haas Unica
Caslon #540

Paper:
Munken Print White, 90 gr. 1.5
Invercote 200 gr.

Lithography:
Mariska Bijl, Wilco Art Books

Printing and binding:
Wilco Art Books, Amersfoort

Publisher:
Astrid Vorstermans
Valiz, Amsterdam, 2018
www.valiz.nl

Distribution:
• NL: Centraal Boekhuis,
www.cb.nl
• BE/LU: EPO, www.epo.be
• GB/IE: Central Books,
www.centralbooks.com
• Europe/Asia: Idea Books,
www.ideabooks.nl
• USA: D.A.P., www.artbook.com
• Australia: Perimeter,
www.perimeterdistribution.com
• Individual orders: www.valiz.nl

V

Fourth print, 2025
ISBN 978-94-92095-40-4
Printed and bound in the EU

Photography:
Courtesy the artists
Ernesto Milsztain (p. 95)
Stephen White, London (p. 103)
Carol Winkel, Amsterdam
(pp. 87, 92, 99, 100, 107, 115, 116, 120, 124, 128)

*Janwillem Schrofer has based his book* Plan and Play *on his many years of experience and encounters with visual artists and their differing ways of thinking and practicing. For me, an important aspect of the book is that it breaks loose from the assumption that artists 'just muck around' or merely develop organically and intuitively. Schrofer takes his subjects (the artists) seriously and analyses how a healthy artistic practice can be built up. Never before have I read an analysis and strategy of this type. The book will be helpful as well as being a source of new ideas for budding and established artists alike. Schrofer's call/recommendation always to return to self-reflection is particularly compelling. The book will reinforce the position of the artist himself, but also his position vis-à-vis his surroundings, society, since the artistic practice can serve as an example of the way in which a practice can be developed based on personal characteristics and preferences.*

Maria Barnas, writer/artist

*I consider* Plan and Play, Play and Plan *to be an important and timely book, because it examines all sides of the artistic practice, from choice and commitment to actual practice, in all its facets—including that of entrepreneur. Schrofer's emphasis on one's own positioning and awareness of it greatly appeals to me. These are aspects that I always communicate to my students as well. The title conveys the thrust of the book and the scope of artistic calling in a nutshell: oscillating between plans (fact-finding, structuring, reflecting and contemplation) and 'play', the creative nature of free creativity, thinking and acting.*

*The book is structured clearly, with frequent references to basic questions. The 'reflections' work well as additional food for thought and in stimulating to consider one's own position and path. The personal account is equally useful as frame of reference, it emphasizes the importance of hands-on experience.*

*Alongside the eleven examples of 'positions', there are eleven with 'mixed practices', which aptly reflect the scope of artistic calling. In all, this is a valuable book, combining practice and reflection, and providing clear insight into the different kinds of practice, the choices the artist makes, but also the pleasure and satisfaction of it.*

*It is, to my mind, a 'must' for anyone involved in the creative and professional practice of artists, ranging from artists themselves (novices or established artists) and those involved in the art world, to relevant authorities. A manual about acting and reflecting.*

Kitty Zijlmans, Professor of Contemporary Art History and Theory, Leiden University

*In the early 1980s I was not entirely clear about how to combine my artistic calling with my work as an organiser of art projects and coordinator at a post-academic institution. This handbook would have helped me to better understand that position. Could I still be an artist if I were to give priority to different activities within the arts? I was young and inexperienced and got no answer to that question. Today I know that, as well as creating artworks, artists can be active in other fields and play parts that also belong in their professional practice. With this book, Janwillem Schrofer provides artists with a tool with which to examine their practice in a pleasurable way and to set it in a wider social context. You can read the book in its entirety or pick out individual sections that are relevant for you. In addition, the book is very informative for people working with artists, or wishing to do so.*

Annelie Musters, coordinator / deputy head Residency, Rijksakademie van beeldende kunsten, Amsterdam

*Pleasantly surprised by your message about your book, of which you had already told me. Great, it's sorely needed. I know: thanks to your help I have many contacts in the world of artists. I am looking forward to it.*

Yvonne van Eekelen, art historian, is researching the Prix de Rome for her thesis

*First of all I wanted to thank you for the meeting we had that day. You believed in my project, thus I believed it too! I have been discussing it with people and I have had some interesting feedback :)*

*I will keep letting you know how it goes! I think this book will help a lot!*

Despina Charitonidi, Athens, graduating student HKU (2016/17)

*At the time I got a lot from your two workshops which I enjoyed at ArtEZ. I also benefited greatly from the way you saw to my CV […]. I'm very enthusiastic about your e-mail: how splendid that there's a publication on its way! That's an achievement that would be worth my last euro; I still bear your lessons in mind in my practice. […]. You've got my backing already!*

Rosanne Jonkhout, graduating student ArtEZ – Arnhem (2017)

*– Very generous sharing of non-intrusive, non-normative or prescriptive navigational tools;*
*– Empowering, in the sense that it provided content that allows for agency, control and the avoidance of exploitation (the part on how to make a budget and how to be correctly compensated for your immaterial labour);*
*– Allowing for space and providing concrete formulations on how alternative possibilities can materialise while being of significance, rather than formatting artists for the 'art' market;*
*– Very happy to see the artist treated as worker and social agent rather than individualistic genius to be randomly selected by the market or not;*
*– The part on how to 'smell' the air and figure out if you should commit in any kind of collaboration beforehand was also very clever, given its hard to read economic collaborations through an affective filter.*

*Very educative and well designed, fitted a lot of important things to say and practice without feeling overwhelming or boring. Thanks!*

Marika Konstantinidou, graduating student Academy of Fine Arts Vienna (2018)